Also by Robert _. ___

Hoaxes, Myths, and Manias: Why We Need Critical Thinking
(with Benjamin Radford)

". . . a good entertaining introduction to critical thinking for the general reader and for undergraduates." — *Contemporary Psychology*

". . . fast-paced and intriguing . . . anyone with an interest in the odd or in critical thinking should read." — *Statesman Journal*

". . . you are certain to be amused and amazed in equal parts . . . an entertaining and enlightening book." — *Psychology Today*

Outbreak! The Encyclopedia of Extraordinary Social Behavior
(with Hilary Evans)

". . . a work of immense erudition and scholarship but also a thumping good read." — Simon Wessely, King's College London

". . . an absorbing and authoritative read and an extremely valuable reference for anyone interested in the field of psychosomatic medicine." — Keith Petrie, University of Auckland

". . . quite possibly the most important contribution to the world of Forteana . . . in a very long time . . . The book is indeed scholarly; but it is also highly informative, insightful, illuminating and witty." — Nick Redfern, author of *Keep Out! Top Secret Places Governments Don't Want You to Know About*

Little Green Men, Meowing Nuns and Head-Hunting Panics:
A Study of Mass Psychogenic Illness and Social Delusion

"The book will interest any reader . . . it is extensively documented and food for thought." — *Australian Journal of Forensic Sciences*

". . . well-documented information to those interested in mass psychosocial phenomena, and as fascinating leisure-time reading to the general public." — Wolfgang G. Jilek, Professor Emeritus, University of British Columbia.

FEB   2013

THE UNTOLD STORY OF
CHAMP

THE UNTOLD STORY OF
CHAMP

A Social History of America's Loch Ness Monster

ROBERT E. BARTHOLOMEW

excelsior editions

AN IMPRINT OF STATE UNIVERSITY OF NEW YORK PRESS

Published by
STATE UNIVERSITY OF NEW YORK PRESS
Albany

© 2012 State University of New York

For information, contact
State University of New York Press
www.sunypress.edu

Excelsior Editions is an imprint of State University of New York Press

Production, Laurie Searl
Marketing, Kate McDonnell

Library of Congress Cataloging-in-Publication Data

Bartholomew, Robert E.
    The untold story of Champ : a social history of America's Loch Ness
Monster / Robert Emerson Bartholomew.
        p. cm.
    Includes bibliographical references and indexes.
    ISBN 978-1-4384-4484-0 (pbk. : alk. paper)
    1. Champ (Monster)   2. Champlain, Lake—History.   3. Champlain, Lake,
Region—History.   4. Champlain, Lake, Region—Social life and customs.
5. Legends—Champlain, Lake, Region.   I. Title.

QL89.2.C53B37 2012
001.944—dc23   2012003676
            10 9 8 7 6 5 4 3 2 1

CONTENTS

ILLUSTRATIONS

FOREWORD

"There are some very strange things in this lake."

A 75-year-old merchant marine, who had crisscrossed the oceans on freighters, swept his hand toward Vermont and let that sentence hang in the air.

I was 13 and standing on the shores of Lake Champlain for the first time in my life.

My family had purchased a summer home at Crown Point, New York and the sailor was filling me in on the basics of fishing the southern end of this beautiful and mysterious lake.

Transfixed by what I had just heard, I could barely breathe. What he said sounded more like an omen than a warning.

Little did I know at my young and impressionable age that the sailor's words would weave themselves into my work as a newspaper reporter as I chronicled the flurry of fascination with all things related to Champ, the Lake Champlain "monster."

My healthy skepticism about Champ would continue unchecked until 7:10 AM July 2, 1983.

The lake surface was glass. My girlfriend and I were fishing from our anchored rowboat in about fifteen feet of water, facing the New York shore.

"Ron, what's that?"

I turned. About thirty feet away I saw three dark humps—maybe 12 inches thick—protruding about two feet above the surface.

The humps were perhaps two or three feet apart. They didn't move. We didn't either.

We watched in disbelief for about ten seconds. The humps slowly sank into the water. There was no wake, no telltale sign of movement.

Unexplained. Eerie. Unsettling.

Get ready for the same spine-tingling, thought-provoking ride as Robert Bartholomew guides you through 400 years of facts, fantasy and controversy surrounding Champ.

Bartholomew has culled interesting and pertinent information from personal journals and correspondence, newspaper archives and interviews with major players in the Champ saga to give us an unvarnished look at a landscape filled with scientists, common folk, and hustlers.

Like any solid reporter, Bartholomew asks the tough questions. He draws you into the vortex of egos of the Champ researchers. He chides his media colleagues for sloppy reporting. He acknowledges the cheerleading by chambers of commerce along the lake that have hitched their wagons to the tale of Champ.

It's all in here, and more.

Whether you're an arm-chair explorer of the unexplained or a card-carrying member of the National Geographic Society, Champ is a fascinating subject of study because of its broad appeal.

This book will answer some important questions and present many more.

If you're fortunate to read this book while relaxing on the shore of Lake Champlain, look up once in a while.

The view is beautiful. It may also be startling.

Is that one hump out of the water, or two?

RONALD S. KERMANI
Albany, New York

ACKNOWLEDGMENTS

Phil and Sean Reines gave generously of their time and took great pains to offer editing suggestions on an earlier version of the manuscript. I had originally intended for Dr. Reines and Joe Zarzynski to write separate prefaces, but as the book began to congeal it became apparent that to do so would compromise my objectivity. In the end, it was necessary to develop my own voice and reach my own conclusions, independent of either Phil or Joe, both of whom I know personally. This emotional distancing was essential to maintain a professional detachment from my subjects of study.

Scott Mardis was remarkably helpful and gave selflessly of his own time and materials to better inform this book. Gary Mangiacopra, with whom I have corresponded since childhood, was also of immeasurable help. Scott and Gary are selfless, dedicated researchers who rarely receive public attention they deserve.

The idea for the title of Chapter 2 is from an article by *New York Times* journalist Peter Applebome. It is used with his blessing. My brother Paul Bartholomew was of great help in locating contemporary materials from his vast files of the unexplained. Mike Pluta also gave freely of his time. I also wish to acknowledge the proofreading skills of Sara Dove.

INTRODUCTION

Things are seldom what they seem, skim milk masquerades as
cream.

—WILLIAM S. GILBERT

Many people think they know the story of the Champlain Monster beginning in 1609 with Samuel de Champlain's famous encounter with a twenty
foot-long serpentine creature with a horse-like head, which he described
while exploring the lake for the first time. But how many people know
that this description is almost entirely fictitious and his encounter never
even happened on Lake Champlain? Surprisingly, much of the history of
America's most famous lake monster remains untold. The public deserves
a book that chronicles the full history of Champ. Throughout the years,
authors, reporters, researchers, and local politicians have blurred the line
between fact, fiction, and speculation to the point where it is no longer
recognizable. People no longer know what to believe. What is the likelihood, as some assert, that Champ is a zeuglodon or plesiosaur: Creatures
that have supposedly been extinct for millions of years? What are we to
make of Liz von Muggenthaler's "discovery" of a mysterious creature in
the lake that uses biosonar to get around? What is depicted in the celebrated 1977 photo snapped by Sandra Mansi? One thing is certain: A
closer inspection reveals that there is more to her story than meets the eye.

In this book I will paint for the first time, a detailed picture of the
serpent's rich, colorful history, beginning in the nineteenth century when
it became a household name across the United States. I will chronicle
key sightings and events through the decades, and reveal the actions and
personalities of the modern-day monster hunters; their egos, obsessions,
and behind-the-scenes squabbles. Their trials and tribulations are not a
voyeuristic sideshow intended to highlight human frailty and sensationalize

the subject; they are every bit a legitimate part of the history as Champ himself. Over the years, Champ has become a chameleon-like figure representing many things to the region's inhabitants: local icon, environmental symbol, tourist draw card, and perhaps a new or long-thought extinct species. But ultimately, the history of Champ reveals more about us than it does about him.

ROBERT EMERSON BARTHOLOMEW

FROM OUT OF THE BLUE

The Early Memoir of a Sea Monster

One measures a circle beginning anywhere.

—CHARLES FORT[1]

Mention the subject of lake monsters at any dinner party and invariably the first creature that springs to mind is the legendary Loch Ness Monster. Yet Nessie's spiritual cousin who is said to reside in Lake Champlain has been startling goggle-eyed witnesses ever since pioneer days, and has a history that is every bit as rich and storied as his Scottish counterpart, with hundreds of sightings spanning at least three centuries. In fact, there is only one difference separating the two creatures: a good publicist. Between 1870 and the early 1930s, the Loch Ness Monster was virtually unknown, wallowing in obscurity, and would have given her left dorsal fin to have received the notoriety of her North American counterpart during this period, as the Champlain Sea Serpent had the spotlight all to himself. Today, buoyed by a lucrative European tourism market that drives advertising campaigns aimed at luring tourists to the Highlands, Nessie has surpassed Champ as the world's most famous lake monster. In recent decades, amid a flurry of sightings and renewed journalistic fervor, Champ's star has risen once again until he now ranks a close second to his media-savvy relative from across the Atlantic and is occasionally referred to as "America's Loch Ness Monster."

WHAT'S IN A NAME?

Throughout much of its written history the Champlain Monster has been referred to as a "sea serpent," although it is said to inhabit a lake. The nineteenth century was characterized by a widespread belief that sea serpents roamed the oceans, and it was thought that some had been trapped in local lakes during the previous Ice Age. Whether or not it is technically or even politically incorrect, the sightings in this book are described using the terminology of the times. The creature is almost always described in male terms and in the singular as if there were only one. Yet if it exists, there must be a breeding population, as it would be absurd to think that there is a single creature thousands of years old cavorting around the lake. Therefore, whenever it is referred to in the singular or as "he," it is done for reasons of literary ease and color; it should be taken as a reference to the entire population, *if* they exist. The same is true of the common use of the word "monster," which is highly derogatory. "Monster" comes from the Latin *monstrum*; an aberrant occurrence within the natural order and often has sinister connotations. It also derives from *monstrare* (to display or show) such as the "monsters" seen in circus sideshows. To most of his neighbors, Champ is a shy, serene figure who simply wants to be left alone. Many local children affectionately cuddle stuffed Champs as they drift off to sleep. If he were to read the papers, he would be aghast to learn that some people refer to him as a monster. The price of fame demands it as the media has been sensationalizing his exploits for more than two centuries.

Since its emergence from the Champlain Sea roughly 10,000 years ago, the natives living on the shores of what is now Lake Champlain have swapped tales of a mysterious serpentine creature that is said to reside in its depths. This denizen of the deep has since been given many names. During the nineteenth century, it was commonly known as the Champlain Sea Serpent and The Great Snake, while skeptics were fond of calling it His Majesty and His Snakeship. Since the mid-twentieth century, it is most commonly referred to as Champ, although other names are occasionally used: Champy, Sammy, and the Champlain Monster. Skeptics often describe it with the words "sturgeon" and "log," whereas believers frequently use the words "prehistoric" and "monster." Whatever *it* is has been evoking wonder and curiosity soon after humans first laid eyes on the lake more than ten millennia ago.[2]

Is it possible that a small breeding population of prehistoric creatures became land-locked at this time, making the lake their home and adapting to the fresh water as rain and inland floods gradually flushed away the salinity? Fossil records reveal that the Champlain Sea was once home to an array of exotic creatures including whales and walruses. Is it too far-fetched to think that a species, still unknown to science or thought to have been long ago extinct, could survive into the twenty-first century? If so, how could it elude detection for so long? Proponents argue that the creature *has* been detected—based on hundreds of eyewitness accounts. Yet it is a conundrum that in more than 10,000 years of human habitation on the lake, no one has recovered a body or fossils of a plausible candidate. There are, however, precedents in nature. In 1938, fishermen off South Africa stunned the scientific world by catching a strange-looking fish in their nets. Dubbed "the living fossil" and considered to have been the zoological find of the twentieth century, the coelacanth (seel-uh-kanth) was thought by scientists to have been extinct for 60 million years. Will Champ become the zoological find of the twenty-first century?

INDIAN LORE

Native Americans living along Lake Champlain told stories of a mysterious "horned serpent" that was said to reside in the lake. In the early seventeenth century, Abenaki guides told French captains to be careful not to disturb the monsters that live in the waters of Lake Champlain. "While in the canoes, the men should not make loud noises or fire their muskets without good reason. Neither should they throw anything into the water."[3] Along the shoreline at the place the Abenaki called *Tobapsqua* ("the pass through the rock"), at Rock Regio or Split Rock south of Essex village, New York,[4] there appear to be pictographs of snakelike creatures resembling modern-day descriptions of Champ.[5] The "drawings" on Split Rock are natural formations of "contorted segregations of silicates that only resemble snakes."[6] The rock and surrounding waters were sacred and believed by the natives to be home to a spirit called *Tatoskok,* which took the form of a giant serpent or lizard.[7] At least one historian thinks that the spirit in this legend refers to a giant fish or serpent.[8] The Split Rock spirit was feared by the natives and while passing nearby in their canoes they would place food, tobacco, or pipes into the water in hopes the offering would

afford them safe passage.[9] This tiny, heavily wooded landmark is situ-
ated near the deepest part of the lake—some four-hundred feet—and
is the site of several significant sightings. For this reason, many locals
consider the waters off Split Rock to be the monster's home. Could
the aquatic spirit that was thought by the Indians to dwell near Split
Rock, be more than folklore, in fact an early reference to Champ?[10]

The Abenaki of what is now southern Quebec and northern Vermont had a name for an aquatic beast they called *Gitaskogak, Gitaskog,*
or *Peetaskog,* the "great snake" that was believed to reside in *Bitaw-
bagok*—the Abenaki name for Lake Champlain.[11] Not being a single
uniform culture and language, there were different traditions and dia-
lects depending on where one lived. The Abenaki (People of the Dawn
Land) were an eastern branch of the Algonquin nation. Joseph Bruchac
identifies another term for this creature: *Padoskoks* meaning "bigger-
than-big snake."[12] Could these Indians have created myths based on
their observation of Champ-like fossils? Fossils of beluga whales have
been found in the Champlain basin and these massive creatures frol-
icked in the Champlain Sea a mere 10,000 years ago, yet none of
their descriptions match modern-day Champ accounts or the tales told
by the Indians. Beluga whales resemble oversized dolphins, are snow
white, grow to an average of fifteen feet and can weigh more than
3,300 pounds. While they swim freely in the northern oceans and the
mouth of the St. Lawrence River, a beluga whale in Lake Champlain
would stand out like Barack Obama at a Klu Klux Klan convention.
It would not stay undetected for long. There is not a single description of Champ that even remotely resembles a beluga.

So how do we explain the legends of a "giant snake" in the
lake—descriptions that closely resemble modern-day Champ reports?
Perhaps it is because there *is* an enormous snakelike creature in the
lake. Yet there are other equally plausible explanations. The natives
may have misidentified large fish such as sturgeon and gar, and their
stories were exaggerated over time. There are several smaller lakes in
New York, Vermont, and neighboring Quebec province where people
occasionally spot aquatic monsters.[13,14] These sightings are most likely
misidentifications, for it is highly improbable that a breeding community of such creatures could survive in such tiny bodies of water
or go undiscovered. Indeed, a major objection by many scientists to

the existence of UFOs as alien visitors is that there are too many sightings and no concrete proof. Without a carcass, and with sightings from numerous lakes around the world, a similar case can be made against the reality of lake monsters. Furthermore, although many Native American tribes had extensive precontact myths about giant snakes ("the horned serpent"),[15] several areas along Lake Champlain are notorious for rattlesnakes that den and thrive there and could account for these beliefs. Split Rock was known by the Abenaki as *sizikwáimenahán* or "rattlesnake island."[16] It is easy to make erroneous assumptions without a full knowledge of local history. During the French and Indian War (1754–1763), a British soldier named Abel Horsmer was stationed along the lake at Crown Point, New York, when in 1860 he made a powder horn carving which included a dragon-like creature. In 1984, Joe Zarzynski suggested that the carving *may* have been prompted by a Champ sighting.[17] By 2009, this vague suggestion had morphed into something entirely different, with mystery writer Michael Newton proclaiming that in 1860 Horsmer "saw a dragon swimming near Crown Point." Even worse, Newton implies that this is why locals named the nearby harbor at Westport, Big Snake Bay.[18] There is no mystery here. Also called Snake Den Harbor, the area also was known for rattlesnakes.[19] Newton's account is reminiscent of Peter Beagle's dedication of *The Last Unicorn* to Dr. Olfert Dapper, who he believed had written an eyewitness account of a unicorn in the forests of Maine. Actually, Dapper never left his native Netherlands—he just collected and published travelers' tales.[20]

Myths are easily spawned and perpetuated. For instance, many people are unaware that the Iroquois or "snake people" never referred to themselves as such until recent times. The word appears to be a French variant of a Huron word that was used to describe their Iroquois neighbors and archenemies in derogatory terms: snake-eaters or snake people. Even the word Huron appears to be of French origin and was used to describe either the tribe's hair style or unkempt appearance. As for the Iroquois, they referred to themselves as *Haudenosaunee* or "People of the Longhouse."[21]

The point is: Europeans perceived and understood the actions and beliefs of these New World natives from their own Eurocentric frames of reference. Even the name Iroquois was used to refer to a confederation of different tribes, each of which had different tribal names and distinct customs. Were stories of a giant horned serpent in the lake a reference to Champ or simply part of the wider North American myth about giant snakes that were once believed to have inhabited the land and lakes? Stories of giant serpents stretched across much of the continent and varied from place to place. No one knows the true meaning behind these accounts, as we are left with oral traditions, stories from early explorers and settlers, and rock drawings from which to piece together a complex system of beliefs—much of which has been lost forever. Abenaki religion is a good example of this. The Abenaki had many gods and spirits and made it clear to the early missionaries that they would not "be so foolish as to give up their thirty-seven gods for the white man's one god."[22] This has implications for the legends surrounding Split Rock as a closer examination reveals that some natives would place food or tobacco overboard to appease *Sen-al Wissa-Mando* ("The Rock's Wind Spirit") and not a giant serpent.[23] It appears that different groups were appeasing different spirits depending on their beliefs at any given time. The modern-day equivalent would be the many people in the region identifying as "Christians," of which there are dozens of denominations, some of which can be at extreme variance in their teachings. By some accounts, there were even two different wind spirits at Split Rock, male and female.[24] Yes, history is complicated and easy to oversimplify.

The Abenaki also told stories of a giant snake (*makwaaskadamôd*) that inhabited ponds, lakes and bogs, and would carry off young maidens. These accounts may have nothing to do with a literal water serpent, but instead may serve as cautionary tales aimed at warning the young and vulnerable of the perils of straying off alone.[25] They may be the Abenaki equivalent of the Boogey Man. A kindred creature was the *Meskag-kwedemos* or "swamp monster."[26] It is curious that some of the early French explorers in the northeast reported that when the Indians "discovered massive mastodon bones and tusks in swamps and streambeds, they also identified them as underwater horned monsters."[27] Surely, dinosaur fossils would have fueled some Indian myths. The Abenaki believed in the existence of enormous rabbits,[28] giant lizards, and diminutive water fairies who were referred to as the "Little People" or *Manôgemassak*. These latter creatures were believed to have lived in rivers and in Lake Champlain and "had faces like axe blades."[29] Although most people today—the Abenaki included—no longer believe in giant amphibians and water fairies, it may be that as these mythical creatures were to the Indians, Champ is to us. In this sense, the widespread belief in creatures like Bigfoot and Champ may reflect the same human desire to believe in an alluring world filled with monsters, only the form has changed to reflect the social and cultural context. It could be said that whereas fairies are no longer believable, they have been replaced by more scientifically plausible creatures. In this regard, Champ could be viewed as a sort of over-grown modern-day fairy.

SAMUEL DE CHAMPLAIN'S ENCOUNTER OF 1609

The first recorded sighting of Champ has been attributed to the lake's namesake, French explorer and cartographer Samuel de Champlain (circa 1567–1635).[30] This is pure myth that was perpetrated in a 1970 *Vermont Life* magazine article by Keeseville, New York historian Marjo-rie Lansing Porter (1891–1973). Porter wrote that in 1609 Champlain was exploring the lake when he saw "a serpent-like creature about twenty-feet long, as thick through as a barrel and with a head shaped like a horse."[31] Her description is mystifying as Champlain never wrote this. We know that Porter had read many early newspaper reports of sightings, and may have come across the claim and used it, without checking the original source. Many early papers reported that the first European to have seen the Champlain Sea Serpent was none other than the great man himself. For instance, on July 18, 1929, the *Ticonderoga Sentinel* asserted that Champlain saw a creature that was twelve feet long "with a hide so tough that a poniard (dagger) was broken in an attempt to spear him." Champlain's log states nothing of the sort. The explorer wrote that he had observed creatures five feet long (not twelve!) and he said nothing about scales so hard that they broke a poniard. As for Porter's claim that the creature was as thick "as a barrel," in Champlain's own words, the creatures "were as large as my thigh," whereas the head was "as big as my two fists."[32] These descriptions are hardly monster-like. Porter also made a second mis-take; claiming the encounter took place on Lake Champlain. In July

1609, Champlain reported seeing a mysterious creature in the nearby St. Lawrence estuary that feeds north into the St. Lawrence River. Shortly after Porter's article appeared, historians began to observe that they had been unable to verify her claim after checking Champlain's writings, and it soon became apparent that it was not true.[33]

As to what Champlain saw, we must consult his log. The "Father of New France" and founder of Quebec did describe a fierce-looking creature that the natives called *chaousarou* (chow-sa-roo) which they said grew up to ten feet long.[34] Based on his own observations, Champlain said the creature possessed "jaws two feet and a half long, and a double set of very sharp and dangerous teeth. The form of the body resembles that of the pike, and it is armed with scales that a thrust of a poniard [dagger] cannot pierce; and is of a silver grey colour. The point of the snout is like that of a hog. This fish makes war on all others in the lakes and rivers."[35] A monster it was not.

Champlain's account is a textbook description of an adult garfish or gar pike (*Lepisosteus osseus*) that still flourish in the lake today—accurate right down to its grey color, razor sharp teeth, and piglike snout. The natives told Champlain that to cure a headache they took the teeth of a *chaousarou* and would "bleed themselves with the teeth of this fish on the spot where they suffer pain."[36] Similar remedies using gar teeth are mentioned by other Native American tribes such as the Huron.[37] In the 1612 edition of Champlain's map, *Carte Géographique de la Nouvelle France*, he even drew a picture of a *chaousarou*; it looks identical to a longnose gar.[38]

In 1664, Louis Nicolas, a Jesuit missionary, arrived in New France and compiled a book of drawings and customs of the native inhabitants and the local flora and fauna.[39] Among the sketches is one that closely resembles a gar pike identified as *chausarou*. This is almost certainly Champlain's *chaousarou*.[40] But how could the creature recorded by Samuel de Champlain be described as growing to ten feet long when a longnose gar only reaches six feet? Fishermen are notorious for exaggerating the size of fish. There is even a name for it: "fish stories" about "the one that got away." Historian John Ross writes: "It would seem that the natives . . . were, themselves, not above telling tall tales to the newcomers with the white skin and the strange beliefs."[41] It is noteworthy that Champlain never claimed to have seen a ten-foot long *chaousarou;* the creature he saw was only five feet long. He said that the natives had *told him* that it could grow to ten feet. The natives also told him other tall tales, such as the existence of a bigfoot-like creature called the *Gougou* that was taller than his ship's mast and lived on an island in the lake.[42]

Ross thinks that many seventeenth-century explorers commonly exaggerated their New World discoveries in hopes of making a bigger impression back home. He contends that Champlain was able to protect his reputation by attributing certain exorbitant claims to the Indians. He writes: "Champlain protected his integrity by saying that eating habits of this fish were described to him by the Indians who said that 'When it wants to capture birds, it swims in among the rushes or reeds, which are found on the banks of the lake in several places, where it puts its [open] snout out of water and keeps perfectly still; so that, when the birds come and light on its snout, supposing it to be only the stump of a tree, it adroitly closes it, which it had kept ajar, and pulls the birds by the feet under water.'"[43] Surprisingly, this part of the story as told by the natives is true. Gar eat birds—not exactly common food for other fish in the lake, and an almost certain indicator that the fish the natives were referring to was a garpike.

Nicolas not only sketched a *chaousarou,* he made a drawing of a "sea monster which was killed by the French in the Richelieu River."[44] As the river is connected to Lake Champlain, could this be an early reference to Champ? His sketch resembles the mythical merman (the male counterpart of a mermaid), and is half human, half fish.[45] Most likely what Nicolas saw was from the pinniped family and could have been a seal, sea lion, or walrus seen at a distance.[46] He also drew a creature that was supposedly seen not far from Lake Champlain in "the River of Chidesak which empties into the St. Lawrence." Identified as a giant seahorse, it has the head of a horse, two front paws, and the body of a fish.[47] Was Nicolas the first European to have sketched Champ—right down to his distinctive horse-shaped head? Hardly. In 1535, French explorer Jacques Cartier sailed up the same waterway, which he dubbed the "River of Horses." These creatures were undoubtedly walruses that were known to inhabit the same river at the time.[48] His drawings bear little resemblance to modern-day images of the Champlain Monster, which are distinctly snakelike.[49]

The association between famous people and aquatic monsters is not uncommon. In the year 565, the Irish monk St. Columba is often credited with having the first recorded encounter with Nessie. But like Champlain's sighting of Champ, this also is mythical. The saint was supposedly watching a man swimming in the loch when a monster allegedly appeared and headed directly for him, its mouth agape. According to the legend, St. Columba is said to have commanded the monster: "You will go no further. Do not touch the man; turn back speedily," at which point the creature immediately stopped, then swam off.[50] The account of St. Columba's feat was written about one-hundred years later and likely never occurred, as the lives of medieval saints are filled with colorful claims of fantastic encounters with aquatic monsters. More to the point: St. Columba's "encounter," if it happened, never took place on Loch Ness, but on the banks of the River Ness.[51] Few people are aware that the first widely publicized sighting of a large, aquatic creature in the Loch was not until 1933![52] Numerous reports of the Champlain Sea Serpent were documented well over a century before this date. Between the 1870s and early 1930s, the most famous lake serpent in the world was the Champlain Monster, and accounts of his antics were reprinted in hundreds of newspapers across the country and around the world.

A MYSTERY SURFACES ON LAKE CHAMPLAIN

The first-known sighting of the Champlain Sea Serpent was published on May 18, 1808, when the New York-based *Public Advertiser* reported: "Lake Champlain—A monster has lately made its appearance on the waters of the lake."[53] It is evident that sea serpent sightings were known to the early settlers in the area, yet with newspapers in their infancy, and the early pioneers having more practical matters on their minds such as staying alive, most sightings would have gone unreported. Even if someone saw a serpent in the lake and wanted to report it, there were no telecommunications in 1808. Assuming they were literate and had the time and inclination to write, a settler would have to deliver their letter to the nearest newspaper in hopes that they would publish it—which was far from certain. Given the fear of ridicule by skeptical neighbors, many settlers may have been content to say nothing.

On Saturday July 24, 1819, there was a spectacular report of the monster on the New York side of the lake. In a letter to the *Plattsburgh Republican*, it was reported that a Captain Crum had been navigating a small scow off Port Henry two days earlier.[54] "On Thursday last, the inhabitants on the shore of Bullwaggy Bay, were alarmed by the appearance of a monster, which from the description must be a relation of the Great Sea Serpent." The letter continued:

Captain Crum, who witnessed the sight, relates that about eight o'clock in the morning when putting out from shore . . . he discovered at a distance of not more than two hundred yards, an unusual undulation of the surface of the water, which was followed by the appearance of a monster rearing its head more than fifteen feet, and moving with the utmost velocity to the south—at the same time lashing with its tail two large sturgeons and a Bill-fish which appeared to be engaged in pursuit. After the consternation occasioned by such a terrific spectacle had subsided, Capt. Crum took a particular survey of this singular animal, which he described to be 187 feet long, its head flat with three teeth, two in the center and one in the upper jaw, in shape similar to the sea-horse—color black with a star in the forehead and a belt of red around the neck—its body about the size of a hogshead with hunches on the back as large as a common potash barrel—the eyes large and the color of a pealed [*sic*] onion—he continued to move with astonishing rapidity towards the shore for about a minute, when suddenly he darted under water and had not since been seen, altho' many fishing boats have been on the look out. . . .[55]

Bulwaggy Bay (now spelled Bulwagga) is a well-known Champ hotspot and has been the scene of numerous sightings since. What are we to make of this extraordinary tale? Given the extreme detail for an object so far away, including a description of its eyes and exact length, the account must be taken with a grain of salt. How could anyone estimate the length of an object so precisely? Perhaps Captain Crum was comparing the length to that of a vessel which he knew was 187 feet long, but you would expect him to have said so, otherwise it undermines any semblance of credibility. Then there is the problem of too little detail, as we are not told Captain Crum's full name or that of the person who supposedly interviewed him. Suspiciously, the story appeared on page two! Imagine, a humungous sea serpent is spotted by a local captain in a major port community, residents are said to be excited and scouring the bay for the creature, and it does not even make page one! Many books cite this case as the first documented account of the Champlain Monster after Samuel de Champlain, yet fail to mention how the anonymous author of the article ends the letter.[56] It is signed "Horse Mackerel." What are we to make of this cryptic name?

In assessing the reliability of this case, a short history lesson is in order. The subject of real sea serpents was well known throughout the world at this time and was long accepted as an established fact. For centuries, encounters of ocean-going ships with large unknown sea creatures were dutifully recorded in their logbooks. Nautical historian Phil Reines observes that during the nineteenth century, many ship captains and naval officers attested to seeing sea serpents. "Too many reports from too many ships and certainly, a plethora of responsible eyewitness accounts over many years presented an impressive body of well-documented incidents that were accepted as fact. By the middle of the 19th century, no responsible seagoing nation doubted the existence of . . . the Sea Serpent."[57] The belief in sea serpents also was common throughout the ancient world and is even referred to in the Bible.[58] Two years before the Port Henry incident, newspapers throughout New York and New England were abuzz with reports of a sea serpent off the coast of Gloucester, Massachusetts. Although scientists have attributed sightings of the famous Gloucester Sea Serpent to everything from a ribbon of seaweed floating on the surface to a whale shark or a sea elephant, spectacular accounts from the New England seaboard would fill papers around Lake Champlain for the next several years.[59] In 1818, there were many publicized rewards offered to whalers along the New England coast for a specimen, dead or alive, and many attempts were made to obtain one; residents around Lake Champlain would have been well aware of it.[60] Amid the numerous reports of a sea serpent frolicking off Gloucester and nearby Cape Ann in spring 1817, a panel of scholars was appointed to examine the sightings and to interview witnesses in hopes of determining the creature's reality.[61] Later that year, the scientists issued a report concluding that the Gloucester Serpent was real.[62] This was big news at the time. Their findings inspired Captain Richard Rich, a legendary local whaler, to mount a famous search for the monster, which he claimed to have harpooned. His sea serpent turned out to have been a Bluefin tuna, commonly known as a horse mackerel.[63] The writer of the 1819 *Plattsburgh Republican* article was almost certainly doing so in jest and making reference to this affair. The article is even entitled: "Cape Ann Serpent on Lake Champlain," and the writer (Horse Mackerel) said that Captain Crum "had sent an express to Capt. Rich, of Boston, communicating this intelligence . . ."

After the Port Henry affair, the Champlain Sea Serpent was not seen until 1826, when he reportedly startled two young fishermen on the Vermont shore. The shaken pair said a thirty foot-long creature emerged from a cave and slithered toward them. Its body was "as round as a common saw log and covered with red and black spots." The next day they returned to find what appeared to be a trail left by the monster and a musky snakelike smell hung in the air.[64] The creature was not sighted again for several decades when a flurry of spectacular encounters would elevate Champ to celebrity status.

PRELUDE TO A MONSTER SCARE

With the completion of the Champlain Canal in 1823, and the Erie Canal two years later, the Adirondack region grew and prospered. The lake's economy was further boosted by the opening of the Chambly Canal in 1843, allowing boats to go around the Richelieu River rapids in southern Quebec, linking boat traffic between the St. Lawrence River and the northern end of Lake Champlain. These waterways, together with the building of new roads and expanding rail lines, opened the vast, unspoiled Adirondacks to the outside world as the area quickly became a magnet for tourists. With its quaint villages and pristine wilderness, it was inevitable that both population and commerce would increase. Commenting on this explosive growth in tourism, in 1886 naturalist William "Adirondack" Murray wrote: "Fifteen years ago [1871], the Adirondack region was an almost unknown wilderness. A few dozen sportsmen visited it each summer. . . . Today, 100,000 people visit the woods each year, and great hotels stand on the shores of the little lakes. . . ."[65]

During the nineteenth century, communities along the lake were experiencing an economic shift that may have contributed to a wave of sea serpent reports in the 1870s and 1880s. Historian Connie Pope writes that the iron and lumber industries were in decline at this time and entire populations were gravitating away from inland villages, dependent on logging and mining, and moving to the new railroad hubs and lake ports.[66] It may be no coincidence that with more people moving to the lake, there would soon be a dramatic upsurge in sightings. Yet, the most curious aspect of these reports remains unexplained: the serpent's fickle personality. Often years would pass without a single recorded encounter, while in other years, such as 1873, 1886, and 1887, there were more than a dozen reports each. Newspapers were no doubt a factor in fueling these flaps, either by encouraging other witnesses to come forward, or prompting residents to scour the lake in the expectation of seeing the serpent. A second possibility is that there *were* sightings during this period but they were not recorded, as people were preoccupied with the greatest social and political upheaval in the nation's history. A sea serpent in Lake Champlain would likely have seemed insignificant in comparison to more serious matters of the day: the War of 1812, the abolition of slavery, events leading up to the Civil War and its aftermath, including the assassination of President Lincoln. But six years after the end of the nation's ghastly war between north and south, the serpent reappeared in 1870, staging a performance before a steamboat excursion from Essex, New York. Astonished passengers told of seeing its head and neck rise from the water, leaving behind a forty-foot wake.[67] During the encounter, it was said that a little girl named Alma "held her ticket clinched in her teeth as she ran frightened and excited with her elders to the ship's rail."[68]

The next summer, passengers on the eighty foot-long, double-decker steamship *Curlew* excitedly spotted a mysterious creature near Barber's Point, north of Crown Point, New York. The St. Albans *Temperance Advocate* reported that it was moving "at railroad speed" and the water was "strongly agitated for thirty or forty feet from the erected head of the monster when in motion." It was too far away

Figure 1.1. During summer 1870, the serpent was spotted by passengers of the steamship Curlew north of Crown Point, New York (Jonathan Clark sketch).

to get a better description and was seen through a field glass.[69] This incident marked the beginning of a series of close encounters that would gradually escalate into a regional panic. Soon the entire lake was on monster alert. In 1873, it came, in spectacular fashion, to the settlements on the New York side of the lake.

THE GREAT SERPENT SCARE

In 1873, the Champlain Sea Serpent came of age, appearing at the southern end of the lake in a series of extraordinary sightings the likes of which have never been seen since. Whitehall, New York was then a busy commercial hub nestled at the base of Lake Champlain. It was a major regional thoroughfare for vessels delivering goods to the many village ports dotting the lake. Founded in 1759 as Skenesborough, it was the first European settlement on the lake.[70] This alone may help to explain the paucity of sightings until this time. There had been few Europeans living on or near the lake, and the early pioneers who were there were in survival mode, dodging Indian raiding parties, living through smallpox epidemics, and eking out a living in the unforgiving wilderness. In the spring of that year, work crews were "beavering away" on the few remaining shoreline sections of the New York and Canadian Railroad line that would soon link New York City with Montreal and result in a dramatic decline in the use of boats to transport goods on the lake. The episode began in the rural, sparsely populated town of Dresden, a rugged region north of Whitehall where heavily forested mountains and jagged ravines meet the lake. Deceptively beautiful yet treacherous, the area was infested with rattlesnake dens and much of the terrain was physically inaccessible. It was within this primal setting during July 1873 that a work gang, laying track, spotted a strange large serpentine creature in the water. The *Whitehall Times* of July 9 reported the incident:

> As he rapidly swam away, portions of his body, which seemed to be covered with bright silver-like scales, glistened in the sun like burnished metal. From his nostrils he would occasionally spurt streams of water above his head to an altitude of about 20 feet. The appearance of his head was round and flat, with a hood spreading out from the lower part of it like a rubber cap often worn by mariners with a cape to keep the rain from running down the neck. His eyes were small and piercing, his mouth broad and provided with two rows of teeth, which he displayed to his beholders. As he moved off at a rate of 10 miles an hour, portions of his body appeared above the surface of the water, while his tail, which resembled that of a fish, was thrown out of the water quite often.[71]

Witnesses said the creature was "twenty or more feet long, and at least twenty inches in diameter" as it skimmed along the surface for a quarter mile before dropping from sight.[72]

A contractor for the New York and Canadian Railroad, C. S. Leonard, quickly came forward with a strange tale of an encounter weeks earlier. Leonard said he had been the head of a work crew filling in a ravine on General David Barrett's property in Dresden when his workers told him of an incident involving "a big snake." Thinking little of it at the time, Mr. Leonard said that his suspicion was aroused a few days later when he found "bones, feathers and remains of a fish, which had probably been left by the monster." He thought that the creature had been trapped, or lived in the deep ravine.[73]

By mid-July, General Barrett himself told of seeing a "sea serpent" poking its head out of the water near the deck of his home. He said he ran to fetch a gun but the creature was gone by the time he returned. His son, David Barrett Jr., and neighbor, Leverett Wilson reportedly gave chase and soon spotted it "dragging its immense length across the tall grass of the marsh. It had something in its mouth which resembled a large turtle." Barrett said he took aim and fired, but the creature instantly slithered into the water and vanished. The two men described it as between thirty and forty feet long with silvery scales glistening in the sun.[74]

As news of the latest incident spread, other residents came forth with their own encounters. Two weeks before the railroad crew sighting, a fishing party from Whitehall said they were at Linley Marsh in Dresden, when there was a commotion on the lake. The startled men said a creature "arose about four feet from the water's surface" which they initially thought to have been "an enormous turtle." Meanwhile "fish were observed to spring from the water in the neighborhood, while a great wave rippled the water's surface of the marsh."[75]

Adding to the alarm was J. A. Parker of Whitehall, who related a close encounter eight years earlier. Parker said he was traveling on the highway two miles east of the village when he spotted "a large snake 18 to 20 feet-long, and as large as a man's thigh emerge from the mountain recesses and move swiftly across the fields at the rate of ten miles an hour toward Jerry Collins' marsh, and take to the water." He said the scales were also "glistening brightly in the sun."[76] The *Whitehall Times* supported his account, asserting: "Any of our citizens who know Mr. Parker know him to be a man who would make no such statement unless he had seen the snake."[77] During this time, one's reputation and social standing influenced public opinion. If the "right" persons claimed they saw something outlandish, it was often accepted as truth. After all, "a man's word was his bond" and seeing was believing.

ESCALATING FEARS

What happened next would thrust the Lake Champlain region into the national media spotlight, and locals into a tizzy. Animals began disappearing, prompting alarm that the sea serpent was snatching them. General Barrett noticed that two calves were missing from his pasture. Inspecting the field, he found what he took to be the serpent's calling card: a trail of matted grass leading to the shore. Neighboring farmers reported missing sheep and fowl, and observed that their cattle appeared nervous and restless at night, bellowing and making a ruckus. The general was so concerned that a watch was organized to keep an eye on the animals throughout the night to ensure they did not become a midnight snack for the serpent. At this point, many were in a state of near panic, surmising that the missing animals had been prey for the monster in their midst.

Local legend further fueled the atmosphere of escalating fear. General Barrett said that there had been stories of a giant serpent near his farm for at least a decade. According to one story, a cave on the nearby Chapman farm was home to a monster reptile. Residents reported seeing "bright and hideous looking eyes" staring back at them from

Figure 1.2. Artist depiction of the Champlain Monster snatching a calf from the Dresden shoreline during the Great Serpent Scare of 1873 (Jonathan Clark sketch).

the darkness of the cave, while another local, Harvey Buel said he had spotted a massive serpent in the area on several occasions over the years.[78] Above Dresden in the tiny hamlet of Putnam, where Lake Champlain and Lake George are just miles apart, the serpent was said to frequent the many dens and caves south of Gull Island on the eastern shore of Lake George.[79] A newspaper correspondent wrote that a man acting on behalf of the great showman P. T. Barnum had once entered one of these caves in hopes of capturing the creature and putting it on display at his museum. As the story goes, screams were heard from inside the cave and the man and his guide were seen rowing vigorously to the western shore, never to return. The same correspondent told of an earlier sighting by six witnesses in which the serpent was said to have been seen slithering toward Lake Champlain in the midst of an advancing forest fire.[80]

On Friday, July 25, there was a spectacular encounter by occupants of the little steamboat *W. B. Eddy*, which was reportedly struck by the great serpent and nearly overturned while en route from Ticonderoga to Whitehall. Startled passengers and First Mate Kin Holcomb said that they could see the creature's head and neck thirty yards away before swimming off at the speed of "a fast sailing steamboat. . . ." The incident occurred as they were passing the Barrett farm at Dresden. At first, it was thought the vessel had struck a log, the craft shifting violently to one side: "The passengers all made a rush to the opposite side of the boat when the vessel suddenly righted and the spectators were horrified at observing the head of a great snake rise from the water about 100 feet to their stern and spirt two jets of water high into the air." Mr. Holcomb said that as the serpent swam away, it "appeared above the surface like great waves resembling mammoth ridges of silver, as its bright scales sparkled in the sun."[81]

The incident with the *Eddy* caused a sensation as residents at the southern end of the lake near Dresden and Whitehall were on high alert. The Whitehall Harbor Inspector recalled an incident several years earlier while fishing at nearby South Bay below Dresden. Mark Doherty said that he hooked a catfish and had reeled it to within fifty feet of his boat when "the head of an immense snake . . . appeared near the catfish. As it disappeared, his line was snapped quickly" and a ripple in the water moved away.[82] He was convinced it was the serpent.

Meanwhile, sightings continued to pour in at the southern end of Lake Champlain. A railroad foreman named James McGue said he watched in disbelief as the serpent entered Blind Bay in Dresden, which extends half a mile into the mountains. Too frightened to follow after it as it disappeared into the thick brush and tall grass, McGue claimed that the creature was more than thirty feet long "and spirted two jets of water from its nostrils, and that its tail looked like the tail of a fish." He said the creature "threw it [the tail] out of the water every few seconds."[83] His description was similar to that reported by passengers on the *Curlew*.

In late July, the serpent swam to the Vermont side in Shelburn Bay (now spelled Shelburne), south of Burlington. J. P. Farmer, the engineer at the Burlington marble mill, was so moved by his encounter that he contacted the offices of the *Burlington Free Press* to recount his ordeal. He said the incident occurred on Monday morning at 10:30 while fishing near the top of the bay, not far from the George Munroe Farm nestled on the eastern shore. According to an account of the ordeal: "The water was very still and was suddenly disturbed by an unusual splashing, when he [Farmer] looked up and saw, not over thirty feet from him, an animal with a brownish body, seemingly from twelve to fifteen feet in length, and having a large head in shape like a bullpout's (a freshwater catfish). The serpent . . . disappeared under the water but came up shortly afterwards and made for the boat. Farmer then pulled away from it, and it again sank, but soon reappeared about twenty feet ahead of him, swimming towards the mouth of the bay." Mr. Farmer rowed to the shore and summoned Mr. Munroe and Amos Page. The three men stood watch for the next two and a half hours in hopes of seeing the creature, but to no avail.[84] Munroe claimed to have seen a similar creature on his farm in about February 1872, in one of his cow pastures where it was thought to have been lying in wait to snatch a fresh meal of veal courtesy of one of his calves. Munroe is said to have courageously driven the creature off his farm—no doubt to the cheers of the populace and relieved moo's of the rescued calves.[85]

Meanwhile, Patrick Childs of West Haven, Vermont, which borders Dresden, was exhibiting symptoms of "monsteritis." Childs said that he was with the party that first saw the monster and was experiencing traumatic flashbacks, being unable to rid his mind of the image of the "bright, scintillating scales" which had left an indelible impression.[86] His symptoms were characteristic of post-traumatic stress disorder—a condition that would not be identified as such for nearly a century.

Anxiety levels climbed further after more mysterious animal deaths. On July 30, the *Whitehall Times* reported that a dead horse, found the previous week at the Dresden farm of Timothy Seight, had its back broken. The serpent was the prime suspect. On the James Bagourty farm, a missing ox was assumed to have fallen prey to the creature. Three dogs that were accustomed to wandering together, one owned by General Barrett, one by his son Silas, and a third by neighbor James Tobin, went missing, prompting concern that the serpent had gobbled them up too. Their fears seemed to have been realized when the carcass of one of the dogs was found in a marsh near the Barrett sted.[87] Amid swirling rumors of a carnivorous monster slithering about the countryside, the beleaguered residents of Dresden and Whitehall were on edge.

AN INCREDIBLE TALE: OF MONSTERS AND MEN

In the midst of the monster panic that was gripping the area, enter stage right, one William A. Wilkins, editor of the *Whitehall Times*, who took the unusual step of organizing a hunting posse to track down the serpent, or so he claimed. Wilkins soon inserted himself as a key figure in the history of the monster, for what he claimed happened next reads like a script from a B-Grade "monster movie" and was almost certainly fabricated.

According to an account written by his own hand and appearing in the *Times*, after organizing the party, he received reports that the great beast was trapped in Axehelve Bay. An axehelve is another term for axe handle, and the bay resembles its name being a sharp, thin gash that juts deep into the rocks opposite Pulpit Point in southern Dresden. Wilkins wrote that he and his companions set off for the bay on the steamship *Molyneaux* and found the area choked with weeds, making it impossible to get a good view of the serpent so they devised a plan.[88] Sometime between Friday August 8 and Saturday August 9, the pilot of the *Molly*, Captain Belden, proposed that several shots be fired into the tangled clumps of swamp weeds and bushes in hopes of flushing the creature out.[89] General Barrett, in charge of the expedition, called for volley firing: "First, that the three men at the head of the line should discharge one barrel [each] of their pieces into the bay. Then, at the second order, the next three in line should discharge three more shots [a volley] in the same manner."[90]

The men soon positioned themselves on the deck of the *Molly* and began firing into the thick bush.[91] With smoke billowing skyward and the smell of gunpowder wafting in the air, the popping of musket fire began echoing through the treacherous nooks, crannies, and ravines of the Dresden countryside. In response to the shots, there was a "crackling and whistling noise." At this point, Captain Belden gave the order to steam out of the bay "as the head of the mammoth snake appeared through the tangled vines and brushwood. The greyish hood upon his head flopped backwards and forwards like the immense ears of an elephant being punished by his keeper." Wilkins certainly had a way with words! Ridges of silver could be seen protruding from the water as the creature was "undulating and scintillating in the bright sun. . . ."[92]

Wilkins reported that the creature's "fanlike tail" was waving back and forth six feet above the water. It was said to have had red eyes that resembled "burning coals" and "rows of long and formidable teeth, pearly white and wicked looking," the sight of which one eyewitness admitted, "sent an indescribable thrill through us, which we shall never forget." Wilkins wrote that the serpent's mid-section was eighteen to twenty inches thick and stretched out forty feet, gradually tapering at both ends. What he claimed happened next would stretch the credulity of even the most ardent of believers. "Our vessel began moving downstream. Shots were discharged at the great moving, waving, mass of silver. Two streams of water arose high above the monster's head, the wind blowing the spray over us on the boat." More shots rang out. The monster was said to have responded by lashing the water "with his fishlike tail, and gave great spasmodic, powerful lurches with his broad flat head." As Charles Hughes and General Barrett fired simultaneously, "the head was seen to turn" and its immense body began to curve.

"Streams of red blood spurted from its head . . . and the creature gave one spasmodic twist of its immense length, forming a circle by bringing its head around towards its tail; then the great serpent, which had caused so much excitement in this vicinity, disappeared beneath the red sea of blood."[93]

What an imagination! Wilkins' sensational tale in his *Whitehall Times*, was widely reprinted in many papers across the country, often with the more sensational parts cut out or summarized and toned down, giving it an air of authenticity. Although some local residents were quick to dismiss the account, others were not so sure, especially in light of recent events. In either case, the Champlain Sea Serpent had become a household name across the country and was the leading subject of conversation by locals, as the customary "Hello" was replaced with, "Have you heard the latest about the serpent?" Railroad crews laying track near Dresden were said to be anxious and staying close together for fear of being snatched from the shore.

During the 1870s, farmers in Dresden were notorious for their fierce independence and unwelcoming attitude to outsiders. Pulpit Point, ten miles north of the village of Whitehall, had been a magnet for campers enjoying the unspoiled outdoors. There was tension between the local farmers and campers at this time, especially when the latter decided to leave the Point in search of fish and game. *The New York Times* described Dresden as an area fraught with danger for any outsider bold enough to encroach on the local farms, and several sportsmen who had dared venture onto farmers' lands to hunt had found their precious dogs shot. This state of affairs was underscored in July of 1878, when 19-year-old Charles Long, son of prominent Whitehall physician Dr. A. J. Long, decided to venture into the area. The young Long and friend Merton Stafford were setting fishing lines late one night when there was a flash, a loud bang, and Long fell into the water—dead. At the same time, there was a voice from the woods: "There—you, you'll not steal any more of my geese!" Such was life in Dresden, New York in the 1870s.[94] General Barrett aside, many Dresden farmers would have been none too happy with Wilkins for writing his story as it resulted in a large, albeit brief influx of even more outsiders.

WANTED: DEAD OR ALIVE

Upon reading the spectacular reports out of Dresden by Wilkins and his band of monster hunters, P. T. Barnum fired off a dispatch to the offices of the *Whitehall Times*: "I hereby offer $50,000 for the hide of the great Champlain Serpent to add to my Mammoth World's Fair Show. You are authorized to draw on me for any sum necessary to assist in securing the Monster's remains."[95] Barnum routinely offered large sums for natural curiosities including exotic animals from around the world. Never one to shun the limelight and with a flair for self-promotion, Barnum entered the circus business at age 61, establishing "P.T. Barnum's Grand Traveling Museum, Menagerie, Caravan & Hippodrome." By 1873 and the serpent scare, it was being billed as "The Greatest Show on Earth."[96] A friend to the ordinary and the privileged alike, his exhibitions helped to popularize museums with the public, transforming them from lifeless displays of fossils and stuffed birds to something more exciting. Barnum was a master of astonishment who gave the public what they yearned for: bizarre creatures, curiosities, and exotic artifacts, many from little known or far-away lands. He also had a well-publicized "seedy side" and a reputation as a shrewd businessman, hokum hawker and "wheeler-dealer." He was particularly interested in exotic creatures and was not above stretching the truth if it translated into profit. At one point, Barnum blatantly displayed "the Fiji Mermaid" (often spelled Feejee) billed as "half fish, half monkey." It was later determined to have been the head and torso of an infant monkey sewn onto the back half of a fish! Barnum was always looking for spectacular animals to display, and the one that he longed for most was that of a sea serpent—dead or alive.[97]

Barnum's reward fueled further excitement on the lake as the hysteria reached fever pitch. By now, armed parties were scouring the bays and marshes in and around Dresden, while hundreds of curiosity seekers were flooding into the area in hopes of catching a glimpse of the creature. Motivated by a sense of adventure, excitement, and with visions of the reward, search parties combed the area in hopes of finding the carcass. Some enterprising residents even used grappling irons to drag the bottom of the lake for half a mile either side of the

Figure 1.3. P. T. Barnum, the great showman, offered $50,000 in 1873 for anyone who could produce the carcass of the Champlain Monster (Jamilah Bartholomew sketch).

Barrett Farm, where Wilkins and his men claimed to have slain the serpent.[98] They found nothing, of course.

Dismissing the monster sightings on the New York side, Vermont newspapers such as the *Rutland Herald* made light of the affair, ridiculing witnesses as "red neck" alcoholics: "The accounts of this 'sarpint' are sad comments on the terrible alcoholic substance that is in vogue on the banks of Lake Champlain."[99] The *Rutland Daily Globe*, no less sarcastic, wanted to know the type of whiskey that created sea monsters.[100] By late August, Vermont's *Argus and Patriot* quipped that sightings were "becoming so common that scarcely a party can go fishing, even on brooks distant from Lake Champlain without returning and startling their friends with reports of the 'big serpent . . .'"[101] Newspapers in other parts of the country took the view that there might well be a sea serpent in the lake.

Meanwhile, the offices of the *Whitehall Times* were being inundated with letters from excited citizens from all over the country. Many were addressed directly to members of the hunting party credited with killing the monster. Amidst this backdrop of excitement and fear, rumors flourished and tongues were wagging. One of the more outlandish claims was that the creature had been found, its skin removed and sealed in a copper kettle and shipped to the State Capital in Albany.[102]

The steady stream of sightings flowing from Dresden and Whitehall convinced some regional newspaper editors that there may have been some truth to the stories. For instance, in Malone, New York, the editor of *The Palladium* wrote: "The Lake Champlain papers for the past few weeks have contained repeated allusions to a monster serpent in the lake, which has been seen and described by many 'responsible persons.' We have hitherto taken no notice of the monster . . . but, owing to the persistence of the interested journals and the increasing number of the witnesses," the paper decided to reprint an account from the *Whitehall Times*.[103] The editor of the nearby *Essex County Republican* was having none of it, pointing out with glee that Wilkins and his party were "unable to substantiate their story by exhibiting a piece of the serpent. . . ."[104]

On August 10, two St. Albans men reported seeing a sea serpent while breaking in a new yacht. Sailing from Burlington to Charlotte, Vermont, Curtis Lyon and William Barker said that the encounter took place a mile off Juniper Island.[105] Five days later, twenty miles to the north, several people attending Camp Watson in the town of Milton on the Vermont side of Grand Isle, reported a strange encounter. It was Friday morning August 15, when a dozen campers piled into three small boats and set off to go fishing near Hyde Point off Grand Isle. The sky was overcast, the water still, and the atmosphere hazy. After rowing for an hour, the group in the boat led by Colonel Fred E. Smith, of Montpelier, spotted an object moving to the northeast, two miles away. One of the campers said: "At first it looked like a large black dog 'sitting' on the water. In a moment it appeared to rise, and draw more of its length from the water, until it bore more the resemblance of a woman dressed in waterproof cloak and hood." Both theories were discarded when the figure bent over and submerged. As the boaters tried to make sense of what they had seen, the object reappeared. "First there seemed to be a black dog or head, apparently looking about and making observations, then its length was drawn up to what seemed about seven or eight feet, perfectly erect, with evidently as much length still in the water," traveling swiftly southward and was soon moving at a "tremendous speed." Suddenly the object again went under the water. Once more it came into sight . . . gradually rising to its former height," staying in view for another eighth of a mile before finally disappearing for good.[106]

The climax came on September 7 when word spread that the carcass of the great serpent had finally been discovered north of Dresden. A work gang on the New York and Canada Railroad were sitting on the shore when someone noticed a mysterious floating object upward of fifty feet long and twenty-five inches thick. Suspecting it was the carcass of the creature slain by Wilkins, three boats of men quickly filled and set out to secure it, with visions of splitting the reward money dancing in their heads. Making their approach, someone shouted to get back—for the creature appeared to be still alive! They scurried back to shore, and after arming themselves with everything from pickaxes to rifles, set off again, this time in a flotilla of about a dozen boats. After slipping a noose over what appeared to be the tail, they began rowing with all their might. As the tiny vessels reached the dock, their quarry in tow, a quarrel broke out as to how the reward money would be split. Some thought that General Barrett and Mr. Hughes would try to collect the money as they claimed to have shot the creature. Others thought that Barnum would pay directly to the editor of the *Whitehall Times,* as the offer had been made to him. The men threatened to destroy the carcass if they were not in on the reward. As the debris was cleared the "serpent" soon became visible: a clump of slime and weeds entwined on one of General Barrett's dock sticks![107] One can easily imagine General Barrett watching these goings-on and having a good laugh.

This farcical incident closed the book on the Great Sea Serpent Scare of 1873. It was the tale of a monster with an attitude; a temperamental creature cavorting around the southern end of the lake poaching farm animals, ramming boats, and frightening the locals half silly. It was a restless creature who seemed as much at home slithering across fields and swamps as he did in the water, and oh how he loved to hide out in caves. After a brief respite, the shenanigans of this now nationally famous sea serpent would continue for the next two decades, for the reports of his demise in summer of 1873 were greatly exaggerated. The Great Serpent Scare is best epitomized by the words of Mark Twain: "You cannot depend on your eyes when your imagination of out of focus."

THE SERPENT, OR AT LEAST ITS TALE, RESURFACES

Don't be silly. Of course there are lake monsters.

—A LITTLE GIRL

One year after the Dresden sea serpent saga, it appeared that the creature was at it again. On July 23, 1874, a father and son from New York City thought they had spotted the elusive sea monster while fishing in a small boat off Westport Bay on the New York side of the lake. Rowing closer, they soon came face to face with the great beast, which turned out to be a seal, prompting the editor of the *Essex County Republican* to joke that residents could now breathe a sigh of relief.[1] In the nineteenth century, the presence of a seal in the lake was a feat in itself. With Lake Champlain far away from the St. Lawrence River and its access to the sea, this made for a long, arduous journey. Occasionally, seals have managed to reach the lake via the Richelieu and St. Lawrence rivers.

The serpent would not be reported for the next several years as a semblance of normality returned to the many communities along the lake. Perhaps he was emotionally exhausted from his many appearances in 1873 and his having been repeatedly shot at and rammed by boats. In either case, his recuperative powers were such that in late summer 1878, he would reappear in spectacular fashion. On August 30, several prominent citizens were sailing on the yacht *Rob Roy* off Button Bay Island in northern Vermont, when they spotted the serpent. On board was Edward J. Owen, principal of the Sherman Academy located across the lake in Moriah, New York,[2] and his friend, Dr. William Marks, a professor of engineering at the University of Pennsylvania.[3] The two men were so impressed by what they saw that they wrote a letter to the *Port Henry Herald*:

. . . a party of six left Westport in the Yacht "Rob Roy" for a sail to Button Bay Island. While returning from the island the yacht became becalmed and lay apparently motionless for some three hours at a distance of about three-quarters of a mile from the island. Not a ripple was to be seen for miles upon the water and the surface was as smooth as glass. While so becalmed, a lady in the party called the attention of the others to an object in the water, appearing to be distant about half a mile toward the Vermont shore. Without any difficulty we could discern a monster proceeding through the water at a rapid rate, having just back of the head two large folds projecting above the water, and at some distance, say 150 feet or more behind, two more folds at what was apparently the tail. As it passed along in its course, the head would go under the water and lift itself above at a distance easily discernable. The motion was similar to that of a snake, sinuous and undulating. We could easily distinguish the head as it appeared above the water and motion of the folds. Its course was from the point north of the Island to Barber's Point on the New York shore. At a little distance north of Barber's point it disappeared from sight beneath the water.

It was within plain sight for some five or more minutes. The smoothness of the lake proves satisfactorily to us that we were not deceived in believing that the object was a marine monster of some description. Of course, if we had had a glass with us, we could give a more particular account of his snake-ship. As it was we were quite satisfied that he was moving from us and not toward us and that he was far off as he was. We did not court any nearer acquaintances. We make this statement with the view of inducing other persons who claim to have seen a similar monster in the lake, to give their statements to the public. We know that others have had a like experience and while we have hitherto been skeptics as to the existence of any such creature in the lake, and have had our joke and laugh over the absurdity of any such idea, we now willingly put ourselves on record as firm believers in the being and existence of His Majesty The Great Snake of Lake Champlain.

—WILLIAM D. MARKS AND EDWARD J. OWEN[4]

In May 1879, a farmer in the town of Maquam, Vermont south of
the Canadian border, reported a strange encounter. It was but one of
a bumper crop of sightings that year. Mr. Holmes Record, whose farm
was on Maquam Bay, said he was working near shore by the main
dock with his hired man, when he heard what he thought was "the
discharge of a gun." Looking out onto the bay, they saw a creature
with a snakelike head "as large as a butter tub" moving northward.[5]
The *St. Albans Advertiser* reported that "apparently the greater part of
the monster was under water, but about fifteen feet could be distinctly
seen. . . . The body was jointed, and appeared like lumps connected
with each other by narrower sections." The creature was in view for
two hours. Mr. Record must have had excellent eyesight because the
serpent was estimated at a distance of sixty rods, or well over three
football fields![6] During the sighting, "it moved slowly, and, at short
intervals, he made a sound like the concussion of [gun] powder, followed by a loud roar." When the wind finally shifted to the north,
"the monster raised his head several feet out of the water, and, turn-
ing round, went south with greater speed, and soon disappeared from
sight." Both witnesses watched as the creature "splashed the water as
he moved along, the propelling motion being apparently concentrated
in his head and tail. He moved in undulations both up and down
and from side to side."[7] The editor of the *Lowville Times* in nearby
Lewis County, New York, quipped light-heartedly: "The atmosphere of
Maquam must have high refracting powers and the water they drink
there has a very peculiar effect."[8]

Two weeks before the incident, three residents of St. Albans, Vermont, reported a huge serpent in the lake. On the afternoon of Friday
May 9, Charles H. Harvey, L. M. Downing, and W. M. Downing were
fishing in a rowboat west of St. Albans when suddenly there was "a
great agitation of the water at a distance, and on looking towards
Butler's Island, some two miles away, they discovered that the water
was lashed into a foam." They said the water had been "dead calm"
and their first impression was that a school of fish had come to the
surface. They quickly abandoned the notion as the spot near the creature began to foam and boil. All of a sudden "the water was thrown
to an estimated height of thirty or forty feet. In the midst of it they
discovered a dark object of considerable bulk, which would rise to the

height of ten or fifteen feet for a minute or two and then go down and come up again. They pulled for the spot as fast as they could, but before they got near enough to get any distinct outline of the object, it dove out of sight . . . for another 10 minutes."[9] The *St. Albans Daily Messenger* reported: "What it was they do not pretend to say, but that it was something one or two feet in diameter and at least ten or twelve feet long, and alive and active and powerful, they positively know."[10]

On June 12, 1879, the editor of the St. Albans *Daily Messenger* published a lengthy article defending the veracity of local serpent witnesses, after the paper received a letter from a Burlington man who scoffed at the idea of a lake monster and made light of witnesses. The editor claimed that the following letter was received and published unedited:

> "I see dat on de paper 'bout a sarpint, and I knows somebody bin fooled. I see dat same ting good many time. Some time he be crooked tree, old log. Some time I see big sturgeon jump, and some loon he try to fly, he make one big splash and dive. Big snake all one dam lie. I live more dan 40 year on de Island. I see all tose tings. De man who start dat story he drink too much . . ."[11]

Figure 2.1. During the nineteenth century, newspaper editors commonly asserted that alcohol was the main stimulus for appearances of the Champlain Sea Serpent (Jonathan Clark sketch).

On Monday, September 15, Major W. W. Scranton, of Scranton, Pennsylvania, was rowing two young ladies to tiny Wood's Island off St. Albans. When they got within 1,000 feet of shore, they spotted a sea serpent moving swiftly through the water. The *Burlington Free Press* reported: "The Major describes it as being of dark color, with a head about the thickness of a man's, and at least three or four feet of body was visible at times, while it was certain that the entire length was at no time to be seen." The creature disappeared from view for ten minutes.[12] Several days later, a St. Albans woman visiting the New York side of the lake at Plattsburgh, said she saw the "lake serpent" near Cumberland Head. Her description tallies with that of the major's but she swore that she had not heard of his sighting until after her encounter. These stories prompted other witnesses to come forward to recount their sightings, such as the Henry Fordham family of Cumberland Head, who reported seeing the creature in the same area a few weeks earlier.[13]

In fall 1879, three male students from the University of Vermont in Burlington were doing what students do best: engaging in leisure-time activities—even if it was the middle of the week. On Wednesday afternoon, November 5, the trio said they were boating near Appletree Point (a needle-shaped peninsula five miles northwest of the city), when the serpent appeared. It was long and twelve feet around. The students agreed that it seemed much longer, as it was only partially visible above the water. The energetic creature swam to the south of Juniper Island, then toward Dunder Rock (a tiny nearby rock jutting from the water) and was visible for fifteen minutes.[14] At about this time, a Miss Gordon of Grand Isle came forward to say that she had recently seen the monster—or at least a part of it—the portion she saw out of water being "as long as a skiff, and as big as a barrel."[15] The *St. Albans Daily Messenger* supported her story, observing: "There certainly seems to be some ground for suspecting that the lake contains something out of the ordinary."[16] Also that November, a ferry pilot reported receiving a fright when the serpent surfaced near Barber's Point, opened its mouth and "came directly towards his scow with lightning velocity from the north bound southward."[17]

The 1880s would prove to be a busy period for the sea serpent. Sometime during the decade, a young man said he was fishing on the lake with his uncles when they had an encounter with a sea serpent feeding on a school of perch. The man, nicknamed Rufus, would later write about the experience as a columnist for the *Tupper Lake Press* in 1934. He said he went on frequent fishing trips with his uncles on the Bouquet River near Wadhams several miles north of Westport. "On one of those trips we had run into an unusually large school of perch. We couldn't get our hooks and lines into the water fast enough and soon had more perch than we could carry home." It was then that a "sea serpent" appeared, "moving about among the small fish and evidently feeding on them. . . . At times the huge undulating body would appear above the surface and the great head would dart down into the water, evidently catching fish for food." He said the "monster" disappeared after the perch dispersed. According to Rufus, his uncles became the butt of jokes after recounting their experience with what some said was a piece of floating wood so they stopped talking about the incident.[18]

During summer 1880, two residents from Quebec Province, a Dr. Brigham of Phillipsburg and Mr. Ashley Shelters of Bedford, reported seeing a sea serpent in Missisquoi Bay on the extreme northern end of the lake. They said the creature was at least twenty feet long, although other portions appeared to be submerged. The head was as big as "a flour barrel," had an "irregular shape," and had eyes "of greenish tinge."[19]

MYSTERY OF THE PETRIFIED SEA SERPENT

In September 1881, a remarkable story swept across the New York communities on Lake Champlain. The body of a "petrified sea serpent" was reportedly discovered at the Champlain Granite Works north of Westport on Barn Rock Bay. The proprietors claimed that the mammoth fossil was eight inches in diameter, fifty feet long, and was found embedded in granite and dirt. The *Springfield Telegram* provided a detailed description: "The surface of this stone bears evidence of the outer skin of a large serpent, while the inner surface shows the entrails. Holes dug at distances of sixty feet, show that it is lying in a serpentine form, under some great upheaval of the earth, worked its way through among the rocks in a winding course, until bound fast.

It is over 100 feet above the level of Lake Champlain, in the side of a Mountain of the Adirondack range."[20] Today, University of Vermont geologist Dr. Charlotte Mehrtens believes the report to be a hoax, noting that the description is "highly dubious because of their reference to finding it in 'granite and dirt' [and] there is also *no way* soft body tissue such as 'entrails' would be fossilized or preserved in any way."[21] The university's head of environmental studies, Mary Watzin, concurs with the hoax theory. "I don't know anything about this supposed fossil, which makes me think it is indeed a hoax. I agree—if it did exist, it would be right up there with the Charlotte whale," Watzin observed.[22] Geologist Pat Manley of Middlebury College also is skeptical.[23] If anyone would know about area fossil finds, Mehrtens, Watzin, and Manley would.

The following year, the *Elizabeth Town Post & Gazette* of June 8 reported that stories "of finding a monster in the limestone deposit of the 'North Shore'" were well known in the region. What followed next was an incredible claim that during summer 1880 a group of people including "scientific gentlemen" went to a cottage at the Granite Works in an effort to confirm the fossil's existence. After some hesitation, the quarry superintendent escorted them into a room.

> On the carpet in an upper room lay six or seven feet in length, pieces of an enormous petrified snake. Some portions were six inches long and some fifteen or more. The pieces were placed together and fitted so nicely that there was no room for doubt of their having been broken apart. The largest end was eight or nine inches in diameter, and only three or four feet from the terminal of the entrails, and two or three feet beyond. The entrails were petrified, but much darker and quite open or porous and containing many bright and glistening crystals. The vertebra was visible at each broken end, and the flesh part showed traces of what had at one time been veins.

The astonished members of the party were allowed access to the remains for a full hour, and thus were able to give a detailed description. The paper continued:

"The skin was readily distinguished from the flesh as would have been had the monster been cut in two whilst living. After an examination of each piece, and comparing the gradual enlargement of the cavity, thickness of flesh and skin on the belly, and the gradual thickening towards the back, left no room in my mind to entertain the thought that it was an accident or freak of nature with molten rock. During this hour of examination at the south side of the window with bright sunlight, the Superintendent had sat quietly and had said nothing but answer a very few questions. I said I did not want to be inquisitive, but would like to know in what kind of rock he was found and his general position. He said he was not in the rock but was merely attached to the limestone, and his position was as if he had placed himself for rest or sleep, and he had traced his body by actual measurement over sixty feet, and his weight to several tons when all removed." The superintendent reportedly told the group that in due time, members of the scientific community would be invited to examine the remains in more detail.[24]

This account is suspicious for several reasons. First, the writer indicates that stories of finding a fossilized "monster" at the quarry were common and may have represented a type of urban legend. Given all of the lake monster sightings at this time, the supposed find of a sea serpent would have been a logical and believable story. It is claimed that scientists would soon be invited to make a thorough study of the remains and publish their findings, but this never happened. What harm would there have been in doing so? If the fossil was genuine, the Granite Works had everything to gain and nothing to lose. Furthermore, none of the scientists asking to see the find are named—and neither is the superintendent or the journalist.

Researcher Jonathan Downes has found a later reference to the "fossil" in *The Burlington Free Press* of November 4, 1886 and reports that it was on show at an exhibition in Vergennes, Vermont and "is recorded on page 39 of the exhibition's catalogue." Downes says that it was reportedly bought by P. T. Barnum and was to be displayed at his museum. "From then on the specimen seems to have vanished. Searches of Barnum's records have so far been fruitless. Barnum's collections were twice ravaged by fire but both of these incidents were before he bought the remains."[25] The authenticity of the "petrified serpent" is almost certainly a hoax given the dubious presence of soft body tissue and that nothing on it appears in science journals. As if that was not suspicious enough, there are no sketches or photographs, and the "fossil" itself has conveniently disappeared!

The inspiration for the petrified serpent hoax may have been the discovery of the Charlotte Whale. In 1849, railroad workers constructing the first train tracks linking Rutland, Vermont with the city of Burlington, Vermont to its north, unearthed massive bones in a field near the small town of Charlotte on Lake Champlain. The discovery of the remains of a beluga whale, surprised scientists who soon figured out that it had once swum in the Champlain Sea thousands of years earlier. The find/received considerable fanfare at the time and was described in several prominent science journals. The "sea serpent" skeleton "find" of 1881 may have been a hoax intended to capitalize on the hoop-la surrounding Vermont's most famous fossil—for if as the whale once did, a serpent was still frolicking in the lake, it was logical to deduce that there must be fossils. In 1993, its luster had not faded when the legislature named the Charlotte Whale the official state fossil. Why would the whale receive such attention from the scientific community while the Westport fossil was ignored? There is one logical answer: It was a hoax.[26]

In 1881, the same year as the supposed fossil find, the daughter of the Reverend John Enright claimed to have witnessed a long serpent from the rear deck of a steamboat sailing out of Swanton, Vermont. She said the creature startled her by its sudden appearance close to the steamer, seemingly following in the ship's wake. Ms. Enright informed the pilot, Warren Rockwell, and the two looked on in amazement. As if sighting the sea serpent was not enough for Ms. Enright, she was utterly shocked by what happened next: Mr. Rockwell pulled out a gun and shot at it, at which point it disappeared![27]

The *Plattsburgh Sentinel* of September 28, 1881, reported that three Burlington students were sailing between Apple Tree Point and Juniper

Island, when they spotted the serpent "making directly from the Island to Port Kent. It was upward of seventy-five feet long, "its head standing out of the water at times from four to six feet."[28]

During summer 1882, the *Sentinel* reported that a Mr. Davis of Grand Isle, Vermont, had a sighting of the serpent while standing on the banks of the lake with a neighbor. After becoming the object of ridicule, an agitated Davis contacted the *Plattsburgh Sentinel* to state *emphatically* that *no*, he had *not* mistaken a passing steam yacht for the creature and that any such conjecture was absurd. Mr. Davis lived near Center's Wharf and said that he was intimately familiar with the lake. He said that the creature made a sound similar to "the bellowing of a calf" and that he rushed to the shore to see a forty foot-long sea serpent lashing about and heading toward shore. The animal was distinctly seen, "as it was not more than forty feet from the shore. It raised its head from the water and made a bellowing noise not unlike the sea lions seen in menageries [zoos], and then moved off, making the same noise while under water, its wake being distinctly visible." He soon turned and ran to summon his family and neighbors, who "hastily gathered their guns and proceeding to the shore saw the serpent disappearing in the distance. . . ." Some suggested that they had seen the tiny steam yacht *Sallie*, and the "bellowing" was in reality, its fog whistle.[29]

Three months later and some twenty miles to the north, two ladies from St. Albans reported an encounter during a visit to High-gate Springs, two miles below the Canadian border. They said "they saw the serpent's head, and saw him dive, saw a long white line as he performed a double somersault and revealed his side."[30] The St. Albans *Messenger* amusingly quipped that when two local ladies of high repute spot the sea serpent, "it is about time that volunteers were called on to capture the 'varmit.'"[31]

THE MOONEY SIGHTING

In summer 1883, one of the most credible sightings in the history of the Champlain Serpent saga took place. On Saturday afternoon, July 28, Clinton County's top lawman, County Sheriff Nathan H. Mooney, reported a remarkable sighting. Mooney told of seeing a large snakelike creature near Cumberland Head. He had left Thomas' Landing on the *Nellie*, a small steam yacht, at 5 PM headed for Plattsburgh. While rounding the Head and one-hundred yards away, he saw a black object protruding five feet out of the water, as big around as a stovepipe. He said the water was calm. Certain of what he had witnessed, Mooney had no qualms in reporting it: "I asked the master of the yacht . . . if there was any buoy ahead of us. He said that there was not. Then it occurred to me that it was a log. Suddenly, when we had cleared two thirds of the distance it disappeared." Soon after, Mooney was glancing off to the northwest when he again saw the creature, this time twenty yards away. His description is one of the most detailed ever recorded: "I then discovered that it was an enormous snake or water serpent . . . with a long jaw, a snake-shaped head, at least eight inches across at the top or flat part, and ten inches from the top of the head to the end of the jaw. The serpent was half a mile inside of Cumberland Head, and the same distance from the shore. Its body, which must have been twenty-five or thirty feet in length, was pointed to the north."[32] Mooney said he was close enough to see the muscles in its neck contracting. He said the neck was curved, resembling "a goose when about to take flight."[33] Inside its gaping mouth were circular white spots.[34] The *Nellie* pilot supported Mooney's testimony.[35]

After the Mooney encounter, on Wednesday August 1, the *Whitehall Times* editor William Wilkins published an account of the incident under the headline: "Our old friend re-appears—We thought he would turn up again—It's the same old snake, strawberry mark and all!" This amused the editor of the *Plattsburgh Republican* who printed a humorous response to Wilkins and suggested it was the same creature that Wilkins himself had created from his own imagination and purportedly shot back in 1873, during The Great Monster Scare. He wrote: "Wilkins . . . was the first editor in this portion of the state to 'interview' the Lake Champlain sea serpent . . . [and] therefore claims to be its rightful owner, by 'priority of invention,' as it were."[36] Getting in on the act, on August 24, a skeptical *Plattsburgh Sentinel* reported that the "Champlain Sea Serpent" had appeared during the week on a bay off Charlotte, Vermont: "He had the same old familiar crested head, and created great commotion in the water as he disappeared from view. Ducks, we'll warrant you!"[37]

Several days later, while at the helm of the excursion boat *The Water Lily,* none other than the famous Captain "Phil" Daniels (1843–1929) spotted the serpent. Nicknamed "Captain Phil," Daniels' full first name was Philomène, and *she* had a reputation as a savvy, no nonsense pilot. Four years later, she would become the first licensed female steamboat captain in the country, a real life version of the famous fictional "Tug Boat Annie."[38] The encounter took place in the evening as she was running the vessel into Otter Creek northwest of Vergennes, Vermont near Fields Bay. The *Plattsburgh Sentinel* reported that her attention was drawn to a twenty foot-long object that she initially thought was a log. But, as the vessel nearly reached the object, "it dove and passed under the boat, coming up on the other side and immediately disappearing." The creature dove with such force that it splashed water onto the vessel.[39]

In early August 1883, there was speculation that the creature had gone on summer holidays in Canada when a large sea serpent was spotted in the Richelieu River, which empties into Lake Champlain. The *Plattsburgh Sentinel* reported that it was seen near Iberville. "The monster is described as having a huge head, large flaming eyes, and the body ten feet long. When seen it was playing round one of the piers of the bridge. They gave it chase, but it was soon lost sight of . . ."[40] At about the same time, residents in Sheffield, Vermont, about sixty miles to the east of the lake, claimed to see a twenty foot-long sea monster in tiny Bruce Pond, just one-hundred acres big.[41]

Sometime that same year, Dr. P. A. Wheeler was driving south of the iron bridge on North Hero Island in Vermont when he noticed a commotion on the lake. He stopped his buggy along West Shore road to get a closer look. A third party would describe the encounter four years later in a letter to the *Plattsburgh Republican*: It seemed to be "stranded in the shallow water, lashing the surface to foam in its struggle to get away. After a short time . . . it rose out of the water to a height of three to four feet. The exposed part which seemed to be the head and neck of a large animal was cylindrical shape from eight to ten inches in diameter and of a dark color." Dr. Wheeler said he was close enough to see its eyes. While the creature was still in sight, he got back onto his buggy and drove to a nearby house where he raised the alarm. By the time he and others returned, it was moving out of sight, leaving a discernible wake in its path.[42]

The creature would take another hiatus and it would be two years before it was reported again, during summer 1885. The encounter was recounted in a letter to the *Plattsburgh Republican* by a respected businessman of Willsboro Point, Mr. E. Brown, the proprietor of The Green Mountain View Home, a popular summer resort.[43] He related that Mr. A. Drew and Mr. Fuller of Chesterfield were in a rowboat, fishing in Willsboro Bay when Mr. Fuller spotted "a huge log" in the water and noted, "that log is worth saving." As he began rowing out to retrieve it, the "log" suddenly disappeared.[44] That December, Mr. Brown said that he was looking out over the lake when he saw what he took to be, at first, a steam yacht crossing over from Burlington to Port Kent on the New York side of the lake. He stated: "when I first saw it, it was between me and Apple Tree Point, as I stood in my door yard. The speed of the object was so great that I called the attention of others to see it, it looked from our place like a steam yacht as large as the 'Florence Witherbee' would [be] from the same place and looked as though it was painted white." Mr. Brown related that the object was moving "four times the speed of any yacht I ever saw." It continued to move along on a "course for Port Kent until it got out near to the middle of the lake and then disappeared all at once," surprising the onlookers.[45]

As always, some residents continued to make light of the reports by claiming outlandish reports themselves. A letter to the *Swanton Courier* in mid-July 1886 is one such example, when George Atwood wrote with "tongue in cheek," of a sighting in the early morning sun near Dead Creek in extreme northern Vermont. "His body was out of the water about 14 feet, his head was well up and his great red tongue kept licking his chops as if expecting a breakfast on the healthy camper; his eyes, as big as powder kegs, glowed wildly; and his teeth looked like polished steel, and his horns were bright and brass mounted, a kind of whalebone mane run down his neck and a big buzz saw ornamented his breast. Scales as big as milkpans ornamented his sides, and his nickel-plated tail was feeling the air for bald eagles." Letters such as this made witnesses think twice before attaching their names to sightings and opening themselves up to potential ridicule.[46]

THE SECOND GREAT WAVE: 1886–1887

Over the next year, the floodgates opened with a wave of sightings up and down the lake. Historian Connie Pope captures the flavor of the period and the intense press coverage it received:

> Reliable, trustworthy men witnessed its appearances, for the newspapers gave space to none but those best known for honesty. They came from all walks of life—doctors, business men, navigators, clergymen, salesmen, schoolmen, and gentlemen. All testified to its existence, having seen it floating, frolicking, or fleeing through the waters of the lake. It appeared in every part of the lake, north and south, east to west. It was seen close to shore, in mid-channel, and twice on dry land. It looked like a serpent, like a large Newfoundland dog. Like a whale, like a log, like a seal. It defied description. It was observed in the morning, at noon, in the evening, under a bright moon, and at 2 o'clock in the morning. Its observers shot at it, chased it, threw stones at it . . . hooked it with a fishing line, flailed it with an oar, shrieked at it, and two claimed to have caught it.[47]

When three men reported seeing the serpent at Cumberland Head in mid-August 1886, the editor of the *Plattsburgh Sentinel* noted humorously that it was seen by a "party of three." The trio was standing on the wharf of the Plattsburgh Dock Company on a calm, sunny morning when twenty rods off shore they saw a creature fifteen feet long with its head and neck two feet above the water as it swam. The head was estimated at fifteen to eighteen inches in length. One evening three days later, three men fishing off a Plattsburgh dock reported hooking the sea serpent on one of their lines while it was taking a leisurely swim. Connie Pope describes what happened next: "Being unequal to the task of hauling it in he cried for help, and his two companions set their brawny backs to pulling with him. Together they raised to the surface the head of a horrible creature, at which point the line broke and the creature disappeared." A third party confirmed their account.[48]

On September 10, 1886, the *Plattsburgh Sentinel* reluctantly reported on the sighting of the serpent by a Massachusetts man camping somewhere on Lake Champlain. Under the heading, "Nonsense," it noted that although the man claimed to have seen the creature through field glasses, a "glass in hand" was "about the only way a sight of the sea serpent can be enjoyed."[49]

In October, the *Plattsburgh Republican* reported on two recent sightings. The first encounter involved a St. Albans man duck hunting at the extreme northern part of the lake near the Missisquoi River. The paper said that as daylight broke, "he saw but a short distance away an enormous serpent coiled up on the swampy shore. . . ." The creature appeared to be sleeping. It was "as large around as a man's thigh." When "he reached back to get his gun and in doing so made a slight noise the serpent reared his head fiercely and ran off toward the tangle of undergrowth, making as much noise, as he went crashing through the bushes, as a large hound would."[50] It is assumed that the word *ran* was "code word" for slithered as there was no mention of the creature having legs!

The second incident involved a husband and wife on a leisurely ride in a horse and buggy along Cumberland Head. They tied up the horse and began strolling along the beach when their attention was drawn to a strange object in the lake: A creature with a snakelike head and neck protruding eighteen inches out of the water. The man, not knowing what to do, picked up some loose stones and began throwing them at the serpent, which swam off.[51]

By mid-October, the *Plattsburgh Sentinel* placed a small article on its front page offering a $1,000 reward "to any person who will bring to this office, dead or alive, the Lake Champlain sea serpent." There was but one stipulation: The creature had to measure at least twenty feet in length.[52]

THE SERPENT GETS A PUBLICIST

On Wednesday December 1, 1886, prominent businessman Solomon W. Clark of Willsboro Point was with several people when they spotted a serpent roughly one mile off the Point that was "about the length of the steamer Vermont."[53] The *Boston Journal* reported that the "water foamed as he swam along with great speed and strength, and

sometimes he threw the water 20 feet into the air."[54] The creature was
first spotted by Mrs. Clark from the roadway, moving rapidly southward
against a south wind. Startled at the strange sight, Mr. Clark raced his
team of horses at top speed to the nearby Blinn residence. Mr. Byron
Blinn and his wife, Valorus, were witnesses to the spectacle. Amid the
commotion, a Willsboro physician, Dr. Stebbins, joined the onlookers.
The group watched as the figure disappeared southeast of Essex near
Thompson's Point.[55]

Spring 1887 would mark the beginning of a "monster year" for
monster reports, which followed fast and furious. On Monday May
2, Lewis Smith was working at a home on Willsboro Point, when he
heard what he thought was the sound of a steamboat and ran down
to the lake hoping to catch a glimpse of either the *Reindeer* or *A.
Williams*. Looking out from the shore between Willsboro Point and
the Four Brothers Islands, he was amazed to see a large serpent. His
boss was none other than Solomon W. Clark, who operated the Clark
limestone quarry on Willsboro Point. He later described the incident:
"He then beheld towards the islands a mile or more distant" an object
the size of a barrel, and "about the height of a man, with head dark,
and white below the water. It was moving rapidly southward, but soon
dived, but reappeared after a minute, changing its course toward the
shore to the west. It produced the same noise, much like a steamboat,
and throwing the swells each way, and causing a tremendous foam."
A minute later it vanished. Mr. Smith was described as "truthful and
trustworthy,"[56] being the son of local Civil War veteran Thurman E.
Smith who belonged to the local post of the Grand Army of the
Republic (GAR), the country's first national veteran's organization.[57]

Mr. Clark had been keeping a local tally of serpent sightings. He
described a number of previously unreported incidents that he was
aware of in the vicinity of Willsboro alone. All of these reports had
gone previously unreported in the press, once again highlighting the
likelihood that most nineteenth century reports likely never made the
papers. Clark wrote a lengthy letter to the *Plattsburgh Sentinel*, pointing
out that some twenty years earlier, the late Renback Smith and Mr. A.
A. Rand saw a huge sea monster in the lake that was moving at great
speed. He also observed that seventeen years ago "some fifty men left

their work in our quarry and rushed to the end of Lagoneer Point [now Ligonier Point], to see what they termed a whale, or big fish, moving with great speed by the Point. . . ." He continued:

A year or two later Mr. John French and family, living on the Essex Road, [at] the old Hoffnagle place, saw a monster, resembling a large tree, as they described it, with raised head moving south against a strong south wind, with great force and speed. Both Mr. French and wife, now residents of Willsboro, have told me as they saw it.

About 1875, Mr. Charles N. Wood, and Rev. J.W. Sands saw a strange looking stick or log, described by them as a tree with the bark on, some 35 to 40 feet in length, laying out on the water near Clark's dock, and Wood went for a boat to go for it; returning, found it had disappeared. He believed it a living monster.

In the autumn of 1882, Mr. George Wilkins and his wife, residing on the well-known Boynton Farm, near Willsboro Bay, saw something which they described similar to the sight we saw December last, and moving northward out of the bay with alike described rapidity.

Mr. Frederick Fairchild, living near the Bouquet River, reports having seen something which looked like a large New-foundland dog, in the early season of 12 years since, on the day of the steamer *Vermont*'s first trip south [he undoubtedly was referring to the *Vermont II*], some miles distant towards and westward of the steamer. It moved much the faster of the two and presently dived, reappearing soon, changing its course for a time, and then disappearing and not seen again.

Mr. John M. Ferris and his wife a few years since saw something monstrous also, near the mouth of the Bouquet River.

Mr. George French, son of the above named French, re-ports having seen something monstrous to him while fishing, decidedly frightful, but seemingly not dangerous.

All these and many other witnesses, including Mr. E. Brown, of Willsboro Point, whose statement of his observations appeared in the Plattsburgh Republican, only go to prove the certain existence of a monster, if not a family of them, in this lake.

I am truly yours,

—S. W. CLARK[58]

Solomon Clark was the first person to systematically record sea serpent sightings on the lake. Along with his brother Lewis and father Orrin, they operated a well-known quarry at Ligonier Point in Willsboro that mined "bluestone" used in the Brooklyn Bridge and the Champlain Canal. He was a man held in high regard, and was the creature's strongest advocate, sending letters promoting the existence of the Champlain Monster to such papers as *The New York Times*.

On Tuesday May 3, 1887, male clerks working for both the Port Henry Ore & Iron Company and the Lake Champlain and Moriah Railroad spotted the great serpent off Cedar Point near Port Henry. They said it was forty to fifty feet long "and as large around as a stovepipe. The head appeared as large as a [railroad] switch target" and was moving southward.[59] During the first week of May 1887, there was another sighting of Champ by a farm boy near Willsboro. Upon hearing strange noises coming from the lake at 2 AM, he ran to the

Figure 2.2. In about 1870, some fifty workers at the Clark Quarry rushed to the shore of Ligonier Point at Willsboro, New York, to see a massive creature "moving with great speed . . ." (Jamilah Bartholomew sketch).

shore and surveyed the water. A mile out was a serpent-shaped object as thick as a rain barrel, making sounds like a steamboat.[60]

THE ADIRONDACK MURRAY SAGA

On Friday May 13, 1887, under clear, calm conditions, word spread through Burlington that the Champlain monster was putting on a show near Juniper Island. Throngs of people packed into Battery Park to watch the aquatic display, which lasted three hours. Witnesses described it as undulating through the water at a rapid pace. Upon seeing the commotion, famous outdoorsman William "Adirondack" Murray looked on as someone shouted, "'There he is! There he is!'" Murray recalled: "And sure enough right in front of me not two miles away, the lake being scarcely rippled, the air clean as plate glass, I beheld the sea serpent, and I must say that the spectacle was truly a most startling one." During a lull in the action, Murray was able to retrieve his binoculars and began to focus, but found it difficult as the object was moving so rapidly before losing sight of it. "Nobody, I said to myself, could ever move through the water as fast as that thing is going." Suddenly a shout: "There he is; there he goes again!" And the "serpent" reappeared. To Murray's astonishment, peering through his binoculars, he saw what appeared to be a flock of short-billed plovers flying just above the lake surface, giving the appearance from afar, of a giant sea snake. Murray explained the deception, noting that they "were flying in a long line, which swung up and down and to the right or left as they flew. The under side of their wings and breasts was snowy white; their backs were slaty brown." From one angle "they were flying at such an angle as regards the gazer that the under side of their wings and breasts were seen, the serpent long and white appeared. When they took some slant at another angle their backs and upper side of their wings were turned toward the gazer, the white line faded out and the monster seemed to sink from view," explaining why the "creature" appeared to quiver. "The quick flutter of their little wings in long line extended, the gradual swoop up and down in their flight, made the appearance perfect. His motion being the motion of quick-winged birds cleaving the air and not of an aquatic monster rushing through the water."[61]

Adirondack Murray was William Henry Harrison Murray (1840–1904), a well-known figure in Upstate New York and nationally during the second half of the nineteenth century. Murray was a major celebrity and had a huge following. A Yale graduate and minister, his writings on spirituality and outdoor life helped to popularize the Adirondacks and Lake Champlain with such books as *Camp Life in the Adirondacks* (1868) and *Adirondack Tales* (1877). His books were credited with drawing scores of tourists to the region and his name carried weight.

Many residents cried "fowl" of Murray's bird theory, countering his observation with sightings from other prominent residents, some of whom also had field glasses and saw something very different on the lake that morning. One such was a Dr. C. S. Boynton. Upon learning of the excitement in the bay, Dr. Boynton climbed atop a nearby roof with several gentlemen and began scanning the lake with binoculars. Before long, he spotted "a long, grey line" off Rock Dunder, Vermont, waving on the surface "hither and thither" like some huge marine monster at play. Suddenly, it moved northward "at railroad speed" while leaving a trail of white foam. When the object was opposite Rocky Point, the trail of white changed direction "and came directly toward us." As the object came to within a quarter of a mile from shore, it rose and sank in a manner "much like the somersault of a porpoise." Dr. Boynton was adamant that the theories suggesting the object was an illusion created by birds were ridiculous. "The theory of a flock of geese or ducks is worthless, because when the subsidence disappeared or stopped, I examined the surface of the water at the spot through a glass and no living object—fowl or otherwise—could be seen though the glass was so powerful that it was available thrice the distance." Dr. Boynton said that he was convinced he had seen a "submarine monster, possibly the much discussed Lake Champlain sea serpent."[62] When Murray's bird explanation appeared in *The New York Times*, Solomon Clark grew irate feeling that many locals were being made to look foolish. Clark wrote to the *Plattsburgh Sentinel* and the *Times* to complain that local residents could certainly tell the difference between a flock of birds and a sea serpent, and what had appeared that day in the Burlington Bay *was no flock of birds*.[63]

On Wednesday May 18, the feathers continued to fly in the Adirondack Murray affair. Winford C. Morhous of Willsboro Point spotted a mysterious object north of the Four Brothers Islands off Burlington, between a quarter of a mile and a half mile east of Willsboro Point. It was as big around as "a full-sized barrel" with its head appearing to be above the water. He called to his parents and their servant girl, who all glimpsed the creature and "the swells it put in motion and threw each way, like a vessel swiftly moving through the water." Morhous said the object was moving "much faster than the fastest steamboats" before disappearing from view.[64] He reported having recently seen a flock of plovers, similar to those described by Mr. Murray, and had no trouble distinguishing the difference between something extraordinary and birds—a thinly veiled jab at Murray.

LOOK—A BABY SEA MONSTER!

As the Adirondack Murray saga was dying down, another debate was brewing with claims of a baby sea serpent being captured. On Saturday May 21, 1887, newspapers along the lake were abuzz with news of a strange find near Plattsburgh, where local soldiers claimed to have captured a baby sea serpent while fishing. It was described in the *Plattsburgh Sentinel* thusly: "The fish or reptile, which is the *first ever seen here*,[65] is about 14 inches long, and has a broad, flat head, a trifle arrow-shaped, something after the style of the famous Lake Champlain sea serpent. It has four legs and the remainder of the body is like that of an eel in shape and color. The head is about two inches broad. Three feathery tufts like prolongations from the mucous membrane projects from the upper part of the throat, passing out thro' openings in the side of the neck. It is a very queer looking reptile . . ."[66] The creature was later identified as a *menobranchos* or Great Water Lizard.[67] In August 1887, Dr. D. R. Byrum of Keeler's Bay wrote to the *Burlington Free Press* claiming to have captured a "baby sea serpent" after pulling up a "something" weighing 175 pounds. Its head, back and side were jet black, contrasting with a white underbelly. The eyes were small and the nose was hooked. The weird-looking critter was feisty and able to whip the water into white foam. Although it was not long enough to claim the reward money offered by Barnum or the *Sentinel*, it was almost certainly a species of known fish, and a few weeks later it was on display at the local fair.[68] Vermont folklorist Michael Lange views this, and other baby serpent stories to follow, as significant because it frames the creature as being of the natural order, whereas many early accounts gave it quasi-supernatural qualities. For instance, the encounter claims by both Captain Crum and Whitehall *Times* editor William Wilkins, sound like something from a 1950s Godzilla movie.[69]

"A MILK AND LEMONADE SERPENT"

On July 9, 1887, residents from East Charlotte were holding a leisurely Saturday afternoon picnic on the Vermont shore when they were startled by a commotion on the lake. It was first spotted from behind a headland—a high, narrow area jutting into the water—in full view of everyone present. According to a *New York Times* reporter, it had a "flat, serpentlike head, and portions of its body were visible at times, while a long trail of agitated water to the rear indicated that a large proportion of its body" lay below the surface, with the full length estimated at between fifty and seventy-five feet. Its body was judged to have been as big as a barrel or milk can. The creature undulated towards the shoreline "at a terrific rate of speed," but within a few hundred feet of the shore some of the women began crying out and causing the serpent to make a rightward motion and submerge. One of the witnesses—a minister—said that none of the party had been drinking anything stronger than lemonade and milk.[70]

A few days later, a farmer living near the southern end of the lake related that he was "pulling" a load of hay to his barn when he chanced to look behind him. What he reported, if it is to be believed, is nothing short of astonishing. He claimed to see a fifty foot-long sea serpent, "gliding along like a snake with its head raised about four feet from the ground." It was no more than thirty yards away. He said it was "gray with black streaks running lengthwise of its body which was covered with scales." As he shouted out to his farm hands back in the field, he said the creature suddenly changed course and slithered into the thick underbrush. The man was not about to follow the still wet trail.[71]

By mid-July, 1887, Mr. O. S. Barnum, the secretary of the Port Henry YMCA, reported shooting at "the Lake Champlain sea monster" at Westport. The Plattsburgh *Sentinel* reported that as he was watching a yacht, the creature "rose and lay upon the water, the waves rippling against it as if it had been a log. Occasionally the end which resembled the flat end of a snake, would rise, and the mouth like that of an alligator be visible." He then pulled out a pistol and fired, at which point "the animal disappeared, leaving the water in great commotion."[72]

During the last week of July 1887, several people claimed to have spotted a "sea serpent on the west side of the lake" north of the Split Rock ore bed.[73] Amid the flurry of sightings during summer 1887, in early August P. T. Barnum reiterated his offer to pay a reward for anyone who could produce the body of the creature—so long as it was a minimum of fifty feet in length. This time, the amount was $20,000 cash, a full $30,000 less than the offer he had made for the same serpent in 1873. Barnum told a reporter for the *New York Sun* that he hoped the money would motivate fishermen on the lake to be more vigilant. "I think when they make a systematic search with boats and Gatling guns, and know that there's $20,000 backing up their guns, that there will be no trouble in getting the creature." Gatling guns! Barnum was certainly no tree-hugger. He was a practical, hard-nosed businessman who wanted to display a fifty-foot sea serpent and did not care how he got it. He stated that if found, the body or carcass was to be taken immediately to his agent in Bridgeport, Connecticut.[74] So much for the sanctity of life! During the 1880s, Barnum had a standing policy of paying $20,000 for the carcass of any sea serpent, so long as it met the length requirement, and was "in a fit state for stuffing and mounting."[75]

On August 20, five residents of Charlotte, Vermont, were in a rowboat opposite Deer Point when they reported seeing the serpent sixty yards away. It appeared twice and was "at least 15 to 20 feet in length."[76] Later that month, the *Plattsburgh Sentinel* reported that "a farmer saw the monster near Miller's Marsh, north of Ticonderoga, New York. He reports it as being 30 or 35 feet long, with a head as large as that of a big dog." He said that it swam from the Ticonderoga area to the Vermont side of the lake."[77]

The following year the serpent seemed to take the year off and began cutting back on his appearances through the rest of the century. In mid-September 1889, a party from Shelburn, Vermont, was fishing near Juniper Island when they noticed an agitation in the water twenty yards off.[78] A "huge fish or serpent" emerged with "many large fins, and head, well out of the water." Witnesses said that at least fifteen feet was above the waterline but its body seemed to be much longer. As it swam swiftly southward the water was "boiling" in its wake. The group gave chase but the creature soon disappeared.[79]

THE 1890S

In 1891, the "sea serpent" was part of a hoax perpetrated by one Lafayette Seavey on unsuspecting members of the American Canoe Association (ACA) at its annual meeting on the lake at Willsboro Point. Seavey, who earned a living by making and managing theatrical props, and a co-conspirator constructed a "float" that resembled the monster and subtly towed it from the end of a canoe.[80] On August 17, the *New York Herald Tribune* reported: "The canoe camp was startled to-day by the arrival of the Lake Champlain sea serpent. It was about fifty feet long" and rose "six feet above the water." The pair felt an obligation to create the serpent as they were members of the *entertainment committee*.[81,82]

Later that same month, the creature was seen on several different occasions at the southern end of the lake in South Bay near Whitehall. A watchman at the draw bridge there, Michael Dunn, had the best view. According to the *Whitehall Times*, on Monday night August 24, Dunn "was sitting in his shanty when he heard a great noise in the water and rushed out. The space between the docks of the draw bridge is about eighteen feet wide. The water was churned up and spattered over the timbers of the bridge. The moon was shining brightly and Mr. Dunn could plainly see up the bay for a considerable distance the wake made by the monster whatever it was. He then made a careful examination and found that the water had been thrown for considerable distance on some timber that lay near the bridge, and that it was fresh water, as all around it was dry."[83]

In 1892, the ACA was again having its annual gathering on the northern end of Lake Champlain when several canoeists paddling near Valcour Island reported seeing a "sea serpent."[84] Unlike the encounter of the previous year, there was no evidence of a hoax. The sighting frightened the canoeists, "scattering the flotilla in every direction."[85]

Not to be outdone, that same summer, there was a *mass* sea monster sighting near Burlington, two miles north of Basin Harbor. Captain Moses Blow (circa 1863–1927), a noted navigator of numerous vessels on the lake, was at the helm of the 132 foot-long (40.2 m) steamship *A. Williams* when the incident occurred.[86] The time was 2 PM. One of Blow's daughters recounts the story: "They were at anchor and all of a sudden the boat started rocking, and they couldn't imagine what in the world was the matter and they're looking all around when all of a sudden, the head, then the neck came out of the water and it looked right straight at them, and then he [the captain] said, 'Let's get out of here,' and then they headed for Burlington. . . ."[87] Among the passengers were several scientists who were attempting to measure the depth of the lake and had reached in excess of four hundred feet without touching bottom. The water temperature was recorded at a chilly thirty-eight degrees. Vermont folklorist Joe Citro continues the story: "The scientists told Captain Blow that if anyone drowned there, they would never come up—the pressure would hold the body in place." In a strange twist of fate, Captain Blow's brother Charles Blow, and nephew Harvey Blow, later drowned near this very spot and their bodies were never seen again.[88] Citro speculates that the depths and cold temperatures may explain why no one has ever found a carcass of the monster.[89]

One day in fall 1894, Luther Hager and his son Timothy grew alarmed. They were returning to their Cumberland Head home from a trip to Plattsburgh on Monday September 17 when something caught Mr. Hager's eye in the shoals east of the Head. It appeared to be "the bottom of an overturned skiff floating just inside the reef" but it seemed odd that he could not discern any oars or oarlocks. Fearing that someone could be in trouble, the Hagers galloped home, hooked up a team of horses, and headed to the shore. Meanwhile, a farmhand named Frank Dominey from the nearby Mastic stead, noticed "a great commotion in the water." His account of what happened next sounds like it came from the pages of a Jules Verne novel. He said that the churning water moved toward shore and a creature emerged, moving six feet onto the shore. Terrified, Dominey ran back to the farm to summon his employer, Ephraim Allen, who arrived only to see the object disappearing beyond the reef. Not long after Mr. Hager arrived and was so affected by the incident that he stood on shore watching for the creature until 11 PM.[90]

In September 1894, Mr. L. M. DeLamater of Flushing, New York (which is located on Long Island), sighted the monster off Cumberland Head with his family. At the time, there was speculation that the creature in question was a "sea dog," a commonly used term of the period referring to an array of small marine creatures, most commonly a seal. One local resident claimed that at this time, it was not uncommon to see seals in the Gulf of St. Lawrence and in the Bay of Fundy, both located to the north of Lake Champlain, the assumption being that one of the critters had made its way down into the lake. It was observed that such creatures were "at home on land as well as in water, and will frequently sail along in company with a boat until startled and frightened."[91] The *Plattsburgh Sentinel* concluded that the creature was in all likelihood, a sea dog, but the rival *Plattsburgh Republican* was skeptical of the seal theory, observing that it could be anything from "a sea dragon or sea elephant or sea cow or sea lion," although a sturgeon was seen as the most likely candidate.[92] During the first half of the nineteenth century, two seals had been seen in the lake frolicking off Cumberland Head; among the witnesses was the Reverend Charles Hagar, who would later also suggest the seal theory to explain the sea serpent sightings.[93]

MAN VERSUS MUSKRAT

Some skeptics have pooh-poohed the existence of the serpent by observing that during most winters the lake freezes over, and assuming it is a mammal, it would not be able to breathe. In April 1895, Harry Tabberah of Cumberland Head claimed to have solved the mystery. While out on the ice on January 29, he noticed a curious mound of ice eighteen inches in diameter, mixed with clamshells and weeds. Peering into the hole, he could see clear to the lake bottom and saw numerous partially eaten clamshells. Tabberah speculated that this may have been the creature's "ventilator or breathing hole." That evening, while visiting the site, he said there was a great swashing sound coinciding with a pungent fishy smell. The *Plattsburgh Republican* made light of this, noting that Mr. Tabberah also had seen "hair" near the hole, and suspected that his monster was a muskrat. The *Republican's* commentary was published under the "humiliating" headline: "How are the Mighty Fallen. The Champlain Sea Serpent Dwindles to a Muskrat."[94] Some readers were clearly miffed by the paper's demeaning tone. Several days later, a man who had accompanied Mr. Tabberah to the hole, wrote to say that it was no muskrat! Based on the noise made under the ice, the strong smell and vigorous swashing, he said there was but one conclusion: It was none other than the sea serpent using a "breathing hole" to survive the winter.[95] Of course, how does one know what a sea monster smells like, or for that matter, what sounds it makes?

A SERPENT ON ICE

Three months later in early spring, the St. Albans *Messenger* reported on an amazing find by a resident of Shelburn, Vermont. This individual claimed that he was on the ice near the Four Brothers Islands on the New York side when a mysterious object was seen *in* the ice. Upon closer inspection, he and a companion claimed to have found a large serpentine creature frozen solid. "With the aid of his companion, he scraped away the crust from the surface of the ice for a distance of 20 feet and revealed a portion of the remains of what he thought must be a gigantic sea-serpent which had become frozen into the ice near the surface and which stretched away no one knows how much farther than he had uncovered." If it *had* been a sea monster, it would undoubtedly have made the person finding it rich. As nothing more was ever heard of this "find," it is reasonable to assume that it turned out to be either the carcass of a known fish—such as an eel, a sturgeon, or a garpike—or it was a hoax.[96]

In early November of the following year, Joseph Barker told a harrowing account of a "sea serpent" that jostled his boat while fishing off Grand Isle east of Plattsburgh. Barker stated that he had paddled into Keeler Bay when he was startled by a mysterious something that jarred against the bottom of his boat three separate times, at which point he spotted "the slimy tail of the monster curled up over the stern of the boat, lowering the craft in the water and threatening to swamp it." According to Barker, the serpentine creature had a flat head and disappeared into the lake after he picked up an oar and whacked it.[97]

On August 5, 1899, it was reported that a prominent New York couple, who wanted their names withheld, saw what appeared to be a sea serpent thirty-five feet long. They observed it in the middle of the narrow channel between Split Rock Lighthouse and the Vermont shore—one of the deepest parts of the lake. The witnesses said that the creature was half a mile away and swimming slowly. "The serpent's head appeared . . . broad and flat—something [like] the shape of one's hand as laid flat on a table. The water washed over its neck, which it was therefore impossible to make out. The body, as far as visible, had the shape of a low arch." Its tail was broad and flat and "protruded from the water at right angles to the body,"[98] extending several feet out of the water.[99] After fifteen minutes, the creature suddenly sank from view and the surrounding waters "seethed and bubbled as when a large and heavy body sinks beneath the waves."[100]

During the nineteenth century, Champ was a sea serpent with an identity crisis and would have been a prime candidate for the remedy of the day: psychoanalysis. It was seemingly trying to be everything to everyone. Its eyes resembled a peeled onion; others swore they were green, another—red. One account describes them as small and piercing; another had them as being the size of dinner plates. It had fins; it had no fins. It had ears resembling those of an elephant, a palm leaf; it had no ears. Its length ranged from 14 inches (a baby serpent) to 187 feet. Its skin had scales. It was alligator-like. It was smooth. It was white, silver, black, brown, and gray. It had spots; it had no spots. It had one hump; it had four humps. The head was flat; it was round. It resembled that of a snake, an eel, a Newfoundland dog, a seahorse, a seal, and a catfish. It moved at railroad speed. It crept along at a snail's pace. It was stationary. It had two horns resembling moose antlers; it had no horns. On at least four occasions it spurted water high into the air, but was mostly well behaved. Its body was fifteen feet above the water; it was barely visible on the surface. Its tail resembled that of a fish; it tapered like a snake; it had no tail. Several times it rammed boats but on most occasions was well mannered. Its eating habits were irregular and it appeared to be on a high-protein diet. It was believed to have dined on turtle, catfish, horse, ox, sheep, fowl, and dogs. It made a sound like a steam whistle, bellowed like a sea lion, even crackled, but most of the time it politely passed through the water without making a peep.

It was seen on the beach, in caves, slithering across fields, and under the ice. Its remains were supposedly found *in the ice*—frozen solid, and in limestone, but the body or what remained, always vanished before it could be secured. Above all, it was elusive.

In the coming century, the creature would fall from grace and play second fiddle to an upstart in Scotland and continue to have an identity crisis after receiving a series of new nicknames. But during the second half of the century he would regain his swagger relishing his new role as the center of attention of an annual festival, as the mascot of a semiprofessional baseball team and as the center of a scientific conference. But more than anything else, he had a flair for the dramatic and a penchant for controversy—qualities that would serve him well as he vied for supremacy in the lake monster world with a new media darling from Loch Ness.

THE COMEBACK CRITTER
The Fall and Rebirth of a Legend

It is important to believe in yourself—even if others don't.
—THE AUTHOR

During the first three decades of the twentieth century, the Champlain sea serpent continued to reign supreme in the world of lake monsterdom. During this time, the creature was able to break his fetish for land and was spending virtually all of his time in the lake. Although the number of reports was nothing on the scale of the latter nineteenth century, the "monster" bobbed its head above the water with sufficient frequency to stay in the spotlight of journalists. That would change in 1933 with the first modern-day report of Scotland's Loch Ness (Nessie) "monster." Although sightings of what would soon be called "Champ" continued, they became more of a regional phenomenon within New York, New England, and adjacent Quebec province. Britain's colonial past would play a part in Champ's decline. In 1933, when Nessie sightings began to appear in key British newspapers, the articles were routinely reprinted in papers throughout the Commonwealth and its vast number of colonies, territories, and protectorates, which numbered several dozen and held nearly one-fourth of the world's population. It was a ready-made international audience. Outside North America, few people were aware of Champ's existence, as memories of its heyday in the 1870s and 1880s were all but faded. Even its popular new names—the Champlain monster and Champy—were derivatives of its more vogue Scottish counterpart. Champ had been eclipsed as the world's foremost lake monster.

But all was not lost. From the 1930s to the 1950s, Leon W. Dean, professor of English at the University of Vermont, helped maintain awareness of the serpent by collecting stories from his students and the public. During the 1960s, two researchers at what is now the State University of New York at Plattsburgh, maintained the legend of the Champlain monster. By 1981, there would be a scientific conference devoted to the critter. A string of television documentaries, the establishment of a semiprofessional baseball team (the Vermont Lake Monsters), and an annual "Champ Day" festival followed these developments.

In 1900, the "Champlain sea serpent" began the new century by appearing twelve miles south of Burlington, Vermont, near Cedar Beach. It was Wednesday morning, July 18, when Mrs. William E. Hagar looked out onto the still waters of the lake and noticed a single "white cap." Three other people witnessed the spectacle: her son Clifford, and Mrs. and Mrs. Everett Towne. They said the head was large and resembled more of "an animal than a serpent" and rose "several feet out of the water. . . ."[1]

In 1901, there was a sighting twenty miles to the north at Colchester Point south of Grand Isle, Vermont. On Tuesday morning, September 17, the *Plattsburgh Republican* reported that "Two young Burlington men whose good habits are vouched for were passing Colchester Point . . . when they saw what they believed to have been this monster floating on the surface of the water and in an instant disappearing. They stoutly declare that they were both sober and the thing is described by them as sprawled out" and of great length.[2]

A HOAX OF MONSTER PROPORTIONS

In 1904, there were several sightings of a mysterious sea serpent in nearby Lake George, which is connected to the southern portion of Lake Champlain and lies a few miles to the west. This led to speculation that the monster had bolted for bluer waters off the more luxurious resorts of its wealthier sister lake. In reality, the sightings were a hoax; the creation of one Henry W. Watrous, a prominent New York City artist with a summer residence on Lake George, who enjoyed hob-knobbing with the rich and famous of Gotham. One of his friends was Colonel William Mann who published *Town Topics*, a popular New York society scandal sheet. The notion that the serpent could access Lake George through an underwater cavern was common during this period, and there were reported encounters in the lake dating back to the 1870s.[3]

Watrous owned a cottage at the north end of the lake and Mann had a residence on an island resort nearby. Watrous and Mann had an ongoing wager as to who would catch the biggest trout in the lake. One day, as their boats were passing, the colonel held up a massive specimen appearing to weigh between thirty and forty pounds. When Watrous learned later that the object was a painted piece of wood shaped like a trout, he was determined to even the score with the old boy.[4] On the week of June 27, while the colonel was on business in New York City, the artistic Watrous used a cedar log to fashion a "sea monster" or, as he called it, a "hippogriff," a legendary creature that was the offspring between a griffin and a horse. "I made a big mouth, a couple of ears, like the ears of an ass, four big teeth, two in the upper and two in the lower jaw, and for eyes I inserted in the sockets of the monster two telegraph pole insulators of green glass."[5] "The idea of using those insulators for eyes was a stroke of genius," Watrous later recalled. "All witnesses of the sea serpent thereafter, told of the baleful effect of the glare of the sea-green eyes. . . . I painted the head in yellow and black stripes, painted the inside of the mouth red and the teeth white, painted two red places for nostrils and painted the ears blue."[6] The log itself was some ten feet in length, at the bottom of which was attached a thin rope that ran through a pulley that was attached to a stone anchor. The pulley line was one hundred feet long and was controlled from the shore.[7] An elaborate contraption indeed.

Knowing Mann's routine, Watrous and his chauffeur anchored the hippogriff along the route that the colonel's boat would have to travel to reach his island. After finding a hiding place on shore, the two men "went out in a boat and dropped the stone anchor, sinking the monster out of sight. Then we rowed back to shore and suddenly let go of the pulley rope, with the result that the cedar log, because of its buoyancy, jumped out of the water for almost its entire length." Even though he was the creator of the serpent, Watrous remarked that even he was startled the first time he ran the fake monster through its trial run. "The rope being twisted going through the pulley gave the head of the monster a sort of twisting motion so that it appeared to be looking from side to side, and occasionally turned entirely around as if to survey the scenery from all angles." After testing the contraption several times, they submerged it and waited for the unsuspecting colonel and his party to leave in the launch one Saturday afternoon.[8]

On this occasion, Mr. Watrous set himself to enjoy the surprised reactions of the guests. "The Colonel had as his guests Mr. Davies, Mrs. Bates and several (others). . . . Hidden behind a clump of bushes on shore I watched as the launch approached and just as it was about ten feet away from my trap I released the monster. It came up nobly, the head shaking as if to rid itself of water . . . it was a very menacing spectacle." Watrous could hardly contain himself when watching the pandemonium that followed: "Mr. Davies, who had a rather high-pitched voice, uttered a scream that must have been heard as far away as Burlington, Vt. Mrs. Bates . . . stood on a seat in the boat and beat the water with her parasol, shouting indistinguishable sentences in her native tongue." Mann could be heard shouting, "'Good God, what is it?' through his whiskers and kept repeating his query as long as the boat was in sight." Watrous did not want to push his luck so he and his chauffeur pulled on the pulley to send the monster contraption under the water. That night, news of the encounter involving the fake monster and Mann's party spread rapidly and people all along the lakeshore were abuzz about the incident.[9]

Throughout that summer, Watrous and his partner in crime moved the monster from place to place under the cover of darkness, to perpetuate the hoax, prompting several other frights. On one occasion, the monster popped up in front of a canoe carrying two newlyweds. "With one glance at the vision and utterly ignoring his bride, the young man leaped into the lake, struck out for the shore and disappeared in the woods. When he sought to make up with his bride, she refused to see him,"[10] or so the story goes. It was not until after one victim reportedly suffered a heart attack from the shock of seeing the "monster," that Watrous decided to permanently remove the serpent from the lake for fear of causing further problems. The practical joke had scared too many people and Watrous did not want to be found out, as the sighting prompted *The New York Times* and several other New York City newspapers to dispatch reporters to the lake in search of the serpent.[11]

At the height of the scare, Watrous noted that many of the summer residents on the shore had African American servants who were frightened by the reports. "Within a few days you couldn't see a Negro within a mile of the lake shore, and many of them departed without leaving a trace." As the hippogriff lay hidden in Watrous' dusty barn, people's imaginations took over. The imaginary creature was said to have left for nearby Lake Champlain as at about this time, several witnesses "swore that they saw it swimming in a sluiceway leading from Lake George to Lake Champlain," Watrous recalled.[12]

In July 1905, Watrous struck one last time with "Georgie" by scaring the bejesus out of two boys who were in a canoe that overturned as it neared the contraption, which was lying in wait. While scrambling to right the boat, they were startled to see a spout of water shoot high into the air. At this point, the boys reported that "a great head appeared above the troubled water, its large green eyes sunk deeply in the head,

Figure 3.1. "Georgie" was the creation of Henry Watrous who caused havoc on Lake George between 1904 and 1905 by scaring boaters with his wooden lake monster operated by pulleys (Paul Bartholomew Photo).

fins or ears the size of a palm leaf fan and horns like elephant's tusks, which stuck out from the sides of the monster's mouth." One of the startled boys grabbed a paddle and, being still in a panicky state, reared back and swatted it. They said the creature swam away, but not before getting in a retaliatory swat, striking the canoe with its tail and sending it flying once more, the boys bobbing in the water, grasping for the boat. They reported that the creature was thirty to thirty-five feet long![13] It was an incredible story, and probably doubted by many, but in this instance the excited boys were telling the truth, although slightly exaggerated with all of the adrenalin pumping through their bodies. The hoax was not revealed until April 24, 1934.[14]

A decade would pass before the next reported sighting, once again highlighting the most perplexing aspect of the monster: its absence for years on end. On Wednesday April 14, 1915, several people reported seeing a "sea serpent" off Bulwagga Bay in Port Henry. It was first seen through binoculars and appeared stranded on the reef at the Bay entrance not far from the Crown Point fortifications. Others would later suggest that it was sunning itself.[15] It was described as forty feet long and soon managed to get free "after a few wild plunges which lashed the water into foam. . . ." The creature then "headed for the Vermont shore in great semicircular sweeps, finally sinking, submarine-fashion, leaving a wake which was well defined on the glassy surface of the lake." One theory proposed by locals was that because the lake water was exceptionally low, the serpent was wandering far afield in search of food. Some residents believed that the creature's normal resting place "is in the deepest part of the lake opposite Essex."[16] The "reef" referred to is the old railroad "fill" that once connected Port Henry with Crown Point. In 1870, a 250 foot-long draw boat was built, complete with a rail track, which allowed the freight train to cross the lake at Bulwagga Bay. The thirty-four foot-wide draw boat was floated into place, forming a temporary bridge connecting two fixed trestles on either side of the lake.[17]

In 1918, Frank Burrough was flabbergasted when the creature made a sortie near his boat on the southern end of the lake. Mr. Burrough was intimately familiar with South Bay in the town of Whitehall, where he lived in an isolated cabin. His decision to go fishing that day would leave an indelible impression on his memory. He said that the bay was still and the creature's body so wide that it could not have been a sturgeon. "There was a sudden upheaval" of water. "It was of immense length and of a ridge of fins 15 feet long and six feet apart on the back. Its skin was smooth, not scaly and it had a round head with jaws like an alligator." It disappeared after twenty minutes.[18]

On the morning of July 24 1918, a mysterious object spotted near the Burlington breakwater caused a sensation as excited spectators lined up along the waterfront to get a closer look. The *Plattsburgh Daily Republican* reported that animated discussions "raged as to whether a sea serpent or a German U-boat on the way to bombard New York was in the offing." The object peeked above the water several times over the span of five minutes, about one mile off the breakwater where "it could be distinctly seen with a white spray thrown on the sides."[19] The *Adirondack Record* later made light of the incident and the initial witness who was fishing at the time, observing: "When asked how long the sea serpent was the dazed fisherman replied he didn't know for sure, but that it had taken it an hour and twelve minutes to swim by him."[20]

THE PROHIBITION YEARS

To the dismay of many skeptics, sightings continued even after the ratification of the 18th Amendment ushered in the prohibition on drinking and transporting alcohol between 1920 and 1933. Ivan Blaney of Windsor, Vermont, wrote a letter to *The North Countryman* recalling a sighting that he had in 1921 at Rouses Point, New York.[21] While fishing with several friends off a dock opposite St. Patrick's Church, Blaney said that they spotted what they thought was a "large bottle" floating in the lake. "Since the fish were not biting very well we decided to spend some of our surplus energy in throwing stones at the innocent appearing object. . . . One of the fellows almost scored a direct hit on the 'bottle' and, to our amazement, it disappeared under the surface of the water and several long snaky coils arose in its place." They dropped their gear on the spot and raced back to town.[22] That same year, a woman from Winooski, Vermont was watching a bridge-opening ceremony from the deck of the *SS Ticonderoga* when the serpent rose to the occasion, lifting his head "as if to salute."[23]

The following year, on October 8, a wealthy New York merchant, Edward Hatch Jr., announced that he was donating his property, the Four Brothers Islands, to the New York Zoological Society as a refuge for the study of bird and fish life on the lake. At the press conference, the society also announced that one of its goals was to capture a specimen of the "serpent of Lake Champlain." Should the creature be captured, it was to be taken to the New York Aquarium on Coney Island for New Yorkers to view. The aquarium also would be stocked with a variety of Lake Champlain fish species—with the serpent being No. 1 on their most-wanted list.[24]

In early September 1925, there were several sightings of a sea serpent in nearby Upper Chateaugay Lake west of Plattsburgh, leading to speculation by those who had seen it that there was a subterranean passageway linking Chateaugay with Lake Champlain. Jack Davis first observed the serpent near "the island." That sighting was followed by several more in Bellows Bay by such respected locals as Andrew Baker, Will Reynold, and L. D. Morrison. The paper speculated that there might be an "undiscovered underground passage which he (the serpent) may have found his way from one lake to the other as Jules Verne's celebrated Nautilus passed through the earth. . . ."[25]

During fall 1928, two men missing from a disabled sailboat were believed to have drowned off Essex, not far from Split Rock. When divers were unable to locate any trace of their bodies, despite intense efforts to comb the waters, thoughts turned to the sea serpent. Local residents had long believed the spot, located in one of the deepest parts of the lake, to be the home of the Champlain monster, leading to speculation that the creature may have eaten the men's bodies after they drowned. Rumors of a carnivorous serpent flourished when *The Adirondack Record* reported that search divers had told of "a hole or cavern near the Vermont shore which is unfathomable and that efforts to sink a plummet to the exact depth have been unsuccessful. A tremendous current of water draws in and out of the hole alternately and every known scientific instrument used for deep sea soundings has also proved ineffective." A more likely explanation is that the cold temperatures at such depths slows decomposition and the production of gases that ordinarily cause bodies to float to the surface.[26]

On Sunday, July 14, 1929, three young men fishing on the lake claimed to see a serpentine creature emerge from the mouth of the

Boquet River near Willsboro Point, New York. What happened next sounds like a scene from the film *Free Willy*. They said that the creature burst through the water, holding its head in the air. Thomas Bridge of nearby Willsboro, and two friends, Davis Riley and Wesley Quimby, reportedly looked on in amazement as the monster began flailing its tail with such violence that a sea of foam was created for several acres. Bridge stated that the sight of the creature agitating the water scared him so that he turned and ran, not stopping until reaching the village store a full two miles away! As for his fishing companions—they scattered. Bridge had described himself as a devout skeptic on the subject of lake monsters—that is, until his encounter, and he vowed never to go back to the spot.[27] Some locals speculated that the incident had occurred because the lake's water level was unusually high at the time. They theorized that the deeper-than-normal river levels may have induced the creature to explore the stream "and he became stranded on the sand bar formed at the mouth of the river."[28]

Also, in 1929, there was discussion of Dr. William Beebe (1877–1962), the world's foremost undersea explorer, coming to Lake Champlain on an expedition to search for the creature. In July, newspapers reported that a group of sportsmen from northern New York would sponsor the expedition, which was steeped in secrecy.[29] So secret in fact, that the spokesman insisted on remaining anonymous. "The reason for the secrecy is that if it got around who was going and who was putting up the money for a sea serpent hunt," he said, "the whole expedition might be laughed out of existence."[30] If captured alive, it was to be rushed to the New York Aquarium; if dead it would be stuffed and donated to the New York Museum of Natural History. The plan was to spot the creature from the air using a special plane and then quickly move Beebe and his bathysphere into position. The expedition never went ahead.

SERGEANT, I'D LIKE TO REPORT A SEA SERPENT . . .

Champ laid low during the Depression years, perhaps because in the eyes of newspaper editors, sea serpent sightings did not seem to matter given the gravity of the times. He appeared in September 1934, when two boaters claimed to have seen a strange aquatic creature north of Plattsburgh and reported it to the police. It is difficult to know what was going through the mind of the desk sergeant—after all, what could they expect the police to do: don diving gear and attempt to make a maritime arrest? Unless the creature had beached itself, there is little the police could do but to make a record of the incident. After all, appearing to boaters is not an arrestable offense. This is how the *Tupper Lake Free Press* described the incident: "The Lake Champlain serpent has been seen again—this time by a Plattsburgh man. Willis Jarvis . . . walked into police headquarters the other day and told Sergeant L.L. LeVasseur of the state police that he had just seen a monster which he believed to be a large lake serpent, off the shore of Point Au Roche, a few miles from there, in deep water. Jarvis said he was in a rowboat with Earl Gonyea, 150 feet from shore, when they saw a large object bobbing about in the deep water not far out. Jarvis reported that he could plainly see the head and a large fin sticking out of the water. The strange creature moved up and down the lake . . . [and] was about 40 feet long."[31]

During the same year, the editor of the *Plattsburgh Daily Press* told of an undated sighting by an area man named Bill Parker, who had "made an affidavit as to having seen the Lake Champlain sea serpent." He said that the creature was one hundred feet long with "the circumference of a sewer pipe and a head like a barrel, [and] eyes like two dinner plates." Parker stated that the mouth was three feet long and had "rows of glistening teeth which looked as if they might have come from an old-fashioned harrow [from which] protruded a forked tongue about the size of a crowbar."[32]

May 1934 marked yet another claim of a baby sea serpent being caught, this time by a St. Albans fisherman who pulled out a hideous-looking creature from Lapan Bay, described as a cross between a sea serpent and a lizard. Joseph Briere took the strange-looking critter home and was displaying it to neighbors where it was being kept alive in a large bowl. "It is about 11 inches long and colored brown with black spots. Its round body, which is smooth instead of scaly, tapers back from an ugly flat head shaped not unlike that of an alligator with a large mouth and small eyes set far forward in the snout. It has four legs about an inch long with claws." The most bizarre feature was the back of its head, which was said to have "six little sprouts which can best be described as celery plants with red fuzz for foliage." It was almost certainly some type of lizard or salamander.[33]

In late winter 1936, an ice fisherman from Malone, New York, also claimed to have captured the Champlain monster. Fred Fellion told the *Malone Farmer* that he pulled up a strange-looking creature weighing eighteen pounds, eight ounces. The critter was said to be sporting foot-long horns. Local fish experts dismissed the idea of a baby serpent, instead suggesting that what Mr. Fellion had caught was either a cowfish or a salt water catfish that had somehow made its way into the fresh water lake.[34]

That summer, Captain Johnny Blair reported seeing a sea serpent off Chimney Point. The *Plattsburgh Daily Press* would not report the encounter until July 30 of the following year. Blair was piloting an oil tanker that was heading south on July 15. As luck would have it, a deckhand had come up from below to speak with the captain when the serpent appeared. Blair would later describe the encounter: "We saw it [for] about 10 minutes, traveling north. We estimated its length to be 60 feet and the height eight feet. It had sharp scales along its back, blew like a whale, had broad, large flippers and the body . . . [which was] covered with hard skin."[35] It was a remarkable sighting observed by reputable witnesses at close range. It is difficult to imagine two experienced sailors misinterpreting a splash for an aquatic creature spouting water. This description also is consistent with many earlier accounts.

MOOSE-LIKE ANTLERS AND ELEPHANT-LIKE EARS

During late summer 1937, the serpent made three dramatic appearances on the New York side of the lake. All three sightings are remarkable for their detail and close proximity to the witnesses. The first incident was at the south end of the lake near Whitehall, the other two were fifty miles to the north at Rouses Point.

On the morning of July 12, three "old-timers" from Whitehall insisted that they saw the serpent while fishing off the lake pier. Gene McCabe, "Coots" Gordon and Pat Harvey said they were startled when a huge creature fifty feet long, suddenly emerged from the lake near the Stafford boat landing. They said it had a "flowing red mane" and eyes the size of dinner plates. There were two protuberances on its head that resembled those of the antlers of a moose and elephant-like ears. The editor of the *Ticonderoga Sentinel* was clearly skeptical, noting that "[t]hen slowly it sank, ears and all." The *Warrensburg News* of July 29 said that the encounter coincided with rumors that the serpent had snatched a calf of South Bay farmer Oliver "Bunyan" Neddo. The second incident occurred in August when Mr. and Mrs. Andrew Weston saw a mysterious-looking creature not far from the Lake Street shore in Rouses Point, where they got a good view of the head and back. The head was dog shaped, the ears protruding above the water. The section of the body that was visible was black and as "big around as a telephone pole."[36]

In September, there was yet another sighting near the first encounter—but more dramatic, as the creature reportedly rammed a boat! On the afternoon of September 2, one of the most *remarkable* modern-day encounters with the Champlain sea serpent took place at Rouses Point. It was broad daylight, the water was calm and the witnesses—a well-respected local couple—would view the creature at point blank range; so close, they could have reached out and touched it. Charles J. Langlois, a local electrical appliance dealer, and his wife piled fishing gear into their sixteen-foot outboard motor boat and headed for the Rouses Point Railroad Bridge. As Mr. Langlois began to throttle down to three or four miles per hour, they were trolling in the channel a quarter mile below the bridge. His wife began casting when suddenly, ripples appeared on the water. Charles was not overly alarmed, assuming that a school of fish was "playing near the surface." According to a newspaper account, "The ripples moved toward their boat and the water grew agitated. "Thirty feet in front [of them] a giant form emerged from the water [moving] toward the little craft. Mrs. Langlois screamed; her husband jerked the tiller [motor] and the form struck the side of the boat, swerved sharply and disappeared under the water."[37]

Badly frightened, the jittery pair headed back to shore where Mrs. Langlois was so shaken that she was ill for the next several days. Mr. Langlois would later describe what he saw for *The North Countryman* of September 9, 1937: "What we saw was the back. . . . It was traveling toward us and was looped out of the water at least 15 feet long. It was black, without scales, as thick through as a large telephone post, and it traveled through the water in loops like a snake. We didn't see a head or tail. When it hit the boat it jarred it considerably and swerved it from its course. I judged it was making between four and six miles an hour. It churned the water and left a wake like that made by a small boat."[38]

Despite such credible reports, there were enough circulating stories making light of the sightings to caution some residents to think twice before making their encounter public. A humorous example appeared in November 1937, when *The North Countryman* told what at first sounded like a serious story of a 173-pound sturgeon that had jumped out of the water and became lodged inside the open door of a railroad freight car as it traveled along the lake. As the story goes, a customs inspector named Bill discovered the giant fish while examining the car at Malone. The inspector claimed the fish then whispered in his ear: "Is this Rouses Point? Tell the folks they finally got me!"[39]

Figure 3.2. During the latter eighteenth and early nineteenth centuries, there were numerous reports of the Champlain Monster ramming boats. Artist depiction of a close encounter by Jonathan Clark.

THE WAR YEARS

During World War II, the sea serpent seemingly did his patriotic bit for the Allies by not causing a stir and scaring the home side. The sudden "disappearance" of the creature for years on end, broken by a sudden resurgence of reports, may have a social explanation. For instance, in May 1945, a local newspaper editor observed that the creature "has been unreported since the outbreak of World War No. 2 and the theory is that hardworking newspaper editors have had headlines a-plenty as a result of Hitler's ill-fated attempt to upset the universe back in 1939."[40]

There were other possible wartime sightings. In 1943, Charles Weston of Rouses Point visited his brother's nearby summer home and began to relax on the porch when his repose turned to disbelief at what he was seeing on the lake. A large creature was using its fins to agitate the water, leaving behind a motorboat-sized wake. Weston grabbed a pair of field glasses and watched in awe as the creature headed toward the shoreline near the Windsor Hotel, before veering east and disappearing.[41] Also, sometime during the mid-1940s, several people who were spending the summer on Cumberland Head, east of Plattsburgh, were startled by a serpentine creature. Miss Minerva Stoughton said that it was a beautiful day, so she and some friends decided to relax on the porch of the Thompson Camp. They were taking in the lovely view of the lake, looking eastward, when the dark creature moved near the shoreline. But when the onlookers became excited and began making noises, it veered away toward Grand Isle.[42]

In 1946, the sea serpent was seen again at Rouses Point. The wife of Henry Augins, a customs inspector, was boating with several friends when she saw the serpent's head rise briefly above the water before suddenly disappearing. The encounter took place in the evening of June 25, two hundred yards from shore and only one hundred yards south of the home of Rufus King. The creature disappeared suddenly but was estimated to have been eighteen to twenty feet long. It caused the lake to churn and made a "bulge" in the water "caused by the rate at which it was traveling."[43] Mrs. Augins was the only person to see the serpent poke its head above the surface. By the time she raised the alarm, the others were only able to see "the enormous wake it left as it sped through the water near the surface and toward the shore."[44]

Not taking any chances, the boat was quickly rowed to shore. Mr. Chevalier, a worker for *The North Countryman* newspaper, was also on the boat.[45] The story may have never made the paper had he not been on board, underscoring the likelihood that many sightings—perhaps most—go unreported.

In February 1947, the *Whitehall Times* reported that a local man named George Rich claimed to have pulled up a "baby sea serpent" while ice fishing with tip-ups on South Bay. The odd-looking critter weighed fourteen pounds, and measured four feet, three inches long and seven inches in diameter. "It had a ridge of fins along its back, a mouth full of sharp teeth and a round head like a turtle. Its skin was scaly and when aggravated it hissed like a snake. . . ." The creature was put on display at a local restaurant.[46] Hopefully it was not eaten! This incident underscores the tendency for residents to assume that any odd or unfamiliar fish or happening on the lake has some connection with the sea serpent.

One Friday in September 1947, Mr. L. R. Jones of Swanton, Vermont, reported an encounter with a strange creature. The encounter took place at 6 PM, while he was fishing with two friends on the northern point of North Hero Island. Jones later recounted the incident: "The bass were biting really well and we were about to hoist anchor. . . . The lake was calm, undisturbed by the slightest ripple, and the air was so clear that Mount Mansfield, Jay Peak, and all the other landmarks were outline[d] against the cloudless sky." Suddenly there was a massive splash to the north. "There was nothing to see at first, save a group of large ripples diverging in concentric circles from a point about 300 yards from our craft. No other boats were in sight. . . . Then, out of the depths, reared a huge dark form which moved swiftly in a northwesterly direction. Three segments appeared, clearly discernable above the water's surface, separated one from the other by about five feet of water, the overall length of the creature being about 25 feet."[47]

The creature appeared as a series of loops in the water, Jones said. "It moved with incredible swiftness—about 15 miles per hour—and disappeared altogether in about two minutes. Presently it emerged once more at a more distant point, about a quarter mile from the area where it was originally noted, only to plunge out of sight again, this time for good."[48] Jones was adamant that he had not seen fish such as sturgeon swimming in unison, making it seem to be one large creature.[49]

One afternoon in summer 1947, a Port Henry resident had an encounter. He would describe it years later. "One day I rode my bike over to the Champlain Bridge. I walked up on the side facing Port Henry and, looking down at the ledge sloping into the water, I suddenly see this . . . huge black snake" some twenty feet long and eight inches thick. It could have been longer as both the head and tail were under the water. "It didn't slither like a snake from side to side, but instead it humpted [sic] up out of the water (like about four humps). Then it straightened out, with a snap, like a rope pulled tight. I've been on the lake many times; I've never seen it again."[50]

"I WAS ONLY ABOUT THREE FEET AWAY . . ."

During summer 1952, a Burlington man was fishing near where the Winooski River empties into Lake Champlain, a few miles northwest of Burlington, when he was startled by a strange creature. Joseph Hubbard of Oak Terrace said he was in his boat on the lake, forty feet from shore when he noticed the first sign of something unusual: A large northern pike raced past his lure. Suddenly, the strangest fish he had ever seen appeared. It was upward of seven feet long and two feet wide and had a tannish-grey fringe on its head and near its end. That was when he noticed another oddity: It had no tail. "The body just sort of rounded off in back," he said. "I was only about three feet away from it when it glided by. It was near the bottom—it's pretty shallow there—but I got a good look at it." He then called to his wife, who also got a good look. Curious, Hubbard started the motor and headed off after the creature, but at his wife's prompting, quickly decided that retreat may be a more prudent option. He said that he knew that some people might think he was crazy, "but I saw it."[51]

On June 19, 1953, the *Press-Republican* reported on "rumors of a sea serpent" in the waters off Essex, New York that were circulating among "the younger set." It was widely believed that what was being seen were sturgeon.[52] Many Champlain monster sightings are undoubtedly rare glimpses of these deep-water fish coming to the surface.

On May 20, 1960, Harold Patch of Hardwick, Vermont, was enjoying a picnic lunch with his wife when they spotted a strange creature off the Champlain Islands on the New York shore. "It was definitely snake-like in form. I could see three or four humps up in the air, but they were vertical—and not lying horizontially along the water like a snake's would." The creature remained in sight for thirty minutes. Patch is adamant that he had not mistaken a large sturgeon or pike for the monster. "I know darn well it wasn't something else. I saw it and I know it's there," he said.[53] Patch described his encounter in greater detail in a letter:

> It was on a quiet, summer day and my wife and I were driving south on U.S. Route 2 through Grand Isle County, with intentions of enjoying a picnic somewhere. . . . As we approached Dillenback Bay off the eastern shore of the Town of Alburg, we noted two picnic tables at a turnout on the left side of the road and, pulling off, we got our picnic basket and thermos of coffee and sat down to dinner.
>
> I sat facing the road; Mrs. Patch faced the lake. We'd just settled down to eating when she remarked, 'There's a fish or something out there disturbing the water.' The lake . . . was perfectly calm, as smooth as a mirror. I twisted my neck around, looked across the bay toward the upper point of North Hero—and I expect my mouth dropped open!
>
> "FISH!" I exclaimed. "That's the 'Champlain monster' we've heard so much about!" Fortunately we had with us a fine pair of 7′ 35 binoculars, which I at once got from the car, and for the remainder of our noon meal we took turns watching the unusual creature. It was at first headed in a northeasterly direction, slowly moving along, and for all practical purposes, basking on the surface of the lake. It would be difficult to ac-curately estimate the length of this unusual creature for it was probably 300 yards away, but . . . it was at least 20 feet and perhaps nearly 30 feet long, and quite a few inches in diameter.
>
> It was definitely snake-like in form, but with one peculiar-ity: The loops of its body, instead of lying horizontally on the surface as a snake's would, humped up into the air vertically. It showed four or five of these vertical humps well above the water. At times it would rear its head up to a height of a couple of feet, take a look around, then continue on its

leisurely way. After a time, and when we were finishing our dinner, it slowly turned and started working back toward the area from which it came.

. . . I've been provoked a few times at the look someone would give me when I told them of this experience, for while they did not call me a liar, quite evidently they did not believe my account. Well—they can do as they like about that. I know what I saw and watched off and on for a half hour through seven-power binoculars, on a day when the lake was perfectly calm!

—Harold Patch
East Hardwick, Vt.[54]

As credible witnesses go, they do not come with much higher regard than Walter R. Hard Jr., who served as editor of *Vermont Life* from 1950 to 1971.[55] Mr. Hard had long kept close tabs on "monster" sightings in the lake but never imagined that he would have one himself in 1962, when he and his wife were relaxing off Appletree Point northwest of Burlington. He said that what he saw that day with his wife, "defies any explanation that I can think of." The couple watched

Figure 3.3. The snake-like creature witnessed by Harold Patch off the Champlain Islands on a picturesque spring day in 1960 (Jamilah Bartholomew sketch).

the creature through binoculars and had a clear view. "The head was the distinguishing feature—large and whitish and round like a beach ball. My wife . . . saw its body above the water in two or three coils. Then, it moved away rather rapidly into the lake." Hard related that they "both saw the head, going against the wind at a pretty good clip."[56]

The next year there was a rare land sighting as Champ went back to his old ways of crawling onto shore. Thomas Morse said he was startled along Northwest Bay in Westport, New York, when he spotted what appeared to be a cable. "When first seen it appeared as a massive gunmetal gray approx. 18 inches wide cable on the shore and out into the lake." He said the creature "appeared to be a monstrous eel with white teeth" and lifted its head four feet into the air.[57]

On an unusually calm summer's day in 1966, a resident of Swanton, Vermont, who wishes to remain anonymous for fear of ridicule, related that he was fishing on Missisquoi Bay when a "large, large snake" popped up out of the water. "The water was like a sheet of glass out there. It was very unusual to have no movement in the water." The man said he could see "three humps about five or six feet apart, but I didn't see a head or tail." He estimated the length at twenty-five feet.[58]

Mr. Jocelin Tremblay of Essex, Vermont, claims to have spotted the creature on three separate occasions in international waters across the border in Canada's Missisquoi Bay, the most prominent being in late summer 1967. Tremblay, a high school teacher, stated that it was a warm day in late August and he was fishing with his brother-in-law when a figure, twenty-five feet in length, appeared. As they approached in their boat for a closer look, its three grey humps stopped undulating and the creature sank beneath the waves.[59]

That same year, Gordon F. Baker of Port Henry was fishing in nearby Bulwagga Bay when he was *instantly* converted into a Champ believer. He was spin casting but nothing was coming near his lure. "This is when I saw a large creature going past the side of my boat, which was 14 and a half feet long (my boat). The front was passed [sic] my boat and I looked back to the back of my boat and it was still coming by." What it was, he could not say, only that it was certainly longer than his boat.[60]

During summer 1968, a Vietnam soldier, home on leave, decided to relax by fishing in the vicinity of Campbell's Bay, three miles south-west of Swanton, Vermont, near the Canadian border, when he noticed ripples in the water about 150 yards off shore. It was 2 in the afternoon. He stated the water was as smooth as glass—dead calm. "Then I saw it: what appeared to be a very large, black snake—a huge snake. I saw no head, only humps that came up above the surface; but this visible portion was 20 to 25 feet long." The young man noted that he had been trained in the Marine Corps as an aerial observer and was "familiar with assessing [the] size, length, depth of things. I was born here. I've fished the lake all my life, but I have only ever seen the creature that one time." He related that the humps were two feet across the base and up to a foot in height. "They were four to five feet apart. I watched for about 20 minutes and all the time it kept going in a circle 120 to 130 feet in diameter."[61]

In October 1970, Christine Breyette of Dannemora, New York, sighted a strange object from the air while flying her small plane over the lake late one beautiful afternoon. On this day, she had excellent visibility and described her account thusly: "I'm afraid I can't pinpoint the location, but it was an isolated bay with no houses around it. This huge dark grey creature just came up out of the water and went back in. The size amazed me. It was about as wide as, but definitely longer than an ordinary row-boat."[62]

By the mid-1970s, newspaper and magazine articles about the monster—almost all of them positive—began to enhance the serpent's credibility in the public eye, as he quickly became known as Champ or Champy, a name that would stick to the present day. During this period, it became vogue to see Champ, and much of the stigma surrounding eyewitnesses, was muted. There was little of the ridicule that had characterized so many of the early press reports. Then again, he had stopped snatching animals from the shoreline and was behaving in a more civil manner. He had also stopped showing off by stretching his body more than one hundred feet. In the eyes of many residents who were getting acquainted with the creature for the first time, Champ was not only possible, he was plausible. Best of all, he belonged to Lake Champlain.

AWASH WITH CONTROVERSY

Shonky Journalism, a Controversial Photo, and a Monster Dispute

Human, all too human.
—FRIEDRICH NIETZSCHE

Summer 1970 would mark the first in a series of magazine articles by the Champ paparazzi that would gain the creature local notoriety, and by the end of the decade, national fame. Through the first six decades of the twentieth century, the monster became shy and reclusive, floundering in relative obscurity and surfacing only intermittently in the public eye in the form of fleeting newspaper reports. Accounts from his glory days of the 1870s and 1880s had faded from the region's collective memory, and except for a few historians who delved into such arcane matters, public awareness of his existence was such that many residents had never even heard of the monster. In short, Champ appeared to be "washed up"; on a downward spiral from national legend to an obscure footnote in history. All that would change in 1970 with historian Majorie Porter's article "The Champlain Monster," which appeared in *Vermont Life*.[1] With its focus on nineteenth- and early twentieth-century sightings, Porter's article exposed a new generation of residents in the Champlain Basin to the colorful history of its famous sea serpent. A summary of the article was distributed by the Gannett News Service and soon appeared in newspapers across the country. The editor of the *Watertown Daily Times* was typical in his praise of the story, noting that *Vermont Life* was "an exceptionally interesting and reputable magazine." He then repeated Porter's claim that in 1609, Samuel de Champlain reported seeing a serpent-like creature that was twenty feet long, as thick as a barrel, with a head like a horse.[2] There was one problem with Porter's account of the lake's namesake: It was not true.

LOST IN TRANSLATION:
FISHY SCHOLARSHIP CREATES A HYBRID CHAMP

Porter's fictitious account of Champlain's log highlights the fascinating interplay between human perception and media accuracy. As early as 1971, regional historians led by Connie Pope began calling attention to Porter's claim, noting that there was no mention of such a creature in Champlain's logs, but the damage was done and the myth was given life by journalists.[3] The description of a "horse-headed" monster made for great copy, and with reporters quoting Porter's article verbatim, it merely compounded the fiction and turned it into "fact." Porter epitomizes the shoddiness of much of the modern-day press coverage of the Champlain monster. She needed only to have consulted the original logs of Samuel de Champlain (which were readily available), and she would have found an accurate English translation that said *nothing* of a horselike head or being the size of a barrel. She also committed a second journalistic sin by failing to reveal her source. Porter's article not only resurrected the legend of Champ, it altered it to the point where people began to see what they expected to see. A classic example of how observers can be mistaken took place in 1978 in Rotterdam, the Netherlands, when a panda escaped from a zoo, sparking hundreds of panda sightings across the region. It was later determined that the creature had been killed by a train near the zoo and had never wandered from the immediate vicinity. Yes, human perception can be notoriously unreliable.[4]

Before the article appeared in 1970, as far as is known, not one reported Champ sighting described the creature's head as horse-shaped. But *after* the publication, there was no dearth of reports describing such a creature in the lake—*a creature that had not been heretofore described.* The print on Porter's article had barely time to dry when later that summer, people were sighting a creature described *almost exactly* as Porter's imaginary monster. On July 23, 1970, Richard Spear and his 13-year-old daughter, Susanne, were enjoying the serenity of Lake Champlain while riding on the ferry from Charlotte, Vermont, to the community of Essex on the New York shore. As the vessel was nearing the dock at Essex, they saw a "dark, olive-brown" creature less than a football field distance and the same distance from shore as the ferry.

It was "the size and shape of a barrel" and moving north. Their attention was first drawn to the object by the appearance of two "bumps" protruding three feet above the water. The bumps were evenly spaced and extended about four feet along the water in total. Stunned, Mr. Spear would later write that "after a lifetime near Lake Champlain and other large bodies of water I can say with certainty that what I saw was nothing like anything I had seen before."[5] He continued: "Perhaps the most startling thing about this whole affair . . . I had been watching the thing's undulating progress through the water for twenty seconds or so with the aid of a . . . binocular when I turned and offered it to Susanne, who had also been watching. My attention was turned to her for a moment while she was trying to locate the creature through the glasses and when I turned to our companion on the deck to ask if she were observing the same thing she had a most startled look and said 'I saw its head!' By the time my daughter had focused on it, it was just disappearing below the surface" and "she distinctly saw the 'horse-like head' before it submerged." Spear continued: "We were all in a state of excitement and before I could ask our co-observer to describe what she'd seen she said 'it looked just like a 'horse's head!'" The woman standing next to them who had witnessed the entire affair would later assure them that she had never before heard of the "Champlain monster."[6]

Mr. Spear would eventually forget the name of the stranger standing next to them that day, but through a twist of fate, she would write a letter to the local paper identifying herself and providing an independent description of the event. Mrs. James Marsh, who related that what she spied through field glasses that day "was a large snake-like creature, swimming with her head above the water, held as snakes do, with coils behind. I am no judge of size, but I should say she was between 18 and 20 feet long. It was black, and swimming slowly. Her head was about three feet long, wrinkled like a raisin, with a small ridge down the back, a snake body and was blackish-brown."[7]

HORSE HEADS APLENTY

Suddenly, it seemed as though everyone was seeing a horse-shaped head on the creature. Among the more prominent accounts during this time was a 1972 report by two scuba divers who saw an equine Champ in Vermont's Maquam Bay, the story appearing in a bestselling book on the Loch Ness Monster.[8] The following year a Hudson Falls, New York family reported seeing a similar creature near St. Albans,[9] while in 1974, retired New York State Police Officer Anthony Lemza told of seeing a creature with a horselike head off Port Henry, New York.[10] The power of journalists to change the story is no more evident than what would occur in 1981 when Hal Smith would write an article on Champ in *Adirondack Life* magazine. Smith would interview Sandra Mansi who claimed to have taken a photo of Champ and quotes Mansi as saying it had a horselike head. Yet Mansi never used this description in her original recorded interview on the incident, and a perusal of the photo clearly shows nothing of the sort.[11] Whatever it is, the object in the photo is snakelike. One could easily image Mansi being talked into saying this.

Reporter: "It had a horse-like head like all of those other sightings, didn't it?"

Mansi: "Why yes, of course it did."

The article only solidified the myth of Champ's equine profile and give rise to more horse-headed sightings.[12]

In 1976, Champ received national exposure in the book *Strange Secrets of the Loch Ness Monster*. In it, bestselling mystery writer Warren Smith describes an encounter by two vacationers from New York State, Frank Shanafelt and Morris Lucia, who were scuba diving at Maquam Bay during summer 1972. The incident took place a few miles below the Canadian border, west of Swanton, Vermont.[13] After breakfast, Lucia went into the water first, and after a couple of minutes, Shanafelt submerged, only to see his partner in extreme distress. "From his actions, I knew we were in some kind of danger," Shanafelt recalled. "After he saw [that] I understood the situation was dangerous, we both started back to shore. I surfaced about 10 feet out, looking back to see what had given Morry such a fright. That's when I saw this thing. . . ."

Shanafelt was adamant that what he saw was Champ, exclaiming that it "couldn't have been anything other than a sea serpent." The men described the creature as upward of fifty feet long, with, of course, *a horselike head*. Lucia stated that the head "was slightly rounded in appearance, a sort of mushroom gray in color. The head sat on a long, round neck that was dark brown or black. The neck rose up about eight feet out of the water at the highest point."[14] The creature began to follow the men to shore, though Lucia believed that it did so more out of curiosity than malice. "Once, it cocked its head in a child-like manner as if it was curious about our appearance," Lucia said. "It didn't make any effort to harm us. I think we could have gone right back in the water without fear of being hurt."[15] Given the sheer size of the creature, the two divers decided not to go back into the water. Smith's book provided "priceless" publicity for a sea serpent making a media "comeback."

Then, in November 1977, *Yankee Magazine* published "In Search of the Champlain Monster" by Brian Vachon. At the time, Vachon held the coveted position of editor of *Vermont Life*.[16] The article marks the first time that a magazine with coverage beyond New York and Vermont had written about Champ. Unfortunately, Vachon never bothered to check Porter's research, repeating her claims about the lake's namesake. He wrote: "The first written report of a monster was offered by . . . Samuel de Champlain" who saw "a creature that was serpent-like, about 20 feet long and as thick as a barrel, with a head that resembled that of a horse." Remarkably, Vachon never cited Porter as his source. If he had, he could have blamed her for the error as an historian who should have known better. By failing to credit Porter, Vachon made it appear as if he had done the research, and in doing so, joined the litany of writers who had not only gotten the story wrong, they helped to perpetuate the myth. It would have taken little effort to consult a translation of Champlain's log from 1609, which could have been confirmed or denied by a single trip to the library or ringing a scholar on Champlain's voyages. Instead, we were treated to another example of armchair journalism. Vachon's article soon caught the eye of the editors at *Reader's Digest*, and in April 1978, a condensed version was reprinted in the influential magazine.[17] Champ had hit the public relations jackpot. The four-page article, "Is There a Champlain Monster?" was read by more than 50 million readers, catapulting Champ onto the world stage.[18]

By July 1978, another popular national magazine, *Argosy*, aimed at the young male adventure market, helped solidify Champ's newfound status as the most famous lake monster in America, with Gregory

Anderson's article, "America's Loch Ness Monster."[19] The article featured an interview with Clinton County Deputy Sheriff Janet Tyler describing her sighting of three years earlier near Westport, New York. The interview was a testament to Champ's rising celebrity and newfound status. Suddenly, it seemed as though anyone who had ever seen Champ wanted to talk about their encounter.

Tyler said the incident happened October 23 on a picturesque autumn afternoon. She walked through the door of her house overlooking the lake, poured a cup of coffee, and sat down to unwind. Glancing out her porch window, suddenly something caught her eye in the small inlet of Great Northwest Bay. "The lake was as calm as glass. Then, all of a sudden, near the mouth of Hoisington Creek, appeared big waves about three or four feet tall; there was no boat in sight to leave a wake."[20] She looked closer and saw a huge object thrashing and flailing about, apparently caught on a sandbar in shallow water. The creature was no more than a few hundred feet off shore. The figure was black with smooth, shiny skin and appeared to rise out of the water by two or three feet. The sighting lasted two minutes. Tyler said that she felt uncomfortable discussing the incident because of the kidding she had received and that if she had it to do over again, she would not have told a soul.[21] Yet, by 1978, she was willing to tell her story in a national magazine.

That November, after nearly one hundred years of publication, *Argosy* folded. Anderson's article had beaten the final deadline, illustrating the incredible wave of good fortune that Champ was on; everything was going right in the push to regain his status as the world's most famous lake monster. Respected people from the right social circles were now willing to discuss their sightings publicly. That same year, the Champlain monster would make more headlines in another national magazine, this one not so respectable, aimed at the young male fantasy and science fiction market, linking it with a most improbable subject: UFOs. Whereas public relations specialists are fond of saying: "Any publicity is good publicity," this adage was stretched to the limit in 1978, when a sensational story on Champ appeared in *True Flying Saucers & UFO's Quarterly*. The article, "Lake Champlain's Spacemen in Green Caps" reported an encounter by a Canadian couple who were supposedly picnicking on the shores of Missisquoi Bay in Quebec

Province in 1953. Suddenly, a spacecraft landed on the water and little men resembling dwarves emerged wearing green caps. The imaginative writer somehow associates this dubious encounter with Champ. The link between the two is not stated.[22]

A MONSTER PHOTO SPAWNS GLOBAL INTEREST

In fall 1979, news began to spread of the existence of a photo supposedly taken of Champ. According to the story that would eventually emerge, it began on a beautiful summer day in July of 1977, when a Connecticut woman named Sandra, and her husband-to-be Tony Mansi, were vacationing in northern Vermont, with Sandra's two children. Known to her friends as Sandi, she had once lived in Vermont and having family there, she invited her then fiancé Tony, to meet them. One day they had decided to go off the beaten path and explore some back roads along the lake north of St. Albans. They soon became lost and eventually stopped along a secluded lakeshore dirt road. They parked the car and walked down to the water to take in the scenery and go swimming.[23] That was when Tony realized he needed his sunglasses and went back to the car. Suddenly, there was a disturbance on the water. "My God, there must be an elephant tuna fish," Sandi recalled, trying to rationalize what she was seeing. Her next thought was: "Well, maybe it's scuba divers."[24] As the object kept emerging, she continued to search for a logical explanation. Perhaps it was a large school of fish, she thought?[25] As the head and neck became visible, she continued thinking, "it must be one heck of a big fish."[26] It then dawned on her that this was no fish. "The rest of the neck came [slowly rising] out of the water and then the hump came out."[27] Her initial reaction was one of shock: "I'm feeling like I shouldn't be there. This is something I should not be witnessing because to me this thing should have been extinct 30 million years ago . . ."[28]

Sandi stated that the creature did not behave like she would have expected of Champ, noting, "It looked around . . . and was the texture like that of an eel. You know how an eel looks slimy and shiny if the light is on it. . . . It was kind of slow-moving and really quite majestic." Despite its beauty, Sandi said she was terrified that it might have legs and come ashore.[29]

At this instant, Tony returned with his sunglasses, saw the "creature" about 150 feet from shore and called out, "Honey, get the kids out of there." He said that the two children—Heidi-Jo aged 11 and Larry aged 12—were wading in the water with their backs turned to the lake and saw nothing. Being around lunchtime and not wanting to alarm the children, Sandra, responding to Tony's command, said, "Let's get a pizza!" and the kids went running up to the car.[30]

Frightened, Sandi continued: "He [Tony] helped me up the bank and he had picked up his camera while he was at the car, and he said, 'Take a picture of it.'" At this point Sandi said that she was so shaken that she fell to her knees. "I didn't focus. I didn't even care if it had film on it. I just wanted to get out of there," she recalled.[31] She took one picture with the Kodak Instamatic 110, and they scrambled back to the car, which would not start! They soon managed to start the vehicle and drove off. Later, when the film came back from a Photomat, she looked at the photo and jokingly decided to call it the

Figure 4.1. Sandra Mansi's controversial photo reportedly taken in July 1977 at Lake Champlain. When it was released in 1981, it caused a global sensation (credit Sandra Mansi).

Figure 4.2. Blow up of the Mansi photo (Photo credit Sandra Mansi).

2,000-pound duck. Why? "It's easier to live with a 2,000-pound duck than something we didn't know what it was," she said.[32]

The Mansis said they decided to keep quiet about the photo until a co-worker brought up the subject of the Loch Ness Monster. Shortly after, she had seen the *Reader's Digest* article featuring Dr. Philip Reines, a media professor at the State University of New York at Plattsburgh, mentioned as a Champ expert.[33] In fall 1979, Reines received an unusual phone call. On the line was Roy Kappeler, a young Mystic, Connecticut man who said that a friend had snapped a photo of the Champlain monster and wondered if he would like to examine it? It was like asking a nun if she would like an audience with the Pope. Reines jumped at the chance and a small package soon arrived with the original photo.[34] Upon opening it and seeing the photo for the first time, his reaction was: "*WOW! What is that?!*" With it was a handwritten note: "Dear Professor, Here are [sic] the photograph of the Lake Champlain Monster, I promised you. I leave it up to you, now, to do what is needed to prove the photograph is authentic, etc.

I hope you are pleased at what you see, I am. The tape will follow in a few days. Please call when you have received them. Thanks for everything you are about to do. Roy N. Kappeler."[35]

Welling with excitement, Reines rang the Mansis to find out as much as he could about the photo, only to become crestfallen to learn that they no longer had the negative. Recovering from his disappointment, he told them that all was not lost—as long as they could pinpoint the location where they took the photo, which they said was just above St. Albans. Real estate agents are fond of saying that the three most important factors in determining the worth of a house are location, location, and location. The same can be said of analyzing monster photographs. Knowing the location is crucial and could reveal valuable clues including the size and distance of the object, and whether the photo was even taken on Lake Champlain. As much as he wanted to, Reines could not take the Mansis' claims on faith alone. They promised to come to the lake that spring, assuring Reines that finding the spot would be no problem.[36] Reines advised the couple to keep quiet about the photo until either the location or the negative was found. Under *no circumstances* was news about the photo to be made public, as without more evidence, the media and skeptics would have a field day with the question marks hanging over it. When he was not lecturing, Reines spent his spare time searching for the site during the late fall of 1979 and early winter of 1980.

Frustrated at not being able to find the spot, he enlisted the help of fellow Champ expert Joe Zarzynski of Wilton, New York. Throughout the remaining winter and spring of 1980, the pair combed the Vermont lake shore above St. Albans, but they were unable to pinpoint the location.[37] Adding to the tension were the Mansis who seemed in no hurry to drive up and point out the spot. The couple waited until July 4 1980 to finally visit the area for a ten-day break at Burton Island State Park.[38] Remarkably, when they arrived, they never looked for the location. On July 17, Zarzynski told Reines the bad news: "For your knowledge . . . the Mansi's did not look for the site. They waited until the last couple of days of their vacation to look and according to them bad weather set in. I guess they could not leave the island. . . . I think it was very poor planning on their part."[39]

Was it *really* poor planning, or did the Mansis know something they were not telling—that the photo was not taken on Lake Champlain after all? Was it a hoax? They had nothing to lose and everything to gain by finding the location, yet they had not even made an effort over ten days. What's more, one of the explicit purposes of their trip was to find the location. On the other hand, there was no evidence of a hoax. It was about this time that the Mansis decided they were going to go public with the picture, and although having reservations, Zarzynski told them he would do whatever he could to help them do it. He told Reines that "it now appears that they wish to make a public statement about their photo through *The Burlington Free Press*. Actually this would be a story about them and the photograph . . . without publishing the photo. Hopefully the article will tempt some action on the part of the media and public to want to see their photo . . . I think this is . . . the best path. . . ."[40]

THE KELP HITS THE FAN

Reines was furious when he received Zarzynski's letter. He saw it as a stab in the back by someone whom he had invited to verify the photo, and who had previously agreed not to go public until the site was found. Furthermore, he had not even been consulted on the decision to go public.[41] Reines was adamant that they should continue working quietly behind the scenes to find the all-important location, away from any media scrum that would surely ensue. He also harbored suspicions that Zarzynski may have been trying to cut a deal with the Mansis to split any proceeds from the photo, noting that he was constantly quoted in the press that he had spent tens of thousands of dollars from his own pocket, researching. Reines wrote to Zarzynski with distain: "Part of the Barnum Ballyhoo you have fostered is the large financial expense you have incurred. It does look foolish and cheapens your image. . . ."[42] Zarzynski contends that he cited his expenditures as a way to convey to the public just how serious he was about his research. Reines viewed it with suspicion and still does.[43] Zarzynski vehemently denied that there was any sinister conspiracy with the Mansis to either benefit from the photo's publica-

tion or push Reines out of the picture.[44] He said that if the Mansis
were going to go public, he had an obligation to help them—after
all, who was he to judge whether their story was true or not—and
although he had earlier agreed to keep the photo secret until the site
could be found, he had no control over the Mansis; it was their decision to make. Furthermore, it was not as if he had signed a binding
contract requiring him to keep the photo under wraps. It had seemed
like a good idea at the time to follow Reines' suggestion, but now
the landscape was different, as the Mansis wanted the world to see
the photo. Besides, how much longer should they wait before going
public? Six months? A year? Five years? At this point, three years after
the photo was supposedly taken, they were no closer to locating the
spot. What if the site was never found? Would the photo remain out
of the public eye forever? Perhaps release of the photo would even jog
someone's memory and prompt him or her to recognize the location.

   At about this time, Zarzynski wrote to Reines that the Mansis
wanted him to return his original print of the photo, either to himself or them.[45] Reines felt insulted and would later say that Zarzynski
had "betrayed a colleague," ceased being a researcher and turned into
a crusader.[46] Reines criticizes Zarzynski for having become a public advocate for the Mansis, while expressing private concerns. For
instance, in his letter of July 13, 1980, to Roy Kappeler, Zarzynski
wrote pointedly "that it is absolutely NECESSARY that this site be
found. Without a positive ID of the site the Mansis' story has a loop-
hole. . . . It is a must that the Mansis find the site in person . . . [for]
without the site you folks are lacking in the two main points. You have
a print, but no negative. And you are not sure of the site. Those two
points against the case will not win over any skeptics. Thus, I would
like to offer a little advice. Before anything goes public the site must
be found. . . . If this letter seems critical it is not. It just points out
what I consider a MUST." The letter ended with a final exhortation
to the Mansis to return during the summer and locate the site. The
next month, Zarzynski accompanied the Mansis to scour the shoreline
north of St. Albans; once again they came up empty. The site was
proving to be more elusive than Champ himself, who ironically, would
have known the location but was not talking (assuming it was on the
lake). Zarzynski felt that he had the right to change his mind—and

besides, it was not Reines' decision to make. It was the Mansis' and they wanted to go public—for better or worse. Reines, on the other hand, was convinced that Zarzynski was deliberately muddying the waters by encouraging the Mansis to get the photo from him. Although miffed, Reines was too tied down with his academic duties to pursue the matter, but expressed private fears that the photo's release could turn into a public relations nightmare for the Mansis. He also worried what would happen should they try to sell the photo, which eventually occurred. Reines believed that in backing the Mansis, Zarzynski was playing with fire because there could be serious repercussions if the photo were proven to be a fake. He points out that when Frank Searle claimed to have snapped several pictures of the Loch Ness Monster in the 1970s, they were later proven to be fakes, leaving many research-ers red-faced and with diminished credibility. Reines was fearful of a media feeding frenzy once the photo was released. He felt that "a sacred trust had been broken" and the investigation was forever com-promised. He also believed that Zarzynski "had become obsessed with the idea of being a lake monster celebrity, and the photo was his best opportunity to achieve it."[47]

In August 1980, Zarzynski again wrote to Reines asking him to return the original photo.[48] He steadfastly refused, saying that he would only return the original directly to the Mansis if and when they contacted him.[49] That December, the Mansis contacted Reines through their attorney, Alan Neigher of Westport, Connecticut, offi-cially requesting that he return the photo.[50] Reines was bemused, observing that after all, the Mansis had first contacted him to assess its authenticity. He felt that because he was unwilling to endorse it, it was being snatched away for all the wrong reasons. Neigher wrote with a sense of urgency: "On the Friday after Thanksgiving, the Mansi home was broken into while the Mansis were meeting with me and another attorney. Every indication is that the intruders were look-ing for the photograph. For this reason we must take every security precaution available to us. Consequently, we must request that you return any prints or negatives of prints that you may have concerning the creature in your possession . . ." Neigher then tried to reassure Reines that the request for the return of the photo was not personal. "Please be assured that the above request has no negative suggestion.

You have been an immense help and the Mansis appreciate it. All we are saying is that it is quite apparent that there [are] those who will take criminal steps to secure the photograph and we want to eliminate that temptation and opportunity. . . ."[51]

Reines saw this as "a flimsy excuse to retrieve the photo" and end his involvement.[52] A few days later, on Christmas Eve 1980, Reines received a business-like letter from Zarzynski explaining that the Mansis' attorney wanted the prints returned, fearing that they may fall into the wrong hands. "Mr. Neigher is worried that the photo might leak out or be stolen by someone," he wrote.[53] By now, Reines was getting the distinct impression that *his* hands were "the wrong hands." He was especially concerned at Zarzynski's next statement: "Mr. Neigher will also be coordinating the release of the photo when the time comes. I believe the Mansis made a wise chose [*sic*] in securing his assistance." But it was the last sentence that particularly irked Reines: "Dr. [Roy] Mackal and the others are fully aware of the loss of the negative and such."[54]

Reines dashed off a letter to Zarzynski expressing surprise that during his recent phone conversation with Professor Mackal, the famous cryptozoologist at the University of Chicago, he was unaware of Reines' involvement with the Mansis. Reines was now even more convinced that Zarzynski was trying to write him out of the history of Champ to have the limelight all to himself. His tone turned acerbic: "Now from your letter and *virtual silence* from the Mansis and then the *insulting* letter from Mr. Neigher, leads me to one of 2 conclusions 1) your nievety [*sic*] and trust . . . is far greater than I ever imagined, or for reasons only known to you, you *do not* want (and perhaps also the Mansis) my continued participation. . . . If so I am sorry to say *I am* involved and will continue to be so, if, for nothing else—but to *ensure objective truth* is not *lost* . . . or garbled. Or this thing *made into an exploitation for $.*"[55]

The Mansis felt that they had every right to profit from the photo. Other people benefit from taking famous photos, so why shouldn't they? After all, people go to baseball games never intending to catch the ball hit in historic home runs, but when they do, it would be a rare person who turned down money in exchange for the ball. Was taking a photo of the monster any different? It was not as if the Mansis could be accused of seeing dollar signs immediately after snapping the picture. They did not secure the services of an attorney to handle inquiries until three years later. However, Reines was against any attempt to profit from the photo, believing that it would ultimately backfire and cast suspicions on the Mansis, whether founded or not. As he saw it, in the eyes of the public and the media—and he was a professor of media studies—image is everything, and one's reputation is priceless. It would certainly have enhanced Sandra's image and the credibility of the photo if she had refused to accept any money for its use. Reines wrote: "The Mansis won't allow publication of the picture until they meet with a *business* agent. *How Crass!*"[56] He then took aim at Zarzynski for, as he saw it, trying to rob him of his Champ legacy. "Why didn't you tell Dr. Mack[al] of our Vermont excursions looking for the location [and] how come Dr. Mackal was *not* asked to return the photo or slide. Ditto Dr. Zug [then head of vertebrate zoology at the Smithsonian Institution, Washington, DC]. Did you return your slide? . . . I asked you that but you did not answer . . . why are you in contact with Mr. Neigher. . . . To what purpose?"[57] For his part, Zarzynski felt that Reines was asking too many questions and it was none of his business how he conducted his affairs; that included supporting the Mansis going public. As far as he was concerned, the photo was back where it belonged: in the hands of the Mansis. Zarzynski, who had reportedly invested more than $20,000 and countless hours researching Champ,[58] was now in a battle for his cryptozoological life because in the same letter Reines said he was soon going to meet with Professor Mackal and had already expressed his displeasure to the famous monster hunter over what he felt was Zarzynski's quest for personal glory. At this point, Zarzynski felt that his disagreements with Reines were beyond repair, as he was not only challenging his intentions and credibility, but also doing so aggressively and in front of other cryptozoologists. As fate would have it, the two men would soon have an awkward meeting at a scientific seminar on Champ held in August 1981.

MONSTER PHOTO FOR SALE

With Zarzynski's media connections, the Mansis went public on November 11, 1980, when the *Burlington Free Press* published a front-page article under the bold headline, "LAKE CHAMPLAIN MONSTER CAUGHT ON FILM." It read in part: "A Wilton, N.Y. man who has been studying "Champ" . . . produced Friday what he described as 'startling new evidence' of the unidentified creature. The evidence, a color photograph . . . was brought to the *Free Press* by Joseph Zarzynski . . . founder of The Lake Champlain Phenomena Investigation . . . Zarzynski said the photograph couldn't be published without the approval of its owners, Anthony and Sandra Mansi, who have obtained a copyright and hope to sell it. Mansi . . . by telephone . . . said he would not allow the picture to be run until he has a conference with his business agent. . . ."

Reines was predictably annoyed by the article, labeling it a blatant attempt by Zarzynski to "hog the limelight," writing: "The remainder of this lengthy article is all about Zarzynski and his efforts to get the photo analyzed, his four trips to Loch Ness in Scotland, and his six years of Champ investigations. The article makes it clearly seem that only Zarzynski is the investigator. No mention is made of anyone else involved, except by inference that this 'mysterious' group he founded, The Lake Champlain Phenomena Investigation group, was actively participating."[59] He was also unhappy that in his many press interviews on his Champ research, there was no mention by Zarzynski of the historical newspaper reports that he had compiled with historian Connie Pope and given to him. Zarzynski felt that Reines was going overboard, and just because he had given him some historical clippings, he was not obligated to pay homage to Reines every time he gave an interview.[60]

On June 26, 1981, Plattsburgh radio personality Gordie Little of station WIRY, phoned Reines to ask him what he thought of the impending publication of the Mansi photo in *The New York Times*. Reines was caught unaware and was shocked and angry that Zarzynski had not told him.[61] On June 30, the photo was finally published. *The New York Times* carried the headline: "Is it Lake Champlain's Monster?" Accompanying the article was a black and white image of the Mansi photo. Touted by Zarzynski as "the first clear-cut photograph of Champ," its placement on page 1 of the coveted "Science Times" section, was priceless publicity. The photo and the lengthy article by Pulitzer Prize-winning writer John Noble Wilford caused a sensation and resulted in a deluge of media stories on the possible, if not likely, existence of the legendary creature.[62] The monster's Renaissance was launched.

The prestigious *Times* article gave Champ renewed credibility and unprecedented publicity befitting a rock star, yet two months later, a bitter Sandi Mansi confided to a journalist: "If I could do it again I would tear the picture up and never tell anyone about it." Mansi said that her private life had been shattered by publication of the photo in the *Times*. Believing that going public would silence skeptics, it had the opposite effect. Reines says that he took no pleasure in saying "I told you so" quietly to himself. In the same interview, Mansi complained: "We have had reporters call at all times of day. What do you say to ABC when they get you out of bed at 11 o'clock at night? . . ."[63] Although the media can be intrusive, what happened to saying, "No!" or changing your number or leaving an answering machine message saying, "Hi, this is Sandi Mansi. Leave a message after the tone, unless it's a question about Champ, in which case—get a life and don't call back." There is no law that says anyone has to answer late night calls or even talk to ABC News. It was not as if reporters were camped on her front lawn, following her every time she drove to the local store. It should have come as no surprise to her that few serious research-ers were willing to accept the photo as proof of Champ's existence without more information. This is especially so, given the questions surrounding the negative and the still unknown location.

Mansi later admitted that she had been seduced by the initial burst of attention from the photo's public unveiling, and that it began to control her and have a negative effect on her family. She and Anthony divorced in 1980, and she found herself struggling to raise her two children. "I learned that it's so easy to get caught up in one thing and let that dictate your life. I lost track of my priorities. This was all new. I went on *The Merv Griffin Show*. A limousine picked me up." She said that reality sunk in when she returned home to Winchester, New Hampshire, where she was raising her two children as a single mom.

"I had my children stay with friends for four days. What kind of mother is that? That bothered me terribly. So I said, 'This is my pri-ority—my family. This is something that happened to me, and I will deal with it,' but I never left my children again."[64]

In her defense, Mansi was no scientist and may have thought that the media should have treated her more kindly. After all, you are supposed to be innocent unless proven guilty. Like it or not, the release of the photo made Sandi Mansi both a celebrity and a target as cynics were quick to point out that she was attempting to capitalize financially from the photo. Was she an opportunist or an innocent victim? Was it a fake intended to get rich, or was she a victim of circumstance? Unfortunately, in trying to sway public opinion in her favor, Sandi Mansi was often her own worst enemy.

Predictably, within two weeks of the *Times* story and accompanying photo, doubters were beginning to smell blood in the water. Noted monster skeptic Dr. Paul Kurtz, philosophy professor at the State University of New York at Buffalo, attacked the credibility of the photo, telling *Time* magazine that it may have been a ploy to build up the local tourism industry. "It's about as real as Bigfoot, UFOs, and the tooth fairy," he quipped.[65] With no negative or location, and having taken steps to get a business agent and sell rights to publish the photo, it was tough to blunt such criticisms, for after all, science is grounded in evidence and verification, and not faith alone. At about the same time, Zarzynski observed that a flurry of new sightings seemed to result from more open attitudes toward seeing Champ. "Now there's a favorable and sympathetic atmosphere, so that people are coming out of the closet," he said.[66] Well-placed photos in *The New York Times* have a tendency to lend credibility to marginal topics.

ANALYSIS OF A MONSTER PHOTO

Without a negative or location, little more could be done to support the photo's authenticity: The believers believed (on faith) and the skeptics demanded to see more evidence. All previous attempts to get experts to validate the photo ran into a brick wall. When in the early spring 1980, a slide of the photo was sent to Dr. George Zug, head of vertebrate zoology at the Smithsonian Institution, it was met with disappointment. "Unfortunately, I can offer no unequivocal identification," Zug replied.[67] Strike 1. The following month, two of the institute's ichthyologists (fish experts) reported that there was *not* enough information to determine whether the object was even alive.[68]

Strike 2. At the same time, Kodak Films in Rochester, New York, was sent a copy of the photo but they refused to render a verdict, saying they were not in the lake monster verification business.[69] Strike 3. Vermont's state naturalist, Charles Johnson, was then sent a copy of the photo but was unable to make a determination.[70] The strikes kept coming. These events left Zarzynski disheartened, and the Mansis under more pressure to find the location.

Not surprisingly, journalists were still getting the story wrong. In March 1981, the photo was analyzed at the University of Arizona where Dr. B. Roy Frieden could see no sign of tampering. Media reports soon followed claiming that experts had determined that the object was alive or genuine. These are media-generated myths resulting from sloppy journalism. For instance, the University of Arizona report concluded *only* that the photo had not been tampered with. This is a far cry from what was claimed by the United Press International (UPI) on April 20, 1981, which appeared in newspapers across the country. The anonymous journalist made a ridiculous assertion: "Experts at the University of Arizona . . . said an analysis indicated that the picture is real and shows the image of a real animal." The report *never* concluded that the object was alive, and it also *could not* rule out a hoax. Someone could take a picture of a hoaxed object without tampering with the camera or the photo![71] In setting the record straight, cryptozoologist J. Richard Greenwell said that he had been *misquoted* by UPI, whose article implied that the photo "proved" the existence of Champ, and as a result, Greenwell was being bombarded with media inquiries. "We only know the photo is not a fake. There is definitely something on the water. Now it is up to the biologists and zoologist[s] to tell us if it is a tree trunk, a plastic model or a living phenomenon."[72] In 1983, Dr. Roy Mackal summed up his views on Champ by noting that although the evidence was impressive the final answer would only come when scientists have a specimen.[73]

CHAMPOLOGISTS GATHER FOR A SCIENTIFIC CONFERENCE

In early summer 1981, Dr. Reines picked up a local newspaper and learned that an international seminar on Champ was planned for August just across the lake in Shelburne, Vermont. Reines was again fuming, this time because Zarzynski had not told him about the gathering, believing that Zarzynski was hoping to mute his reservations about the Mansi photo, and for his own personal glory. Reines quickly contacted the Lake Champlain Committee—the main seminar sponsor—and was invited to speak. He would later write with some bitterness at nearly missing out on such an historic event, noting that "at no time did I receive any communication from Mr. Zarzynski . . . in any form inviting me or telling me about the event" despite having given him much of his research collection and inviting him to join in his investigation of the Mansi photo.[74] Zarzynski was not on good terms with Reines by this point and had abandoned any hope of ever working with him in the future. It was unlikely that Reines was ever going to miss out on the conference. Being the other active Champ researcher, Reines was almost certain to find out—and he did. At the seminar held on August 29 1981, at the Shelburne Museum, Reines said that Sandi Mansi expressed surprise to see him, given his college workload had caused him to drop out of the investigation, something Reines contends was untrue.[75] He then met with Zarzynski and put him on the spot, asking him why he had not invited him. His answer, Reines wrote, was that he had decided to work alone. "He also stressed the importance of 'faith' in people and the acceptance of 'truth' in the Mansi adventure. At this point he noted my continued skepticism as the major reason for his non-contact."[76] Privately, Reines did not believe his explanation, feeling that his motivations were driven more by a quest for fame. The behind-the-scenes "undercurrent" between the lake's two Champ experts remained out of the public eye. It was in both their interests—and certainly that of Champ's, that the conference be accepted as a serious scientific endeavor and treated with respect by the media and public. It was.[77]

About two hundred people attended the conference, officially dubbed: "Does Champ Exist? A Scientific Seminar." Although the idea of such a conference had been percolating for years, the Mansi photo helped create the political momentum to make it a reality. With Zarzynski's prodding, the Lake Champlain Committee, working with Vermont representative Millie Small of Quechee, organized the event and lined up sponsors. Some sponsors were motivated more by economics than altruism, hoping that the seminar would enhance regional

tourism. Among them were the Plattsburgh, Clinton County, and Port
Henry chambers of commerce, the latter staking the identity of their
small community on the rising popularity of Champ. Other financial
donors were the University of Vermont Environmental Program, the
Lake Champlain Committee, and the Shelburne Farms Museum. These
organizations tend to be conservative in lending their names to marginal topics, but the possibility of Champ seems far more plausible
than other borderline topics. Let's face it, they were most unlikely to
sponsor a conference on local psychics, Bigfoot, or UFO encounters.

Zarzynski gave an overview of the history of Champ and the
importance of legislative protection, while Mackal said that Champ
might be a primitive whale called a zeuglodon, thought to be extinct.
J. Richard Greenwell, optical science professor at the University of
Arizona, pronounced the photo genuine (i.e., it was not a fake). But
he also noted that he could not tell whether the figure in the photo
was even alive. Another prestigious speaker was Dr. George Zug who,
at the time, held one of the most coveted jobs in science: director of

Figure 4.3. Dr. Phil Reines addresses the press conference at the 1981 "Does
Champ Exist?" Conference. (Gary Mangiacopra photo)

Figure 4.4. Panel of experts at the August 29, 1981, Champ conference. From right to left: Roy Mackal, Joe Zarzynski, Sandra Mansi, Phil Reines, George Zug, and J. Richard Greenwell (Gary Mangiacopra photo)

Figure 4.5. Photo of Joe Zarzynski with Sandra Mansi in 1981 (Gary Mangiacopra photo)

zoology and biology at the Smithsonian Institution. Zug would not say whether he believed Champ existed, only that there might be a population of large "somethings" in the lake, but whether they were a new species or a recognized creature, he could not say. Dr. Reines emphasized that the most important task was to validate the location and demanded its corroboration from the Mansis: "That location must be found! There's no question about it!" Reines exhorted. "I want that photograph to prove to me the existence of Champ . . . but I have got to find that location. I have to satisfy my own criteria."[78]

During the conference, many eyewitnesses recounted their sightings. One of the most memorable was Elsie Porter, a long-time resident of Port Kent, New York, who shared her sightings from the 1920s and 1930s. Reines also informed the audience that he was the original investigator of the Mansi sighting, but stopped short of revealing his turbulent relationship with Zarzynski. A panel discussion of the "experts," with questions from the audience, ended the conference, which was well received and was picked up by wire services and reported on around the world.[79]

Although the conference attracted national attention, it changed little and soon faded from local memory, except for cryptozoologists. It was essentially a rehashing of what was already known. Bernard Carman, then editor of *Adirondack Life*, would later observe "frankly I heard nothing there which struck me as especially new or different in kind from that which had already been said and published. . . ."[80] Although cynics might argue that there was no difference from your run-of-the-mill Bigfoot or UFO conference, the seminar had two big points in its favor. First, it featured a prestigious zoologist from the Smithsonian Institution, and another from the University of Chicago. Second, the topic of Champ is far more credible than say, a conference on Sasquatch or reincarnation. When Reines inquired into the possibility of SUNY Plattsburgh hosting a second conference the next year, he hit a brick wall. The director for the university's Institute for Man and the Environment, James Dawson, was fearful of harming the SUNY's reputation by associating with such a marginal topic. Dawson, who attended the Champ seminar, tactfully expressed "reservations about the true scientific nature of some of the approaches," suggesting instead that perhaps the SUNY History Department could hold a second seminar with a folklore theme, or the Psychology Department could sponsor it "as an exercise in perceptions." In the end, the academic support for another conference at SUNY Plattsburgh was underwhelming and met a quick death. Short of a body to analyze, there was little to be gained given that the best evidence for Champ is all "soft," in the form of eyewitness testimony and inconclusive photos.[81]

A TURF WAR REIGNITES

Just days after the seminar, Reines read a copy of *Pursuit*, a publication of the now-defunct Society for the Investigation of the Unexplained, which had an article by Zarzynski touting the Mansi photo's authenticity.[82] In it he wrote that the photo's existence "remained a family secret until autumn, 1979, when they copyrighted the photo and then looked for help in getting it analyzed and authenticated. Shortly after this time I [Zarzynski] was told about the photo's existence, and thus began the lengthy and slow process of verification." Reines complained that Zarzynski made it appear as if the verification process began only after Zarzynski became aware of it. The article lists no less than six experts who were consulted about the photo's authenticity. Reines said he was stunned to read that he was not on the list, despite having been the original researcher for both Champ and the Mansi photo.[83]

Furious, Reines (who had the unusual habit of underlining words for emphasis), fired off a letter to the journal's editor, Fred Wilson, protesting that Zarzynski had left him out of the Champ biography, "*adroitly side-stepped truth, mis-represented* himself and, in doing so maligns me by fabricating an incident which *never* occurred. . . ."[84] Reines was now convinced that Zarzynski was on a quest for personal glory by trying to portray him as an amateur who knew little on Champ. In his article on the photo, Wilson wrote that Zarzynski told him in a phone conversation that he had recently "interviewed" Reines and listened to his "red flags" about the photo but that he "did not take his objections more seriously than those of other non-experts. . . ."[85] This infuriated Reines who was adamant that Zarzynski had never interviewed him.[86] "Please be informed for the *record* that Mr. Zarzynski *never* at any time *ever* interviewed me and . . . was *originally invited* by me in Fall, 1979, to participate in the Mansi case. His outrageous statement to you in placing me with 'other non-experts' and claiming communication with me in a fictitious interview . . . reflects the length he has gone to aggrandize his personal position in this matter *after* he broke off all communication with me in December, 1980. After a 5 year association, his attempts to place himself in P. T. Barnum style ballyhoo as the foremost expert of Champ phenomena on Lake Champlain is *absolute poppycock*."[87] In Zarzynski's defense, whether or not he had formally interviewed Reines, the two men had exchanged letters detailing their opposing stances, and by Reines' own admission they had a frank discussion over their positions on the photo at the recent Champ conference.

On September 17, 1981, Fred Wilson replied by trying to smooth the matter over: "Your letter of September 3 and the 24 attachments was quite unsettling on first reading; less so, second time around, and on third reading the personalities seem to drop back, the objectives come forward, and you and I are found sitting in the same car on the same train on the same track: We look back and we see a flawed investigation imperfectly conducted. . . ." Wilson then asked Reines to write a new letter for publication—dispensing with the behind-the-scenes fracas with Zarzynski. "Would you be willing to write another (much shorter) 'letter to the editor' which would summarize your objections to past procedures in the 'Champ' investigation and your views as to what course the investigation should follow?"[88] The original letter was not published and remained hidden from public view.[89]

THE POST-MANSI MEDIA FREE FOR ALL

After the Mansi photo appeared in *The New York Times*, Reines felt that his fears of a media circus were coming true. The article and photo triggered an avalanche of Champ articles—many of which infuriated Reines. "With very few exceptions, what is being printed is a rehashed reworking of previous magazine articles and newspaper accounts which are outdated or inaccurate and misleading and, in some cases, composed of wild speculation and fantasy," he lamented. "In almost every instance, the author is merely a self-styled 'professional' writer who knows next to nothing about the subject."[90] In reality, shoddily written

Champ articles, especially of the magazine variety, were nothing new. They were simply appearing in greater volume.

Reines then took aim at a regional icon: *Adirondack Life* magazine, sending a letter to editor Bernard Carman, protesting the use of an "outsider" who knew next to nothing about the subject matter, Hal Smith of Windsor, New York, to author a feature article about Champ. Reines complained that he had been plagued by writers such as Smith, "who in some magical manner have been contracted to write the story of 'Champ' with all it's [*sic*] wealth of detail and history without: (1) having any prior personal or objective knowledge of the subject matter, (2) not [being] local to the area where it takes place, (3) [having] no significant scientific expertise, (4) utilizing as the basis of source, only what they have read, in which largely outdated, inaccurate and biased information becomes the basis for their understanding of the phenomenon."[91] To make matters worse, Reines said that Smith had not even attended the Champ seminar. He viewed Smith as a literary mercenary who was simply doing a job for an indifferent editor. Smith's biggest error was to perpetuate the myth that Samuel de Champlain had spotted a twenty-foot Champ that was as thick as a barrel and had a horselike head.[92] "I am absolutely appalled at this dismal display of journalistic ignorance, to what is a respectable (albeit exotic) and exciting subject worthy of impeccable research and mature comment," Reines wrote.[93] Carman staunchly defended the use of Smith by noting that all reporters have biases, and tried to lighten the tenor of the debate by writing that "perhaps we can debate all this one day over a glass of Olde and Mellow hoisted in a congenial waterfront setting."[94] They never did.

In fairness to Carman, having a local writer handle the story would likely have made little difference in the quality of the article. When local historian Marjorie Porter, from Reines' own town of Keeseville no less, wrote her 1970 article in *Vermont Life,* it was not exactly a journalistic masterpiece. Despite being a local and a monster expert, her account contained major errors. Newspaper and magazine articles often contain mistakes. Part of the blame rests with the time pressures that many reporters face as they are expected to be instant experts on a variety of topics. Although that can be used as an excuse for newspaper reporters, we can be less forgiving of magazine writers.

Yet, no less a professional publication than *Time* magazine also got the story wrong, stating matter-of-factly in 1981 that "the lake monster . . . was first reported in 1609 by the French explorer Samuel de Champlain."[95] Of course, the anonymous reporter did not give a source, which means it was most likely taken from an earlier magazine or newspaper article. *Time* is a weekly, meaning that they have more time (no pun intended) than newspapers. Three months later, another national weekly, the *Grit*, said that Champlain had spotted a creature that was "serpentlike, about 20 feet long, and as thick as a barrel."[96] Again, no source is given. Magazine writers often have deadlines that stretch months, and yet journalists for such publications as *Adirondack Life* and *Yankee* all got this basic element of the story wrong.

It is a concern that even when reporters have more time to devote to making the story accurate, they do not, and that includes locals who should presumably know better. Plattsburgh *Press-Republican* reporter Lohr McKinstry has written dozens of stories on Champ spanning at least three decades and is based in the Port Henry area. Yet, despite all of his interviews and local knowledge, he has repeatedly made the claim that the first reported sighting of Champ was by Samuel de Champlain in 1609,[97] a claim challenged as early as 1971 by local historians.[98] Even later books by Champ believers such as Zarzynski (1984) and Dennis Hall (2000) cast suspicion on the claim, suggesting that he saw a gar pike. But that has not stopped McKinstry from reporting this popular myth over the years. In this sense, stoking the mystery has proved to be a cottage industry for local reporters. In 2009, McKinstry went further, writing that the "first sighting was in 1609 by French explorer Samuel de Champlain, who noted in his diary that he had seen a 'sea serpent.'"[99] There is no excuse for this kind of journalism. Even in the unlikely event that McKinstry has never read the books by Zarzynski and Hall and was unaware of the gar explanation, one could argue that area Champ hunters have a responsibility to let him know that the sighting is highly dubious and to stop reporting the claim. Then there is the Village of Port Henry board of trustees, which as recently as 2012, continue to oversee a sightings board which lists as the first witness, Samuel de Champlain in 1609. Surely, for a community that touts itself as "The Home of Champ," village board members and residents would be aware that

Champlain almost certainly saw a garfish. Why haven't local residents jumped up and down in protest and forced the village to take down the Champlain sighting? Why haven't Champ researchers insisted that they remove Champlain's name from the sighting board? Perhaps the story continues to be repeated because it just sounds too good—and as the old adage goes—"Why let the facts get in the way of a good story?" The inescapable conclusion is that there is an air of complicity among many locals who are driven more by dollar signs and local pride than truth. At the very least, there should be an asterisk next to Champlain's alleged sighting. The one local who escapes guilt here is Phil Reines who wrote to area magazines to point out their errors. It has changed little.

Numerous books on the unexplained that carry sections on Champ also continue to spin the myth, as do general interest books. For instance, in their 1994 book, *Day Trips, Getaway Weekends, and Vacations in New England*, Patricia and Robert Foulke write: "Way back in 1609, Champlain wrote about a creature he spotted that was twenty feet long, as thick as a barrel, with a head like a horse and a body like a serpent."[100] What is striking about the voluminous coverage of Champ in books, newspapers and magazines is how very few ever attempt to verify the facts; they simply repeat the Samuel de Champlain myth from other erroneous sources. It is an indictment of modern journalism.

November 1983 saw more skirmishes between the two leading Champologists. After reading Zarzynski's article on Champ in *Adirondack Bits n' Pieces* magazine, Reines sent a strongly worded personal letter to the editor:

> I have read with interest Mr. Zarzynski's article entitled 'Champ A Zoological Jigsaw Puzzle' and offer in the interest of accuracy and objective investigative journalistic reporting the following comments. On page 45 I find my name used and referred to in a derogatory manner as a "self-proclaimed nautical phenomenologist." Well, what then is Mr. Zarzynski, a school teacher who has founded an "exclusive" society entitled rather grandiosely, the "Lake Champlain Phenomena Investigation . . ."? . . . composed of five "select" members. Is this a

scientific society proclaimed and recognized by credentialed scientific associations? No, it is not! Mr. Zarzynski refers to my status as an "instructor . . . at SUC." I am not an instructor but a senior member of the Department of Communications at S.U.N.Y. (State University College of Arts and Science at Plattsburgh and a student of nautical phenomena since 1950).[101]

Two days later, Reines wrote directly to Zarzynski, breaking their long silence. ". . . Joe, what you *don't* say (in the article) regarding *our* involvement in the Mansis' photograph, and your *cutting off* any association, speaks volumes . . . Also, the frankly 'shoddy' manner in which you tried to make believe that I don't exist. I very much appreciate the fact that you never intended to let me know that a scientific seminar had been planned. Frankly, I enjoyed your obvious discomfort caused by my presence."[102] They have not spoken since.

The differences between Reines and Zarzynski pale in comparison to other brouhahas within the cryptozoological community. During the 1970s, one infamous turf war between two competing Bigfooters nearly culminated in fight at a McDonalds. Zarzynski and Reines were certainly never going to come to blows at a McDonalds; it was not in their character, and besides, Zarzynski was a vegetarian—although a salad bar fracas was a possibility. That many cryptozoologists do not get along with their colleagues is a far too common reality. Reines saw himself as the elder statesmen on Champ, and Zarzynski as a young "Johnny come lately" who showed disrespect and disloyalty by his siding with the Mansis in their going public with the photo, even after Reines had invited Joe to join him in trying to verify the picture. Zarzynski felt he owed no allegiance to Reines, who had received the photo to analyse through pure chance, and that although grateful for Reines' help, the Mansis were in charge of the photo, not Reines. Over the past three decades and even today, Reines has harbored suspicions that Zarzynski was involved with Champ, at least partly, for the money. In 2010, he even wrote a short poem about it. "Oh! Joe, Sandi . . . If only T'were so! How sweet T'would be (For thee and thou) To reap the gifts of Lake Champ's 'Fat$ cow!'"[103] There is no evidence that Zarzynski ever received money from the Mansi photo, and as far as his now defunct newsletter *Champ Channels* is concerned, at just a few dollars per year for a subscription, he certainly was not getting rich off it. For Zarzynski, Champ appears to have been a labor of love, if not an obsession, which drained his finances. Reines also was suspicious of attempts to turn Champ into what he termed "a cash cow." He once wrote that "good intentions and altruistic attitudes sour, as greed, hunger for fame and overblown egos, abetted by lawyers and financial gain take hold."[104] Here his fears may be justified, for many people have been benefiting from the Mansi photo.

HOW MUCH IS A MONSTER PHOTO WORTH?— OR CHAMP AS A 401K PLAN

When asked about her famous photo in early July 1981, Sandi Mansi repeatedly declined to say how much *The New York Times* had paid for it, proclaiming, "The price isn't important." She then created a cloud of suspicion over her character by remarking: "One of the national scandal sheets offered us 10 times what the *Times* did but we felt our reputations and the reputation of Lake Champlain, was more important." That figure was reported by the *Press-Republican* to have been $10,000.[105] When news of the story got back to William Stockton, the *Times* science news director, he fired off a letter to the editor of the *Press-Republican*: "We were amused by the report in the July 9 issue of the *Press-Republican* claiming that the *New York Times* paid $10,000 for use of the photograph of the Lake Champlain 'creature.' . . . Had your reporter checked with us, he would have been told that the *Times* didn't pay for use of the photograph; that, in fact, a condition for printing the photograph was that the *Times* not be required to purchase it."[106] The man who wrote the story accompanying the image, John Noble Wilford, later observed, "$10,000 is way out of line. The picture was not that good, nor the story worthy of such an investment."[107] Plattsburgh radio station WIRY seem to have done its homework, as it had been reporting since late June that the *Times* was going to print the photo for free.[108]

This matter is perplexing for someone who claims her primary interest is altruistic. Sandi stated at the same 1981 press conference: "The important thing is that everyone works to see that Champ is protected. We don't need bounty hunters out on the lake shooting at anything that looks like it might be the creature."[109] Mansi's veiled statement claiming that the *Times* had paid for use of the photo, whether true or not, placed her in a questionable light. After all, who is the public going to believe: Mansi or *The New York Times*? With the possible exception of conservative Republicans, most would have sided with the *Times*. Couple this with the claim that she no longer had the negative and could not recall where she had taken the photo; doubts grew about Sandi's motives. It would only get worse.

In 1979, Mansi was working as a sheet metal worker at the Electric Boat Company in Groton, Connecticut, which designs and builds nuclear submarines for the U.S. Navy. She recalled that one day General Dynamics "wanted to send me to Scotland, and I didn't want to go." A workmate spoke up, offering to take her place. His reason: He was keen to see the Loch Ness Monster. That is when Sandi said she retorted: "You don't have to go to Scotland to see it; you can see it right here in Lake Champlain." According to Mansi, when the colleague expressed skepticism, she brought the photo in to show him, swearing him to secrecy, but unfortunately, he told one other person, who in turn told another, and before long, word had spread and her phone was ringing off the hook.[110]

Mansi's co-worker tells a different story. Roy Kappeler said that one day at work he told Mansi about an article on Champ that he had seen in the April 1978 *Reader's Digest*, "Is There a Monster in Lake Champlain?" Much to his surprise, he said that Mansi brought the photo to work. Upon seeing it, Kappeler said, "I nearly hit the floor. . . ."[111]

Kappeler convinced Mansi to let him serve as her business manager to represent the image. Soon after the photo appeared in *The New York Times*, Kappeler claimed that he was short-changed by the Mansis' attorneys. He said they "told me I was fired, right when things started looking good." He continued: "I've got a piece of paper in a safe deposit box that says the money gets split in thirds, between the Manzis [*sic*] and me."[112]

Kappeler painted a picture of Sandi Mansi as an opportunist hoping for a big payday. "She would come to work and say things like, 'Are you ready to get rich kid?' and we'd talk about it most every day. I thought their lawyers were supposed to cover all three of us. I was kind of surprised with the way things worked out when I met with them. . . . I'm the one who brought this whole thing out," a bitter Kappeler recounted.[113] Regardless of what was paid, the affair raised questions about her motives. It would be safe to say that Sandi Mansi should not go into a public relations career.

Now to answer the question posed earlier: How much is a monster photo worth? In October 1981, Mansis' agent for the sale, New York-based Gamma-Liaison, said that one-time publication rights for the photo cost $500.[114] After filing suits in both federal and Connecticut State courts, by mid-1982, Roy Kappeler settled his case out of court, receiving 6 percent "of the royalties of any sales of the photograph. . . ."[115] Kappeler said at the time that he was not only hoping to cash in on any sales of the photo to be published in print, but also images appearing on Champ paraphernalia. "If it does explode, I've still got my hands in the pie," he said. His ultimate goal was to be able to quit his day job and live off his Champ earnings. "You might want Champ on the bottom of your ash tray. Post cards, knick knacks, everything. That's where the money's going to be. If you were up there and you wanted to send a post card, what would you send? Champ!" he gushed.[116] Kappeler had dreams of Champ rivaling Loch Ness, where Nessie is the main tourist draw to the Scottish Highlands, generating a hefty income for many locals through souvenir sales. Clearly, he was not thrilled with his settlement, but at least it was some reward for his involvement in promoting the photo. Kappeler says he was offered up to $5,000 to buy out his 6 percent. "As it is I've lost money. But in the long run, I'm sure it will pay off," he said. The settlement took effect on July 15, 1982, and by December he said he had received a total of $83 for his 6 percent—all coming from its showing on *The Merv Griffin* show. That means the show had to shell out just under $1,400 to air the image.[117] Keeping in mind that the photo has appeared in such high-profile publications as *Time* magazine and *Macleans* (a prominent Canadian publication), and in numerous books and TV documentaries, the image has almost certainly generated tens of thousands of dollars over the years. When Champ skeptic Ben Radford asked to include the photo in his 2006 book, *Lake Monster Mysteries* with Joe Nickell, he was told the going price was $1,000![118] Of course, Kappeler and Mansi do not receive all of the money, much of which appears to be going to lawyers. In 1982, the prime business agent for the photo received a 40 percent cut, while Kappeler's attorney, Timothy Bates of New London, Connecticut, was reportedly getting a 3 percent cut.[119] When I first emailed Kappeler and Bates to ask for their comment on the photo dispute, I thought it odd that they never responded. After all, it seemed in Kappeler's best interests to present his side of the story. I later realized the likely reason why: They had resolved the dispute and were both receiving a cut from the photo.

In 1992, Sandi Mansi told a journalist that she had received less than $3,000 after licensing the picture.[120] Without a doubt, the photo has generated a considerable sum of money that is being split many different ways: Sandi Mansi, Anthony Mansi's estate, Roy Kappeler, Kappeler's attorney, Mansi's attorney, and who knows who else! Such rewards may have come with their own price tag in terms of Mansi's credibility. If, as the saying goes, "Possession is nine-tenths of the law," then in the world of public opinion, perception is nine-tenths of reality, and in the case Sandi Mansi, her willingness to accept money for the photo is one more reason to view the image with suspicion, however unfair it may seem.

THE MARKETING OF A MONSTER: CHAMP INCORPORATED

In Hollywood, townsfolk carrying torches, pitchforks, and shotguns typically gang up on monsters to drive them out of town. In 1980, a curious thing happened: The Village of Port Henry, New York, actually embraced Champ with open arms and undertook an organized attempt to cash in on the creature. On October 6, the Board of Trustees adopted a resolution to protect Champ. At the prompting of Mayor Bob Brown, it read in part: ". . . all the waters of Lake Champlain which adjoin the Village of Port Henry are hereby declared to be off limits to anyone who would in any way harm, harass or destroy the Lake Champlain Sea Monster."[121] Brown officially claimed that the reason was out of concern for the critter's safety. "We had received reports of people shooting at the Lake Champlain Sea Monster," he told *The New York Times*. The move was clearly motivated more by economics than altruism, and village officials conceded as much. Chamber of

Commerce president Bob Dubois admitted that the community was placing its faith in Champ to pull them out of the economic doldrums that began six years earlier when the last of the nearby iron ore mines closed.[122] After supporting the community for more than one hundred years, the local industry dried up in the late 1960s as 1,100 miners received severance notices. By 1975, the industry was dead, leaving the area economically destitute.[123] The tiny community was soon floundering and financially adrift, in search of a new industry to serve as an anchor to draw tourists. That's when the idea of cashing in on Champ was devised, with the prompting of Zarzynski, who had made several visits to Loch Ness, a textbook case of how to market a monster. Nessie is estimated to attract upward of $12 million annually to the Scottish Highlands, which actively promotes the No. 1 draw card.[124] Of course, the Scottish Highlands has advantages that Port Henry and Lake Champlain do not, such as Europe in its backyard. For decades, numerous films and TV shows have touted Nessie's possible existence, amounting to a free advertising campaign. In 1992, the small town of Seljord, Norway even sent a task force to visit the area and learn how they could market their own lake monster.[125]

Before adopting Champ as its mascot, the local Chamber of Commerce had been heading in a very different direction and was considering naming the village "the ice-fishing capital of the world." Champ won out.[126] The chamber even had stationary printed with a smiling Champ, as if the point needed to be underscored,[127] and a Champlain Valley Bank began giving away a twenty one-inch stuffed Champ for anyone opening a new account of at least $300.[128] From the mid-1800s to the early 1970s, Port Henry was a thriving community due mainly to its rich iron ore deposits. But with the closing of Republic Steel in 1971, an era had passed. By the 1980 Census, one in every fifteen residents had left Port Henry, and many of those who stayed were forced to travel up to fifty miles just to get to work.[129] Anthony Mydlarz thought the move to adopt Champ was much ado about nothing. "It's a goddamned watersoaked log, and all the people who see it are soaked too," he sniped, while another local, campsite attendant Peter Tromblee, referred to the hoop-la as "that lake monster crap." He estimated that 90 percent of locals were Champ atheists.[130] Over the years, residents from neighboring communities have made

light of Port Henry for billing itself as "The Home of Champ." In
nearby Westport, Charlotte Jones called Port Henry's move to adopt
Champ "a beautiful fraud," quipping: "That's all they have to do (in
Port Henry) and that's all they have going for them. It's a shame."[131]
One Port Henryite took exception with another resident of Westport
who expressed resentment over attempts to capitalize economically on
Champ, observing that it was not surprising as "they also got upset
when we got to give sandwiches instead of them to the Olympic
torchbearers on the way to Lake Placid" (in 1980).[132]

The Port Henry Champ resolution received national exposure
including a mention on the ABC Evening News.[133] An article in *The
New York Times* published the following month aptly summed up the
situation: "Village on Lake Champlain Seeking Its Fortune in Tale of a
Fabulous Sea Monster," proclaimed the headline.[134] Soon the legislative
floodgates were opened. On April 20, 1982, the Vermont House of
Representatives voted 77 to 28 to adopt a resolution protecting Champ.
The New York State Legislature followed suit in April 1983. The resolutions were heavily watered down (no pun intended) and were useless
as practical documents. For instance, New York State lawmakers held
"that 'Champ' should be protected from any willful act resulting in
death, injury or harassment. . . ." They affirmed that both New York
and Vermont encourage scientific inquiry into its existence, and that
witnesses "are encouraged to report sightings of such animals or associated phenomena and photographic evidence whenever possible."[135]

Like the measure passed in Port Henry two years earlier, these
efforts were more show than substance; more symbolic than concrete.
The mystery was no closer to being solved. The resolutions did not
protect the creature; they only *suggested* that it should be protected!
The significance was from the national and international exposure. All
three resolutions amounted to a free plug for communities along the
lake that were trying to capitalize on their proximity to the "monster."
Perhaps someone in Connecticut or West Virginia would decide to
rent a local boat and search for Champ—ideally while munching on a
Champburger and Monster Fries and wearing a newly bought Champ
T-shirt.[136] What would really happen in the unlikely event that someone shot Champ? The fine would be "chicken feed" compared with
the money and notoriety that they would likely receive for securing

the carcass—if it could be accomplished. Let's face it, few people are going to spend much jail time for "bumping off" Champ—although reckless use of a firearm is a distinct possibility. They might even be able to dodge that charge by claiming self-defense, arguing Champ was on a collision course for their boat! If someone were to shoot Champ and produce the carcass, for all the tragedy, they would be on every major morning TV show and on the front page of newspapers around the world. One could envision the shooter being interviewed on *The Today Show* with PETA (People for Ethical Treatment of Animals) activists protesting in the background, their cries drowned out by chants from NRA (National Rifle Association) supporters.

By 1987, the lake monster business was starting to wear thin on the political front. On March 17, the Vermont House of Representatives passed a resolution calling for the Lake Memphremagog monster to be protected, prompting some politicians to grumble, having grown weary of passing perfunctory resolutions. When it came time to vote, many responded with an emphatic "No!" to reflect their irritation at passing what they deemed to be frivolous legislation. Democrat Frank DaPrato of Swanton was part of the anti-monster contingent: "If we keep this up, we'll have monsters in every pond in Vermont. I think it's ridiculous that we get involved in something like this. I think we should be doing something more constructive with our time." Proponents claimed that the resolution boasted something that the Champ legislation had left out: the recognition that Memphre held dual citizenship as the lake extends into Canada.[137] Once again, the legislation was entirely impractical and toothless, having two real purposes: to boost tourism and keep a small constituency happy. By the late 1980s, even the State of Vermont jumped onto the Champ bandwagon when they came out with "Search for Champ" scratch-off lottery tickets. One probably had more of a chance of winning the $1,000 prize as of seeing Champ himself.

Starting in the early 1980s, Champ-related cottage industries cropped up along both sides of the lake, but nowhere more evident than in Port Henry, where shopkeepers peddled Champ mugs and an array of trinkets and bric-a-brac: The typical tourist fare included hats, aprons, tea towels, baby bibs, key chains, bumper stickers, calendars, coasters, fridge magnets, pens, and postcards. There was even a Champ shot glass that could be used to induce sightings. For the person who had everything, there was a hand-blown glass sculpture of Champ retailing for several hundred dollars.[138] One of the more novel items was "Champ Pro Wheat Pancake and Waffle Mix" sold by Anne Johnson in Westport, New York.[139] Another local cottage industry involves the many people who claim to have taken Champ videos, only to run to an attorney to try to profit. After capturing a possible Champ on video in 1992, Frank Soriano of Ticonderoga tried selling it to TV shows including NBC's *Unsolved Mysteries*, and was reportedly intending to sell Champ T-shirts at Champ Day.[140] Although there is little doubt that Soriano honestly videotaped something in the lake, his credibility, and that of others who claimed to have videotapes, would be enhanced if they stopped trying to profit from their images. On the other hand, they have every legal right to make money. Soriano's credibility is not enhanced by his claim, six years later, that on July 2, 1998, he videotaped a UFO flying over the St. Mary's Church steeple in Ticonderoga. When he had difficulty remembering what happened that day, he contacted famous UFO author Budd Hopkins who reportedly placed Soriano under regressive hypnosis and went back to the time of the sightings. Soriano recalled being abducted by space aliens and having his conscious memory of the event erased.[141]

In recent years, the annual Champ festival has resembled more of an annual crafts and entertainment fair than anything to do with Champ. By the mid-1990s, Champ the magic money dragon was puffed out as the monster mania waned. To date, there has been no golden egg. Yet, given his complicated past, one cannot discount the possibility of Champ making yet another comeback. It would not be surprising to see Champ resurface again with a major media splash, for he is only one spectacular sighting or mobile phone image away from renewed fame. The waxing, waning history of Champ proves that there is a fine line between celebrity and obscurity. One is reminded of the old public relations adage: "What is the difference between a rat and a squirrel?" Answer: A fluffy tail and a good publicist. With a lucky break here and a twist of fate there, Champ could be front-page news again.

By the mid-1990s, it was evident that the promised prosperity had not materialized as Champ was proving to be more of a novelty and a sideshow than a tourist draw. By 1996, Susan Green observed that

Champ appeared "to have plummeted from glory" after having been a source of recent regional pride. "Although depicted as a grinning cartoon on T-Shirts, mugs, and other tourist-trap trinkets, this creature radiated dignity befitting an ancient legend. Books were published on the subject. Experts theorized about paleontological origins. Newspapers carried reports of the latest sightings, as Champ caught the spotlight of international celebrity." Green wrote that sadly, the magic and allure were all but gone. "Today, apart from lending his or her name to a local car wash and radio station, there's barely a whisper about the big beast. . . . After fading into semi-obscurity, can Champ now be resurrected?" In short, Champ had lost his mojo. Aside from the occasional newspaper report and TV documentary, in the absence of any compelling photos or video, interest was steadily waning.[142] Some attempts to market Champ over the previous decades were imaginative and must have sounded good on paper, but ended up looking goofy. For instance, at one point, the village of Port Henry had installed coin-operated telescopes along the lake for tourists. Perhaps at night they could have used them to spot UFOs. Of course, not every idea was accepted. One man tried to get the former mayor to sign on to a tacky "Styrofoam-and-wood dragon boat, complete with blinking red eyes and nostrils that snort smoke" to be used as a kiddie ride.[143] The economic prosperity promised by Champonomics has never materialized, and by the end of the first decade of the twenty-first century, interest in the annual Champ Day Festival could best be described as subdued.[144]

Throughout the 1980s and 1990s and into the early twenty-first century, tabloid journalists had a field day with Champ. *The Weekly World News* seemed to have a fetish for the critter. One memorable series of tongue-in-cheek stories chronicled several purported ongoing altercations between Champ and Nessie in the Atlantic Ocean. They were apparently made up because on at least one occasion, Champ was alleged to have impregnated the Scottish lass. The far-fetched story ("Nessie Pregnant—and Champ's the Daddy") appeared on page 2 of the same issue that carried the headline: "Three-Legged Skater Banned!"[145] Although these accounts were silly and unrealistic, they also were hilarious. Like "professional wrestling," the storylines were so outlandish that no one would have believed them (at least we hope

Figure 4.6. Champy is the official mascot of the Burlington-based Vermont Lake Monsters minor league baseball team (Shane Bufano Photography).

so!). Mercifully, *The Weekly World News* went out of business in 2007. It was known for printing farfetched stories at the time such as "Ross Perot Space Alien," complete with pointed ears! Ridiculous as it was, these stories helped to keep Champ in the national public eye.

EGOS, OBSESSIONS, AND THE QUEST FOR FAME

The Monster Hunters

When we have strong emotions, we can easily fool ourselves.
—EVERYBODY SAYS IT

There are no university degrees for cryptozoology, although a few real scientists from a variety of disciplines dabble in the subject, mostly in the fields of zoology and biology. The search for hidden animals lies on the fringe of orthodox science, attracting a large number of amateurs who lack training in the natural sciences. This is the case in the search for Champ, where the leading researchers have no degrees in zoology or biology, resulting in an array of differing approaches and opinions. Dennis Hall thinks Champ is a Tanystropheus; Joe Zarzynski is convinced it is a plesiosaur; Phil Reines opts for an ancient sluglike creature. Biologist Gary Mangiacopra concludes that Champ is likely none of the above, but a misidentification of known creatures. Given the wide-open nature of the field, it was inevitable that cryptozoologists would end up squabbling. The history of Loch Ness is also filled with sordid encounters between rival factions, each hoping to be the first to prove the existence of the elusive Nessie. Rivalries, jealousies, and misunderstandings pervade cryptozoology. Champ is no different and anyone hunting the creature has to develop a thick skin to be able to handle the inevitable ridicule that comes with the territory. But even more challenging is dealing with rivals and the tension that arises when there is more than one hunter for any given monster. This is evident in the discussion in Chapter 4 about the dispute between Zarzynski and Reines. To be fair, other branches of cryptozoology are far worse. For instance, for the sheer volume of disputes it would be hard to beat the Bigfooters. At any given time, most of the several dozen Bigfoot groups that have sprouted up across the United States seem to be in a state of perpetual squabbling. The issues range from whether or not to shoot the critter and obtain a specimen to who should be privy to the location of the latest secret Bigfoot stomping ground that is under surveillance.

A typical example of what is wrong with the field is the New York-based Northeast Sasquatch Research Society. While the organization purports to be scientific, the first tenet is: "BELIEF in the existence of the awe inspiring hominid creature known alternately as Sasquatch or Bigfoot."[1] Pardon me, but as much as I would like to believe, and although there may be compelling "soft" evidence, the existence of Bigfoot is not yet proven. How can this group expect to be taken seriously when they make such assumptions? A more appropriate tenet would be "to gather evidence to prove the *possible* existence of the Big Guy." The members are not the problem but the egotistical structure of the organization is. The society is anything but democratic. The bylaws state that members can only be approved by the director, and are strictly forbidden from engaging in independent research, sharing or discussing their research with outsiders without the director's permission. The director and godhead leader of the group, Bill Brann, writes:

> No member, new or old, will be permitted to engage in in-dependent field research of reported sightings of creatures, or their spoor without first obtaining permission to do so from the Director. Failure to comply with this most serious of restrictions will be cause for the most severe censure, which might include expulsion from Northern Sasquatch Research Society.[2]

Organizations like this are part of the problem because they foster secrecy and the underlying goal appears to be taking credit as the first group to prove the existence of Bigfoot.[3] What is wrong with conducting independent research? What is the big deal about sharing and discussing your research with others? If Bigfoot investigation groups want to be taken seriously in the eyes of the public and credible scientists, they could begin by being more open and transparent. Just imagine what would happen if most scientists conducted their research like this. We would still be living in the dark ages.

Even when sympathetic mainstream scientists try to get involved to lend more credibility to the field, human nature rears its ugly head. The events of May 1978 are a case in point. That is when the University of British Columbia (UBC) agreed to host a Bigfoot conference. What transpired is a testament to why scientists are hesitant to embrace cryptozoology as a full-fledged discipline. For anyone familiar with the field, the outcome was as predictably absurd as it was comical. As Bigfoot researcher Rene Dahinden appeared before a scrum of reporters, journalist Richard Louv recorded what happened next:

> "Peter Byrne [a rival Bigfoot hunter] is a 5 lb sack of sh★#."
> The reporters scribble.
> Dahinden rattles off accusations against Byrne; his words spill out and run together: "Borrowed copy of Patterson film off me . . . slides . . . showed all over the goddamn place . . . "Mike Douglas Show" . . . a $25,000 court action . . . Byrne countered with a suit of $30,000 . . . poor Mrs. Patterson . . . a criminal suit . . . son of a bitch is always running off hiding." The reporters have stopped scribbling and are slowly looking up at one another, confused. What's going on? [At this point, Dahinden points his finger at another researcher, Jon Beckjord, who is setting up a display nearby.]
> The reporters turn in unison and look at Beckjord. . . . "That Beckjord doesn't even have class," Dahinden continues, shaking his finger. "He's just a nut."[4]

Later tensions boiled over; at one point it appeared a fistfight might break out as Beckjord took his finger and poked Dahinden in the chest. A diminutive, bearded UBC professor rushed in to separate the combatants. "Gentlemen. Gentlemen." A more physical confrontation was averted—at least for the moment.[5] Meanwhile, the appearance of anthropologist Grover Krantz of Washington State University evoked bitter feelings among amateurs. Krantz was a vocal advocate of shooting the creature to prove its reality. "I want to rub a few faces in the corpse," he said with indignation, telling anyone who would listen to "shoot it, cut off an arm or a leg or anything you can carry and get the hell out."[6] It will come as no surprise that there was no second

Bigfoot conference at the university. Although the 1981 Champ Conference was civil as cryptozoology events go, as outlined in Chapter 4, it was not without its tensions.

Over the years, several Champ chasers have made their indelible marks in the search for the elusive creature. Their messages were essentially the same—Champ exists—but they went about trying to prove it in different ways. In the case of Dennis Jay Hall, who will be introduced shortly, it is the tale of a man with a Walter Mitty imagination, who saw himself as The Anointed One in a quasi-religious quest for individual glory in trying to prove Champ's existence. For Zarzynski, it is a story of frustration and comically bad timing—although his preoccupation with the creature would eventually result in a marriage proposal—not to an inflatable Champ, but his eventual wife. For Elizabeth von Muggenthaler, who claims to have heard Champ on several occasions, it is the account of an amateur scientist engaging in wishful thinking. Another investigator, Phil Reines, retired SUNY Plattsburgh professor, has been a fiercely outspoken opponent of attempts to sensationalize the topic or exploit Champ for financial gain. This led to his inevitable fallout with both Zarzynski and the Mansis when they went public with their now famous photo.

JOSEPH ZARZYNSKI: CHAMP—A LOVE STORY

In 1974, Zarzynski took a job as a social studies teacher at Saratoga Springs Junior High School. Known to his friends as "Zarr," the Endicott, New York native stood out from the crowd as a six-foot-six-inch tall vegetarian with an interest in Loch Ness. Lured by the mystery and enthralled by the beauty and romance of the Loch, he flew to Scotland in 1975 to experience the wonder firsthand. A self-admitted fitness fanatic, he once jogged the entire length of the Loch—approximately 28.5 miles, from Fort Augustus to Lochend, completing the run in 4.23 hours. And no, he did not sight Nessie.[7]

When he began to hear stories of a similar creature on his doorstep in Lake Champlain, he made his first visit to the lake in 1975. He was smitten, and the rest as they say, is history. From the mid-1970s to the mid-1980s, Zarr was Champ's personal PR agent, giving hundreds of media interviews and countless talks to area schools, libraries, museums, even village boards and both the New York and Vermont state legislatures. At parties, he was routinely introduced as "That guy on the news who hunts monsters." He did more to put Champ in the public eye than any one person. During the late 1970s and early 1980s, he was married to his cryptozoology work, focusing his affections on Champ. For most of the previous decade he corresponded on specially printed stationary with the banner: "Courtship with a Lake Monster." That changed in 1984, the year he became involved in a love triangle of sorts, a threesome sparked by his love for Champ. For eight years he had been asking the Saratoga Springs school librarian, Pat Meany, to help look up information on Champ and other lake monsters, in addition to the more mundane world of social studies. Then they began dating. Although Zarr had caught her eye, Meany was not sure it would ever happen, recalling: "I figured he would never take an interest in me because he was so obsessed with Champ," she later recalled.[8] They were married in April 1985.

His unusual stationary habits aside, Zarzynski cannot be described as eccentric by any means, though during the mid-1970s he had a

Figure 5.1. Joe Zarzynski assembling a sonar tripod near Button Bay in 1980 with Paul Bartholomew. He believed that this was the most likely site of the Mansi photo (Robert Bartholomew photo).

pair of specially designed glasses made up with a hand-painted picture of Champ in one corner. Although he rarely wore them, he would joke that it allowed him to have a sighting any time he felt like it. Throughout his years of Champ hunting, Zarr had one major characteristic in his favor: He exuded normalcy. He was well aware that some would brand him a weirdo but that rarely happened. His position as a schoolteacher and his quiet demeanor and good looks, lent credibility to the cause. In 1981, NBC filmed a segment on Zarzynski the monster hunter to be featured on the popular NBC TV show *Real People*. Doing the show was a double-edged sword because although it offered Champ national exposure and the possibility of more people coming forward with their sightings, it also was known for making people look peculiar or creepy. During the taping, the producers wanted him to sit in a rowboat donning a Sherlock Holmes hat. He refused. Good for him. Documentary makers, especially those exploring marginal topics like Bigfoot and lake monsters, are notorious for portraying their subjects in all sorts of compromising ways if they think it will boost audience numbers. When the show finally aired, it did portray him as somewhat obsessive, but it is the risk one runs when going on national TV on a show designed first and foremost as entertainment.[9]

Zarr says that he once saw Champ in a dream. He was scanning the lake when Champ appeared before him. At that moment he realized that he had left his camera in the cabin. Playing amateur psychoanalyst, Zarr thinks it is a cautionary tale about being prepared. From that day on, he began to carry a camera around his neck religiously.[10] In 1988, he says he *might* have caught a glimpse of his elusive quarry, but by his description, it sounds more like wishful thinking. He reported spotting, through binoculars, a dark, animate object thrashing on the water.[11] The trouble is, it was up to a mile away and could have been anything from a somersaulting Champ to a frolicking beaver.

Life is not always fair and has played its share of cruel tricks on Zarzynski, like the day in 1983 while he and his wife to be were staying in a cabin in Vergennes, Vermont. Each day as they sat patiently on the cabin porch overlooking the water, a fisherman would pass by in his boat and give a friendly wave. The only day they left the porch was to attend a meeting. As fate would have it, the next day the man came by to tell them of the strange commotion he had seen in front of their cabin that very evening—including three huge black humps rising above the water! No one can fault him or Pat for not trying. During their stay they even ate meals on their porch—not gazing into each other's eyes as newlyweds often do, but facing the lake in hopes of maximizing the statistical probability of glimpsing Champ.[12]

Two years later, during summer 1985, the couple stayed at their Vergennes cabin, scanning the lake for any sign of Champ despite winds and rain making their task more difficult. Then on June 29, Zarr packed up their belongings and headed back to their Wilton home. That afternoon—a quiet, overcast day in Vergennes—Champ was sighted not far from their cabin! The lake was quiet; there was not a boat in sight. Peg McGeoch was babysitting some pets at a house on the shore when she noticed a commotion on the lake. "I was facing north in a chair by the window when I saw what I thought were three big fish doing a ballet. Then I realized it was only one." She turned to her friend and co-worker from the Basin Harbor Gift Shop, Jane Temple, who confirmed that she wasn't seeing things. The creature then went under the water, only to pop back up and put on a show for upward of ten minutes as the pair looked on in disbelief. As it resurfaced, she said, "the front end came out of the water about five feet." She could clearly see two humps. "It was like a caterpillar going along a table, and under the water it was wiggling. Its disturbance was not a wake like a boat makes. It was more like sideways ripples," she said. When asked by a journalist what she would have done if she'd been alone, McGeoch had no hesitation: "I wouldn't have talked to you!"[13] It was as if the cosmos were playing with Zarzynski, who could only shake his head in frustration.

Champ: Beyond the Legend

Zarr's book, *Champ: Beyond the Legend*,[14] was published in 1984. A more apt title might have been: *The Case for Champ*. The book focuses on the Mansi photo and the modern-day search. The fundamental problem he faced was in reaching the masses, as Bannister Publications was a small regional company based in Port Henry, New York. Bannister lacked both the marketing power and distribution network to elevate the book beyond upstate New York and Vermont.[15]

The book polarized readers. Believers loved it; naysayers attacked it. In the latter category was Plattsburgh librarian Tim Hartnett who condemned the book's crusading style, noting that "it seems the author can barely contain his exuberance. The book's overall tone is that of a celebrity biography written by an adoring fan."[16] Hartnett takes Zarzynski to task for treating the Mansi photo as the Holy Grail of Lake Monsterology. Journalist Jack Downs expressed similar concerns, writing that the book makes "sweeping generalizations that have turned off some sceptics—persuading them to shelve his book beside 'Chariots of the Gods' and several pseudoscience adventures."[17] In Zarzynski's defense, the book was anything but pseudoscientific, but it was distinctly uncritical and pro-Champ. Critics who charged that the work was one-sided were correct, but so are most cryptozoology books. The title was an accurate portrayal of its contents: the search for Champ. It was never meant to be a definitive study or even a scientific treatise.[18] It was what it was: A broad overview of the evidence for Champ, intended for popular consumption. In this regard, the book was a success and was endorsed by noted cryptozoologist Loren Coleman who "found his research thorough and his method enthusiastic."[19] Underwater explorer Clive Cussler, author of *Raise the Titanic!* also came to his rescue, calling it "a stunning job of research and investigating . . ."[20] Probably the biggest criticism was the conspicuous absence of the many nineteenth-century sightings, most likely because to have included them would have raised a sticky issue: How to explain the many incredible reports of the serpent slithering across land.

In a 1986 interview, Zarr acknowledged that the excitement and allure of pursuing Champ was fading. "The mystery is gone for me already," he said, given his certainty in the creature's existence. A few years later, he had dropped out of the search altogether. He said that there's one part of him that does not want Champ to be found because then the mystery and the thrill of the chase will be over. "I wouldn't throw away my camera. But for a cryptozoologist, finding the animal means losing it. It's not hidden anymore. Then it belongs to the zoologists."[21] By the early 1990s, with his faith in Champ beginning to erode, he admitted to Vermont mystery writer Joe Citro: "I used to be 99.9% sure Champ existed. Now I'm down to 95%. Why? I suppose it's the seventeen years of effort, with little to show but three hundred Champ sightings, a few photos, and some rather poor video."[22]

Zarr's major contribution to the history of Champ was his documentation of sightings from the mid-1970s to the mid-1990s, and his role during this time as the creature's No. 1 PR agent. No one person has done more to raise the profile of the Champlain monster than Zarzynski. He projected an image of charm and boyish enthusiasm. His one shortcoming was his preoccupation with the Mansi photo and his willingness to accept the couple's claims on faith alone, which became fodder for critics. He would later become an apologist for the Mansis. For instance, he once said when they tried to find the spot of their famous photo two years later in 1979, "They were a little bit disoriented. But to their credit, things *had* changed. What was once a field were now condos and houses. Dirt roads had been paved . . . and there'd been a general facelift."[23] But it was not as if there had been a massive economic boom in the region north of St. Albans in the intervening two years, and even if there had, it is hard to image this having any bearing on the inability of the couple to locate the spot. In reality, it was the Mansis who were at best apathetic about trying to find the location.

During his search years, Zarr was fond of saying that men had been hung on much less evidence than there is for Champ.[24] This is a good point that proves two things. First, there are some people in prison who should not be, and second, the Mansi photo is compelling to look at. Neither of these points alters the fact that the negative is still missing and the Mansis cannot find the location. It is perhaps ironic then, that after Zarzynski devoting much of his book to the Mansi photo, Sandi Mansi would later part ways with him, after he kept urging her to try to locate the spot where she took the photo. The fallout happened after Sandi received a letter from Zarzynski pleading with her to keep trying. Mansi later recalled that when she received the letter, she turned it over and wrote: "no, no, no, no, NO," and mailed it back. That was the last time they had contact.[25]

Although Zarr has been criticized for having been seduced by the Mansi photograph and moving from researcher to advocate, it is fair to say that most cryptozoologists believe in the reality of the creatures they are stalking. Zarzynski never claimed to be a scientist, and taking such a stance is not a crime. Sir Arthur Conan Doyle (1859–1930), creator of one of the most logical minds the world has ever known—Sherlock Holmes—believed in fairies. Like Zarzynski, a photograph convinced Doyle—several in this instance. Two young girls from Yorkshire, England took the photo in 1917. The girls, 16-year-old Elcie Wright and her 10-year-old cousin Frances Griffiths, who later confessed to the hoax as elderly women, had fooled him. The ultimate irony is that the book that the photo images were cut from, *Princess Mary's Gift Book* by Claude Shepperson, contained a short story by none other than the great man himself: Arthur Conan Doyle.[26] He would almost certainly have received a copy of the book, but never made the connection. Reines points out that after having lost a son in the Great War, the grief-stricken Doyle turned to spiritualism and the belief in fairies, hoping to prove the reality of life after death. He wanted desperately to believe. In a similar vein and by his own admission, Zarzynski had an emotional and financial investment in proving the creature's reality. Like Doyle, he too wanted to believe and acted on faith to accept its existence without definitive proof. Both stories serve as cautionary tales for cryptozoologists and scientists alike, of the caveats of getting too close to the subject of study.

THE CURIOUS CASE OF DENNIS HALL

In 1992, an enigmatic figure emerged as the leading Champ chaser, picking up the mantle of Champ champion as Zarzynski was leaving the field to take up underwater archaeology after twenty years of searching in vain. That's when Dennis Jay Hall of Panton, Vermont, created the nonprofit organization ChampQuest in an effort to identify the Champlain monster and prevent the spread of zebra mussels—a lofty if somewhat odd combination. He even had a Champ hotline for witnesses to call in their sightings (0-700-SIGHTED). In 1997, Hall launched a high-profile website by the same name.

If Hall were to write an autobiography, an apt title might be *The Chosen One*. To hear him tell the story, at an early age he was seemingly destined to search for Champ. He claims that as a 9-year-old boy an aunt and uncle had a close encounter while boating in Plattsburgh

Bay. But that was only the beginning. By 1999, Hall boasted of having spotted Champ on no less than twenty occasions! In 1985, he claimed to have videotaped Champ while feeding near Basin Harbor, Vermont, and claims to have taken other video and photographs of the creature. During a later encounter on July 6, 2000, he claimed to have videotaped no less than two long-necked Champs.

The Scientific Discovery of the Century—or Not

Although Mr. Hall's enthusiasm for Champ was undeniable and at times boundless, his claims often were so extreme and ludicrous that they would destroy any semblance of credibility that he may have had. Although a charitable interpretation could place him in the category of the "overly excitable type," there were other claims that should have started alarm bells ringing for anyone with an inkling of common sense. For instance, he makes the preposterous claim that in 1976 he was standing next to his father when the elder Hall captured a baby Champ!

The strange-looking specimen was supposedly discovered in a marsh bordering the lake. He told members of the Champ Trackers blog: "It was twelve inches long, held itself up on four sturdy legs, omitted a hissing sound and had a forked tongue. I was lucky that the man who caught the baby was my father, William H. Hall and that I was there. I have much more to say about this catch, and you will be able to read about it in '*The Ultimate Search.*'"[27] Presumably if one did not want to buy the book, they would miss out on the details of this extraordinary episode in world zoological history. However, it contains little additional information except for a description. Hall writes that it resembled "a snapping turtle without a shell. It held its body well off the ground as it walked out of the water. The gait was that of a turtle. The tongue of the animal was forked and darted in and out as it tested the air." He described the head as "a cross between a snake and a turtle and was attached to a short neck. The body was slender with a medium length tail. The feet had five web clawed toes."[28] After reading the book, Ben Radford contacted Hall to find out what happened to the baby Champ. Hall said that scientists at the University of Vermont examined the critter, proclaiming that it resembled no known living reptile. Failing to identify it, the scientists sent it to

Vergennes Union High School where it was kept in the science lab, where, years later, Hall said it was accidentally tossed out when the room was upgraded![29]

Later, while leafing through a book on dinosaurs, Hall said he saw a creature that looked nearly identical to the one he found: Tanystropheus, a long-necked aquatic reptile that fed on fish and is believed to have been extinct for millions of years.[30] Think about it. You catch what appears to be a living baby dinosaur and take it to a university where scientists proclaim it is like no other reptile they have ever seen. Is this not worthy of a press conference? When in 1938, fishermen off the coast of South Africa caught a coelacanth, a fish thought to have been extinct for more than 60 million years, it was dubbed the find of the century. Would this discovery be any less significant? Who are the scientists involved? Why are they not named? Surely such a find would be the crowning pinnacle of any scientific career and perhaps merit an honorary doctorate in zoology. Imagine—you catch what you believe to be a baby aquatic dinosaur—the zoological find of a lifetime, and there is not a single photo of it by either you or the examining scientists! And what happens to this extraordinary find? It is mistakenly thrown out after languishing on the shelf of a high school science lab.

There are more red flags in Hall's story than you would expect to find at a communist convention! You may recall that in 1873, P. T. Barnum offered to pay $50,000 to anyone who could produce the carcass of the Champlain sea serpent; an enormous sum for the time. Surely, finding the carcass of Champ today—to say nothing about a live baby serpent—would be the equivalent of hitting the lottery and would catapult the finder to global fame. Papers would pay huge sums for an exclusive photo of the creature. One could picture the headlines: "Living Fossil Found by Vermont Man and His Son!" or "Baby Dinosaur Found in Lake" along with a captioned photo of the young Hall cradling the little serpentine critter. But alas, despite the enormity of the occasion—a landmark event in modern history—no one thought to snap a photo!

HallQuest: The Ultimate Search

One day in 2007, something strange happened. Without warning, the head of ChampQuest became more elusive than the creature he had been stalking. Famous cryptozoology writer Loren Coleman was one of the first people to break the news on Hall, noting on June 20, 2007, that he had seemingly disappeared from the face of the earth. Coleman wrote: "The virtual vanishing of Dennis Hall . . . is upsetting seekers and friends. For months, [the] Lake Champlain Monster hunter . . . has not been able to be located." He had apparently pulled the plug on [his] old website, ChampQuest.com, which was posting the message: "Gone. The requested resource is no longer available on this server and there is no forwarding address. Please remove all references to this resource." Attempts to reach Hall by phone were also unsuccessful. Coleman said that members of the email group Champ Trackers were baffled by Hall's sudden disappearance. The group's moderator, Sean Clogston, noted that his email address was bouncing: "Dennis Hall mystery deepens. Does anyone have any idea what has happened to Dennis Hall?"[31]

Perhaps Hall dropped out because he could no longer sustain his ever-growing list of startling claims. His sudden departure, without telling his followers anything, certainly created anxiety and hard feelings from those who had supported him. Hall had grown highly sensitive to anyone questioning his views or actions. On one occasion, Coleman had politely questioned Hall's so-called video proof of Champ's existence. Coleman is known for his friendly, nonconfrontational demeanor, and professional approach to the subject. In response, Hall punished Coleman and other Champ Trackers blog members by keeping his latest findings to himself and only revealing them to those who showed loyalty. "It is really something when no one has anything to say about solid evidence presented to them. There will be no more info coming from Lake Champlain until this group starts to live up to its name."[32] The problem was, Hall's research conclusions were based on hope, faith, and wishful thinking, not science, and anyone who questioned him was seen as a Champ denier. He then wrote about being the world's only *true* cryptozoologist and as such, was not receiving due credit or respect. "Nessie is not a Plesiosaur . . . it is a Tanystropheus (reptile) and the sooner that is excepted [*sic*] the sooner Loch Ness research will catch up with that being conducted by Champ Quest. The BBC is a joke. The Discovery Channel is a joke," Hall snapped. "I learned more about and captured 6 clear video clips of Champtanystropheus in one week (June 2–9 2003) than all combined research and evidence gathered at Loch Ness to date . . . during that same week Fauna Communications recorded three echolocations at three different locations. The locations were based on my research . . . the idea was one that I had given the Discovery Channel last fall." He then ended his rant with a "modest" observation: "How many active (daily) Cryptozoologist(s) are out there? 1."[33]

By May 2006, Hall was growing increasingly frustrated with his fellow Champ Trackers and their annoying habit of asking for evidence and politely questioning his calcified views on Champ. Before his abrupt departure, he tolerated no opposition, as illustrated in his May 23, 2006, acerbic response to a question put forth by one of his Champ Trackers to others in the group, who were asked whether they thought Champ may be a Nothosaur (an extinct aquatic dinosaur with webbed feet).[34] For years, Hall had repeated the mantra to his followers that Champ was a Tanystropheus. How dare anyone express an opposing view and poll *his* followers with the "silly" notion that Champ was possibly a Nothosaur. It was heresy. Hall's reaction to this seemingly innocuous poll was swift. He wrote on the following day: "Who created this poll? They best do some homework or find another group to join. There is one man in this world looking for Champtanystropheus . . . Dennis Jay Hall. What is needed at this point in the search is money not opinion polls. I have financed 30 years of searching for Champ. . . . I am done! . . . The group would not exist otherwise. If you enjoy the armchair search make it real and help me set up webcams . . . its only money and the trip to the lake and back . . . now cost(s) me 20 dollars a day . . . Im done! [sic]."[35]

Hall also claims to have developed a special bond with the creature that was reminiscent of a cross between the 1970s TV show *Flipper* and the film *Free Willy*. His secret: spending countless hours on the lake in the same area until he was one with the scenery. "By returning to the same spot over and over you become part of the background [and] an expected sight. Its [sic] then and I am not talking days or weeks, it may be the third or fourth summer, that the animals will accept you as non-threatening [and a] part of their habitat. That is when the REAL fun begins," he wrote on his website.

Curiously, in 1996, Hall's ChampQuest co-director Richard Deuel also inexplicably left the field of Champology, leaving friends to ponder whatever became of him and why he left without saying goodbye.[36] In 1992 he told a reporter: "I'm here to stay. ChampQuest is here to stay."[37] During a 1997 Champ Day festival in Port Henry, Deuel's home for several years, there was excitement when at least two attendees reported spotting Deuel. Although much like the young Hall and his father, no one thought to snap a photo so the sightings could not be confirmed. When Hall was told that Deuel was apparently in attendance, he responded with bemusement. "I don't know what happened to him. Two people came up to me and said they've seen him here. He hasn't come over. You'd think he would if he was here."[38] One would think that Hall himself would have informed his fellow Champ Trackers bloggers and ChampQuest followers that he was getting out of the monster-hunting business. Deuel had reportedly become frustrated over his inability to spot the elusive critter even once, whereas Hall had been blessed with numerous sightings. Perhaps Deuel was literally distancing himself from Hall after a string of sightings that stretch credulity. In the end, we are left to speculate given that both men have left ChampQuest in bizarre circumstances, up and leaving without bothering to say where they are.

Despite all of his sightings over the years, one would think that Hall would have taken a clear photo or video at close range. He has any number of excuses as to why he has never snapped the definitive Champ photo. On one occasion, he says: "While on watch one evening I saw one of these animals herd a school of fish into the shallow water off a state owned island. It happened just as I was arriving. I had to make a quick decision, watch the animal or get the camera and take my eyes off the animal, I watched. The animal guided the school of small fish into shallow water. It then slapped its neck back and forth against the surface of the water, stunning the fish. This sighting also left me stunned." Here is a man who has devoted thirty years of his life to proving the existence of Champ,[39] the creature appears in front of him—there is a camera nearby—and he chooses to watch! With the possible exception of Ghandi or the Dali Lama, it is difficult to imagine anyone with such self-control.[40]

In describing the incident, Hall said that after Champ slapped the water, "there were hundreds of fish just floating on the surface stunned. A couple of minutes later it was . . . completely dark out and I could hear the animal came back [*sic*] and was feeding on the stunned fish. The fish that it didn't eat regained their senses and swam away unharmed."[41] For such a specific feeding strategy, it is curious that of the hundreds of Champ reports, no one has reported a similar episode. One would think that if Champ feeds in this manner, there would be numerous sightings of it stunning, then feeding on the helpless fish. Also, if it was "completely dark" as Hall affirms, how could he be sure the creature was feeding on the fish or that the uneaten fish swam off unharmed?

Unpronounceable Words

My high school English teacher always said, "Never use a big word when a small one will do." It is advice that Dennis Hall would do well to heed. Not one to wait for approval of the scientific community, Hall has given Champ his own, albeit unpronounceable name: *Champtanystropheus*. He relishes in both using and making up his own scientific language. His name for a baby Champ is Tanystropheus. Here is how he describes it in semi-comprehensible jargon: "Tanystropheus is a member of the Protorosaurs family (they live in Charlotte) which in turn are members of the Archosauromorph family (I believe they moved to New York) and they all pre-date the Archosaurs (yes there are still a few up in Forrestdale) better known as Dinosaurs. The Protorosaurs were a lizard type reptile (absolutely no relation to the Charlotte Protorosaurs) that lived in the deserts of Europe toward the end of the Permian Period. Its long legs were tucked under its body, allowing it to chase after fast moving prey-mainly insects. Its neck was made up of seven large and greatly elongated vertebrae."[42]

Hall goes on to claim to have discerned characteristics of Champ right down to its birthing habits! "Tany [his name for baby Champ] and the Elasmosaurus look similar but there are major differences. The Elasmosaurus had flippers. Tany has feet. The Elasmosaurus is 46 feet long. Tany is 25 tops." Hall confidently proclaims that Champ gives birth to live young. "The most important difference is that the Elasmosaurus was an egg-layer and would have laid her eggs much like the modern day turtles (in open sight of humans). The Champtany gives live-birth. Unusual for a reptile, but she was not alone, other reptiles including the very ancient Ichthyosaurs, were live-bearers as are some modern day reptiles."[43]

Among Hall's unconventional ideas: the most important factor in determining when he searches for Champ—the phase of the moon. In 1999, he reported having made a major breakthrough in Champ research enabling him to issue Champ sighting forecasts with a 75 percent accuracy rate.[44] The best times to spot Champ were supposedly the five days before and after a new moon. This is amazing if true. In 2001, Craig Heinselman tested this theory by plotting the specific dates of all known Champ reports from 1878 to 2000—141 sightings in all. Using a five-day window before and after a new moon, he found that more than 60 percent of sightings fell *outside* these days. Heinselman's conclusion: "the 75% success rate does not hold up over history."[45] Aside from Hall, even the most ardent Champ believer would concede that most sightings are a result of misidentifications of all sorts of things: freak waves, boat wakes, birds, otters, logs, reflections, large fish, and the list goes on. This being the case, even if there was a strong correlation with sightings before and after the new moon, any such figures would be meaningless.[46]

Hall also makes the ridiculous claim that the Indians once routinely dined on Champ! In 2000, he told *Sports Afield* magazine: "See, the Indians killed 'em off. That's why there's not more of 'em. These animals competed for the same food sources as the Indians. They're built for snapping salmon out of the air."[47] How can anyone possibly know that our ancestors had Champ on the menu? It is surprising that Hall did not also claim that the flesh tasted like chicken or that the natives preferred it broiled, with corn meal and maple syrup![48] On the bright side, Hall asserts that they don't eat humans; it seems that we are too big.

In July 1999, Hall recorded his twentieth Champ sighting.[49] The following year he had four more, bringing his total to at least twenty-four. For instance, he claims that on Thursday, July 6, 2000 at "7:54 p.m. two Champtanys surfaced and yes I have the video to prove it. This is very good footage that will definitely prove that an animal 16–18 feet in length inhabits the lake. I have 45 minutes of video. . . ."[50] The encounter supposedly took place on the Vermont side south of where Otter Creek meets Lake Champlain. Hall claimed to not only see and hear the creatures, but to smell them. So what does Champ smell like? Apparently like a snake. A few days later he writes: "On July 23 at 5:00 pm I took several minutes of video as a single Champtany stuck its neck out of the water." This incident is reported to have occurred off Kent's Island.[51] Then on October 4, 2000: "I spent the afternoon at the lake and watched two objects all the time I was there "I do have video footage of todays [sic] sighting . . ."[52] On October 11, 2000: "I am almost embarressed [sic] to say—I had another sighting Oct 6."[53] In this same email, Hall complains that the *Burlington Free Press* was no longer taking him seriously. One wonders at which point they had stopped doing so: sighting number nine or twenty-four!

For someone who claims to have taken numerous videos of Champ, his book is filled with fuzzy photos. In a 1999 interview, Hall is quoted as saying that some of his better video, once "released, has the potential of drawing a million or more people to Lake Champlain." Presumably, he decided not to make the video or stills public, yet the interview in which he states this is with U-Haul International, a company that rents trucks and trailers for moving. Hall did the U-Haul interview after they placed a giant picture of Champ on the sides of several of their vehicles, publicizing its existence![54] The U-Haul campaign was not undertaken because U-Haul executives were smitten by the evidence for Champ. In 1998, U-Haul launched a nationwide campaign featuring two hundred regional mysteries around the country, including images of everything from ghosts to space aliens, hoping that the local connection would boost sales.[55]

Dennis Hall tried to run ChampQuest like a cult leader, expecting absolute loyalty and devotion to "The Great One" and his strange, far-fetched views and incredible encounter claims. Like a prophet, he and he alone claimed to have developed a special bond with the creatures, enabling him to take close range videos that stretched credulity. His writing has a quasi-religious tone as he asserts in *ChampQuest*: "They are here for a reason; this is their chosen home."[56]

His self-published book was written to be the Bible of the Champ community, and when people challenged his pseudoscientific claims, even mildly, it was blasphemy. In the end, ChampQuest and its accompanying Champ Trackers blog collapsed under the weight of Hall's inflated ego and grandiose claims, which were not sustainable. In July

Figure 5.2. In 1999, U-Haul launched a promotion campaign involving Champ (Ben Radford photo).

2009, he resurfaced to take part in a study conducted by acoustics expert Elizabeth von Muggenthaler, who had reportedly detected mysterious sounds coming from Lake Champlain. This triggered several emails from relieved Champ Trackers bloggers, but Hall remained mum, telling friends that he was maintaining a low public profile.[57]

ELIZABETH VON MUGGENTHALER: CHAMP WHISPERER

Another Champ hunter is Elizabeth von Muggenthaler, who in 2003 led a research team that reported detecting the presence of echolocation on Lake Champlain.[58] Also known as biosonar, it is the same principle that bats use to navigate without eyes to guide them. Many aquatic creatures use a similar process as they emit vibrations that bounce off objects. The returning echoes allow them to move around and also find food. Muggenthaler says that the echoes heard in Lake Champlain were ten times louder than any fish species that are known to be there, leading to the inescapable conclusion that there is an unclassified species in the lake. To many, it seemed that the long elusive

proof had again been found. Muggenthaler's monumental discovery was
reported with great hoop-la on the Discovery Channel later that year.

In 2005 and 2009, Muggenthaler recorded more mysterious readings on Lake Champlain. She is adamant that the sound was not caused
by human devices such as a fish-finder or a boat. She proclaimed with
confidence: "We know it's not a beaver, an otter, a deer or a moose.
It's not a sturgeon or a turtle, and it's definitely not a zebra mussel.
Can you imagine that? And we know it's not a man-made signal." She
says it is a freshwater mammal, most likely a carnivore about fifteen
feet long that moves slowly through the water (up to five knots) and
has an advanced brain.[59] Muggenthaler contends she wants nothing to
do with the label of monster hunter. However, when the Discovery
Channel offered her an undisclosed sum of money to study the lake
in 2003 as part of their "Monster Quest" series, she agreed, but as a
no nonsense scientist. "That monster stuff, that's just drama. That's not
science," she said in 2009.[60] Midway into the one-week stint on the
lake on a fifty-foot boat filled with an array of listening equipment,
she claimed to have had a breakthrough. "I thought, that sound should
not be in the lake. It was clearly echolocation. It's unmistakable. It's
clearly a biological signal. It was just too bizarre," she said.[61] The first
signal was recorded at Vermont's Button Bay, followed by readings at
Hunter Bay in Essex County, New York, and then near Thompson's
Point off Charlotte, Vermont.

Champ skeptic Ben Radford, also on the boat, was cautious of
her claims. "At several points in their search, strange biosonar readings
yielded no creature sightings at all. The Discovery Channel documentary shows Muggenthaler's crew detecting an unusual high-frequency
pitch and immediately dispatching two divers to investigate the source
of the sound," he wrote. Despite searching the area for an hour, they
saw nothing out of the ordinary.[62] At this point it appeared to be your
run-of-the-mill disagreement between experts, with Radford on one
side and Muggenthaler on the other; then something odd happened:
I wrote to Muggenthaler and asked her to respond to Radford's cautious remarks. Her response was strange to say the least. She fired back
scornfully that Radford and his fellow skeptics "are boring, and in the
real sciences no one listens to them anyway," claiming that their main
purpose was "to make money and create a fuss" as they are "paid

heartily by TV companies to pester real scientists."[63] Her response immediately raised red flags because few scientists correspond with such loose language. I quickly sent off another letter explaining that I was simply trying to learn more about her research—and received a similar vitriol-filled response. It was time to do more digging into her background.

Muggenthaler's echolocation research resonates with many of the region's residents and has been embraced as one of the most exciting developments in the history of Champ, but her claims are fishy and have little grounding in real science. The first red flag is that most of her publications are conference papers. These presentations are not typically peer-reviewed; they are more of a sounding board. I then noticed something unusual: None of the copies of her presentations lists her degrees. I contacted her alma mater, Old Dominion University in Virginia, and learned that she graduated in 1991 with a mere bachelor of science degree in psychology, after which she immediately founded her own institute, Fauna Research Communications.[64] Although a higher degree is not a prerequisite to doing good science, let us take a closer look at her evidence. Muggenthaler's research on the mysterious creature that is purportedly echolocating in Lake Champlain was supposedly presented to a meeting of the Acoustical Society of America (ASA). She admits that it is preliminary and more data is needed to produce a convincing scientific paper.[65] She sent me an abstract of her paper that was listed in the 2010 ASA Conference outline. The paper was supposed to have been presented on April 21, 2010 at 9:30 AM. I contacted the co-chair of the session, Dr. Susan Parks of Pennsylvania State University, asking what she thought of the presentation. Her response: "Elizabeth von Muggenthaler never showed up for the session, and the presentation was withdrawn, so no one ever saw any presentation of the data reported in that abstract."[66] Abstracts alone are virtually meaningless because they are brief summaries and do not include data. People can present at conferences on just about any topic. The scrutiny comes when they get up and try to justify their claims in greater detail before a gathering of other experts. This begs a question: If Muggenthaler never presented the paper, why did she send me the abstract, which gives the impression that she did? When I asked Dr. Simone Baumann-Pickering of the

Scripps Institution of Oceanography in California, what she thought of this behavior along with Muggenthaler's website, she said bluntly: "The described method is missing details and the data presented does not show her claims convincingly. The language used to describe the work seems unprofessional. It is very odd to submit an abstract and then not present at a conference."[67]

In 2012, Muggenthaler was listed as president of the Fauna Communications Research Institute in North Carolina. One of the institute's staff members is listed as Champ researcher Dennis Jay Hall! It is far from a scientific institute but sure sounds like one. Anyone can found his or her own institute. I could found the Robert E. Bartholomew Institute for Marine Anomaly Research on Lake Champlain, but that does not make me an expert on either marine anomalies or Lake Champlain. Muggenthaler identifies Dennis Hall as a "naturalist" and she seems to have an "us against the world" paranoia. She writes: "These naturalists [lake monster researchers] have gathered scores of information from all over the world, have seen this creature living in Lake Champlain, and should not be ignored by the rest of the scientific community. We believe in studying every *anomaly* which is the true definition of science, and we are unafraid of losing tenure. We don't need any, we already have our degrees."[68] Losing tenure for publicly expressing the possible existence of Champ seems far-fetched. Bigfoot, space aliens, and Chupacabras—yes. Champ—no. Champ and Nessie are arguably the most plausible "monsters" in the world, and are the poster children of the cryptozoological community. For a scientist to suggest that an unclassified species resides in Lake Champlain, is not exactly scientific heresy. Securing funds for a research grant to study the existence of such creatures—that's another story. Another concern is Muggenthaler's reaction to scientists who pose legitimate questions about her research, as science works through peer review and verification. When I politely asked her to respond to Ben Radford's concerns about her Discovery Channel research (which were very tame), she threatened to cease all correspondence and proceeded to scold me for having the "poor judgment" to associate with such a "disreputable" character. Whatever her personal feelings are about Radford, he is a respected scholar and drew different conclusions. He also was present for the Discovery Channel shoot that Muggenthaler was featured on. Her website also is excessively harsh toward scientists who reject the existence of an unclassified creature in the lake. "The mainstream scientific community should be ashamed and deeply embarrassed for dismissing these intelligent and diligent individuals [Champ researchers], along with the judges; [sic] pastors, police officers, firemen; [sic] the general public and avid fishermen that have seen this creature as well."[69] That her website was riddled with grammatical and punctuation errors, did not help her cause.

Aside from these red flags, a key question should be asked: Is what Muggenthaler is doing good science—which works by being transparent and allowing others to evaluate their data? When I have asked for more detailed information than appears on her website, she has refused to provide it. Vermont geologists Pat and Tom Manley report asking "her to send us her recordings so that we could do some investigations on it and she would not release it."[70] It is not common for scientists to make bold claims over several years and not allow their data to be scrutinized. A key problem with evaluating her claims is that few people are experts on animal acoustics; even fewer specialize in marine bioacoustics or how creatures communicate under water. I therefore contacted several specialists and asked them to look at Muggenthaler's claims. Dr. David Mann is one such expert at the University of South Florida. His views are enlightening:

I remember being at an ASA conference where she presented a talk on cats purring and healing in bones (in fact, I may have chaired that session). I think she is sincere and means well, but she is definitely not critical in her approach to science. She seems to have a conclusion in mind before she collects data. She had little concept of the difference between acoustic and electrical energy. I thought her starting point was interesting . . . why do cats purr? But, then she goes off comparing frequencies of electrical stimulation of muscles in physiological studies to acoustic frequencies in purring cats.

I spent a few minutes looking at their website on Champ. There are a lot of random things on it (what does blue-green algae have to do with it?). . . . Under the analysis section, whatever they are showing in the top picture is not the same signal as what is shown in the spectrogram below that. Honestly, in the top figure it looks like a lot of 60 Hz electrical noise to me, but you can't tell for sure because there is no time scale on that plot. . . . There is no way you can tell the total length of the animal from acoustic recordings if it was echolocating.

I find it odd that they go to great lengths to go through outlandish possibilities, while not spending much time thinking about other sources of noise. In any case, their comment about transducers not being able to make these kinds of signals is not true. . . . The fact that there were fossil cetacean bones discovered near there [Lake Champlain] means nothing. There are fossil whale bones all over the place where there are no living species today (e.g., in Florida there are fossil river dolphin bones, but no river dolphins today).[71]

Dr. Mann said that there were several alternative possibilities for the sounds Muggenthaler recorded, both mechanical and biological, noting: "One possibility that comes to mind are gas bubbles released by some species of fish (clupeids) which can produce a series of high frequency clicks."[72]

Dr. Peter Madsen, a bioacoustical expert at Aarhus University in Denmark, is also cautious. "I am very skeptical of this. As Carl Sagan said 'Extraordinary claims require extraordinary evidence.'" He noted that to claim the sounds were "from a large unidentified mammal seems bold unless she really has strong data to back that claim."[73] Presumably she does not as she admits that she has been unable to publish an article in a journal for want of more evidence! Madsen's colleague, Dr. Kristian Beedholm looked at Muggenthaler's website and concluded that she did not know what she was talking about. "Many of the facts about echolocation on the page appear to be something she just glanced off Wikipedia. And a sentence like this: 'The echolocation we recorded goes up to 140 kHz, this is 7 times beyond our hearing range. There are no underwater speakers capable of creating this high frequency sound, indeed there is only one or two that can accomplish this, . . .' immediately tells you that she knows absolutely nothing about acoustics."[74]

It is always good to get a variety of opinions from different experts, so I contacted yet another echolocation authority—Dr. James T. Fulton, a specialist on dolphins, which emit similar sounds to those Muggenthaler said she had recorded. He was unimpressed: "I am afraid the web page presentation will disappear into the 'dustbin of History' in the absence of better results," he lamented.[75] Then there is renowned whale and dolphin researcher Dr. Erich Hoyt who has written numerous books involving biosonar. After looking at Muggenthaler's web page he noted "a number of red flags that make me think it probably is pseudo science."[76] Biosonar expert Dr. Craig Radford of the Leigh Marine Centre in New Zealand, said: "It all seems very strange to me!" He questions her use of "vector sensors," which are notoriously difficult to access as they "are heavily embargoed by the US Navy and can't just be used like this." But even if she had managed to access them, "they would not be able to listen simultaneously, which they stated, when recording using vector sensors. More than likely they used normal hydrophones and not being able to tell the difference between these raises more alarms." He says her use of digital audiotape (DAT) recorders makes no sense. "DAT's have a maximum sampling rate of 48 kHz which only allows the recorder to record sounds below 24 kHz, which is outside the range of echolocation signals."[77] Given that Muggenthaler's degree is in psychology, I even solicited the views of the chair of the Psychology Department at the University of Southern Mississippi, Dr. Stan Kuczaj, who also is an acoustics expert. After looking at Muggenthaler's website claims he said: "I doubt that her 'data' would stand up to any sort of scientific scrutiny."[78]

Muggenthaler also claims to have developed a special relationship with animals that goes beyond your normal dog fetching a stick, to where she seems to think she can talk with some animals, prompting one journalist who interviewed her to describe her as a modern-day Doctor Doolittle. In 2002, she told a reporter: "For almost 12 years I have been recording animals and, for some reason, I think they know why we are there. I have had tigers that will lie down two inches from me and 'chuffle,' grumble and just 'talk' for hours. I have had a serval [an African wildcat known for its almost constant movement] come right up to me, put her front paws on my knees and purr directly into the microphone for 2 minutes and 35 seconds without moving."[79] Does this eccentricity mean that her claims about an unidentified creature echolocating in Lake Champlain should not be taken seriously? Of course not, but when you combine it with the assessments of world-class experts in biosonar who say that many of her research claims are dubious or flat out wrong—then yes, it raises red flags galore. Other researchers have probed the depths of the lake without finding Champ. Geologists Pat and Tom Manley of Vermont's Middlebury College have used sophisticated side scan sonar to make a detailed map of the lake. Their equipment is powerful enough to detect everything from logs to ship wrecks. To date they have detected no evidence of Champ.[80]

Both Muggenthaler and Hall have maintained high media pro-files and made startling claims about the likely existence of Champ. Although this makes for entertaining TV, too often what is presented is unbalanced and these so-called experts are given more credence than they deserve. Their claims stray far from the path of mainstream science. Champ may exist, but neither Hall nor Muggenthaler has come close to proving it as their research is based more on wishful thinking than science. I would stop short of labeling Muggenthaler and Hall frauds or hoaxers. They are perhaps best seen as honest, well-intentioned people, who lack proper scientific training in their areas of claimed expertise, and who are overly enthusiastic to the point where they began to see (and hear) what they wanted to. Part of the blame in publicizing their dubious Champ-related claims lies with the media for uncritically accepting their proclamations. For instance, in July 2003, as Muggenthaler's claims were first being reported, Sam Hemmingway of the *Burlington Free Press* did what a reporter is supposed to do: contact a local expert on the lake to ask what he thought of Muggenthaler's remarkable claim of echolocation. He contacted the Burlington-based Leahy Center for Lake Champlain, and talked to director Steven Smith. His reaction: "I just don't know," he said.[81] The trouble was, Smith did not specialize in bioacoustics, and Hemmingway had to move on to his next story. So why did the Discovery Channel contact Muggenthaler to do the underwater recording on Lake Champlain when they could have gotten a recognized authority on bioacoustics instead of someone who has only a BS in psychology? The answer seems obvious: Sensa-tionalism sells. Like the *Burlington Free Press*, if Discovery had queried real bioacoustic experts, the wishful nature of Muggenthaler's claims would have been exposed. This begs a second question: Was the real purpose of this documentary to inform viewers or to entertain them by creating a buzz around the episode in order to raise ratings and ultimately increase revenues?

In July 2011, Muggenthaler was scheduled to give a presentation on Champ to a symposium in Vergennes, Vermont. Her website provided what was billed as a "scientific abstract of one of the lectures." It was the same abstract she submitted, but never presented, to the 2010 meeting of the ASA. In that abstract, which she withdrew from the ASA meeting, she claimed there was a large, mysterious creature echolocating in the lake. The abstract appears misleading as it gives the impression that it was presented to the society when in fact it never was, and that there was some scrutiny of her claims.

PHIL REINES: CHAMP POET, PIONEER, AND PONTIFICATOR

Another pivotal figure in the history of Champ is the flamboyant and confrontational Dr. Phil Reines who has been searching for Champ since the mid-1960s, when he begin teaching media studies at what is now the State University of New York at Plattsburgh, retiring thirty years later. A gifted speaker with an acting background who grew up on the streets of Brooklyn, "Dr. Phil" had the ability to wax profound without any notes on any subject—often totally unrelated to media studies. Between 1965 and 1975, he embarked on an ambitious project with the college librarian Connie Pope to gather nineteenth century press reports on Champ and gave occasional public talks and media interviews.[82] Never one to shy away from an argument, Reines actively confronted Joe Zarzynski and members of the media during the early 1980s, complaining of the inaccuracies in many news reports on Champ, and worried over attempts to exploit the creature for financial gain.

An avid sailor, Reines once owned a 1929 speedboat and has had two "close encounters of an aquatic kind" on Lake Champlain. The first incident took place in August 1975, while he was snorkeling near Valcour Bay south of Plattsburgh. It was on a clear, sunlit afternoon that he came face to face with a massive eel. "It was at rest in twelve feet of water with its tail trailing down to the sandy bottom, its body stretched in a large flattened S-curve, and its head just submerged under the surface of the water." The creature was at least ten feet long, and some ten inches in girth. It looked like a huge snake. "If this eel was . . . a juvenile, then it is possible that I 'said hello' to a young Champ."[83] Is it possible that many Champ sightings are eels?

Reines thinks that what he saw was not a one-off. Historical record supports this view. On January 26, 1887, the *Plattsburgh Morning Telegraph* described a sea serpent sighting involving a "20 foot long snake" with an "eel-like head and body thick as a man's, and snake-like tail that was eel-like" that was observed from a railroad embankment in Essex, New York. The description is remarkably similar to Reines' encounter in Valcour Bay. But is it possible that Lake Champlain could harbor eels upward of twenty feet long? Would they not wash up on shore? Then again, how many people come across a dead sturgeon or gar, or a dead deer or bear in the woods? According to a report in the *Fair Haven* (New York) *Register* of August 9, 1900, such giant eels may be more common than is presently thought: "For several years it has been reported that there was a sea serpent in Seneca Lake. Recently a Geneva man set a strong net and ensnared the creature, which when landed, (and after being shot) proved to be an eel thirteen feet long." Reines believes that reports like this one may be vital pieces to the Champ jigsaw puzzle, observing: "This particular incident is important because it documents the presence, in a small lake of an unusually large eel. Using this as a rough yardstick of size, it is not unreasonable to project the existence of an eel much greater than thirteen feet in Lake Champlain, a body of water that is bigger than all of the six Finger Lakes combined."

On another occasion during the 1970s, something slammed into Reines' one and a half ton, twenty-seven foot sloop, *Beau Geste*, causing it to pitch sideways.[84] He was off Schuyler Island in Willsboro Bay and is adamant that he had not struck an underwater rock as he was well off shore in forty feet of water. He is equally certain that it was not a log or piece of floating debris such as a tree stump. "I didn't strike *it*. *It* struck me!" Had Reines' vessel given Champ a massive headache, or was it a large sturgeon? Like Zarzynski and Hall, Reines has come tantalizingly close to what may have been Champ. "There is an absurdity factor with the many sightings yet no one can prove anything. You have to look at it with a wry smile," he says.[85]

He is more philosophical about his personal search for Champ. Concerned about the human propensity to pollute the planet, he says that if he were to spot the creature today, and even take a clear photo, he would have second thoughts about making it public. For over the years, his attitude about proving the creature's existence has come full circle after being hot on its trail since 1965. He now harbors grave fears for the lake's health, and with it, the creature's continued survival—if it exists. He is in no doubt about Champ's greatest threat: humans, and worries that its discovery could trigger its demise. "Once we categorize it, once we identify it and put it in a tank . . . it's a goldfish," he cautions.[86] "The ultimate irony would be if Champ is found, only to become extinct at the hands of man."[87]

Reines thinks that Champ is the name used to describe a variety of large fish and mammals in the lake along with a number of unusual natural phenomena such as odd wave action and light reflecting at just the right angle at just the right time and place. "Many people see different things in the lake. All are taught to be Champ," he says. Yet ultimately he is a believer, convinced that a small percentage of sightings represent a large sluglike invertebrate (creatures without backbones) that once roamed the oceans. Extraordinarily large eels are another possibility. "Of course, Champy lives. There is no question of that in my mind. Evidence is overwhelming that there are large unidentified creatures that somehow have survived."[88] He points out that all of the evidence for Champ is "soft," such as eyewitness testimony and photos that are open to a wide range of interpretations. His position is that science cannot take people's word for things. "The phrase 'seeing is believing,' was once thought to be infallible, but is no longer the ultimate yardstick of truth. All people can be fooled. People hoax. People are imperfect observers. Science must be based on objective analysis of the available evidence," he says. He is quick to observe that this does not necessarily mean that the Mansis hoaxed their photo. Reines' personal and professional stances on the Mansi photo have never wavered. "My own position is that no matter how visually impressive the Mansi photo is (and it certainly is!), absence of a negative and no proven location precludes me from total acceptance of the incident." He is convinced that it is genuine but not necessarily "the real McCoy." "The photo is genuine. I have no doubt. But of 'what and where?' as Hamlet states, 'is the question.' No one is more frustrated than myself in this matter because the photo promises everything, but ultimately delivers nothing (as yet)."[89]

Reines has written a romantic poem to express his feelings about the mystery. His words underscore the deep personal attachment that many people have with the creature—be it real or imaginary. It is a connection that is often passed down from generations and continues to resonate today strongly as ever—of beauty, mystery and wonder.

"To Champ: A Love Song"

Year after year, alone in my boat,
I seek the prize-sitting-sailing-afloat.
That perfect moment of Triumph's gloat
The finding of Champy and—so attain,
Deserved Glory, Honor, Adulation, Fame!
All Mine!
At Long Last when Champ
Is awarded his Zoological Name.
Ah, for this Grand Prize, do I strive—
Final Proof that Champ is Alive!
O Champ, you elusive, diffusive
All-inclusive Thing of the Mind.
I search and seek but—
Alas, still cannot find.
Are you Blue—Are you Green?
Are you Fat—Are you Lean?
Are you Kind?
(I hope you're not Mean.)
Why and Wherefore?
From Me do you Hide?
Alas, You cannot know that I'm on your side.
Oh! My Champ! Pray tell me so—
Are you a Creature born of night,
To frolic with Joy in the Moon's silver light?

Or, do you serenely repose
In the Sun's yellow bright;
Enjoying your rest far from our sight.
Why! do you vex me as you do?
It's enough! Colleagues brand me Fool
To defend the wonderful Legend of You!
Ah well, right or wrong—however I might,
I cannot give you up without a fight.
For You are my Holy Grail.
So, Avaunt! To the Surface!
And come fill my cup!
I will persist—until you desist.
Your living reality is a must,
Which, of course I insist!
I will seek you by day and at night
Until that Moment of Bliss, Sublime
When I enter Your lair and Make You Mine.

In recent years, Scott Mardis of Winooski, Vermont, has become the most prominent Champ hunter. He began researching in 1994, the same year he began hosting his own local public access TV show on Champ and other aquatic mysteries. Although Champ is a major part of his life, Mardis says he makes a conscious effort not to obsess over it. "There's a lot of researchers that have just concentrated on this and become obsessed with it and their cheese starts to slide off their cracker. I don't want to wind up like that," he cautions.[90] He is not your typical monster hunter. An electronics expert with IBM, Mardis is a meticulous record-keeper of Champ sightings. He regularly culls the scientific journals for information on the geology and biology of the lake that is potentially relevant to Champ. A self-admitted Jerry Garcia look-alike (of Grateful Dead fame), Mardis plays in a rock band, Red Triangle, and has a propensity for understatement. During one interview, when asked what a typical day in the life of a Champ researcher was like, he replied that it was "basically just standin' there starin' at the water lookin' for stuff."[91] Mardis is quick to point out historical instances where scientists have seen their careers take a hit after endorsing the existence of an anomalous creature. For instance, in 1960 when British zoologist Denys Tucker publicly asserted that the Loch Ness Monster was real after his own sighting the previous year, he soon found himself without a job at the British Museum and blamed his unemployment on Nessie.[92] However, in the twenty-first century, one would hope that scientists have more liberty to express their views without fearing for their jobs.

Another researcher who deserves honorable mention is the more armchair-based Gary Mangiacopra, a Connecticut native who in 1992 completed a master's thesis on Champ and kindred lake monsters of North America.[93] He thinks that if Champ is a species yet to be classified by science, it may be an invertebrate (lacking bones), which explains why a body has not been found as it rapidly disintegrates after death. He also thinks that there must be a minimum breeding population of ten, although he believes it may even "be a hermaphrodite, possessing both male and female reproductive organs."[94] Mangiacopra did a statistical analysis of Champ sightings and found that most (21%) occur on Saturday, followed by Sunday (17.5%). This is probably because people have more free time on the weekend and are more likely to spend it on or near the lake. As for the most likely weekday to spot Champ: Thursday is the clear winner at 16.1 percent. The poorest day for Champ watching is Monday, comprising just 9 percent of all sightings.[95] As for the most popular months, July and August account for just over half of all sightings. By far the peak time to see Champ is between 7 and 8 PM. Perhaps the most surprising finding is that only about 25 percent of all sightings involve lone observers.[96] Taking these statistics into account, the best chance of seeing Champ would be on a Saturday evening at 7:30 in July. You would be least likely to spot him at 3 AM on a Monday in January (even Champ doesn't like to go out when it's cold and dark). During summer 1985, Mangiacopra joined an expedition to look for signs of Champ on Lake Champlain, which included dumping a container of Purina trout feed overboard in hopes of attracting a school of fish that Champ might eat. On the morning of July 21 in rough conditions at Whallen Bay, one of the researchers nearly drowned, leaving Mangiacopra shaken and content to continue his research from the more mundane confines of his home.[97]

IN THE EYE OF THE BEHOLDER
In Search of Answers

More light!
—JOHANN WOLFGANG VON GOETHE

Two people stand meters from one another on the shore of Lake Champlain, glancing at the same object on the water: one sees a log—the other—a prehistoric creature. Both are equally sure of what they have seen. What motivates one to believe and the other to interpret what he sees more skeptically?

Prior beliefs and expectations play a big role. Believers tend to believe and skeptics tend to be skeptical. People want to believe in Champ for a myriad of reasons. Few will deny that they *hope* Champ exists—"Champ" referring to a breeding community of creatures, for the possibility that sightings reflect a solitary creature are scientifically and logically absurd. Perhaps first and foremost for the many gift shops, marinas, and restaurants on the lake, there is an urge to believe that is motivated from the obvious economic benefit derived from curiosity seekers who visit the lake hoping to catch a glimpse of the legend, divesting themselves of their money in the process. Then there is the appeal to the human sense of wonder, excitement, and adventure. It is exhilarating to think that a prehistoric creature that is unknown to science or was long ago extinct could be frolicking around the lake. And oh the irony: right under our very noses for centuries, outwitting our ancestors and ourselves. Then there is the human propensity to root for the underdog in the face of so many naysayers who pronounce Champ to be a figment of our imaginations—some of whom have never even visited Lake Champlain.

An illustration of why some people believe and others don't can be found in the events of Sunday afternoon, June 21, 1992. It was Father's

Day and 75-year-old Lawrence Gameline of Champlain, New York, south of the Canadian border, decided to go fishing, something he had been doing since he was 10 years old. But on that day, he would see something that had eluded him for the previous sixty-five years. He was in a fifteen-foot motorboat fishing for perch on the Vermont side of the lake at 2:20 PM, facing the bridge leading to St. Anne's Shrine on Isle La Motte not far from Light House Point. That was when he spotted a long, dark log floating about four hundred feet away and with eighteen inches above the surface. "Then this long, round part came up out of the water" and "appeared to be attached to the hump." He estimated the creature to be sixteen feet long. Gameline couldn't get a good view of the head as it "was even with the water" and difficult to discern. After watching it for five minutes, he decided to get a closer look and started his motor, instantly scaring it away. Once he calmed down and resumed fishing, he noticed something he had never experienced before at that spot: The area was barren of fish. "I kept casting for fish, but there was nothing, and usually you can almost always catch perch and bass there. I've gone back to that same spot several times since then and I have caught fish. Maybe this creature feeds on fish and . . . it scared the other fish off," he said. Gameline received the backing of the Champlain town justice and former police chief, Jack Favreau, who said: "When this man tells you something—no ifs, ands or buts." Favreau said that several years earlier, his wife Carol spotted a similar creature out on the lake, and had received considerable ridicule.[1]

By all accounts, Mr. Gameline was a pillar of his community, well respected and known for his honesty. He undoubtedly saw *something*. The Plattsburgh *Press-Republican* reports that Mr. Gameline was "certain that what he saw . . . was Champy, the Lake Champlain monster." But did he? By his own admission, he had a poor view of the head, and the object was well over a football field away; he never got closer than four hundred feet because as soon as he started the motor to get closer, the object submerged. It is notoriously difficult to estimate the size of objects on water at a distance, and his estimate of sixteen feet could have been considerably smaller. A major reason why he believed he saw Champ was the single hump. He noted, "there's not a sturgeon alive with a hump on its back." It is well known among fish experts that sturgeon have ribbed backs that are often mistaken for humps.[2] So why did Mr. Gameline believe he saw Champ and not a large fish—perhaps a sturgeon? Ultimately it comes down to faith, for without conclusive evidence, the existence of Champ is in the eye of the beholder.

The word *cryptozoology* is derived from the Greek word *kriptis* (hidden) and zoology (referring to the animal world). The literal translation is the study of hidden animals. Cryptozoologists search for animals that are either previously unknown or thought to have been extinct. Over the past one hundred years, the scientific community has witnessed a series of remarkable discoveries in our oceans and lakes—of creatures we either never knew existed or were thought to have been long-ago extinct. Will Champ be added to the list? Does a prehistoric creature frolic in the waters of Lake Champlain? The consensus of scientists is a resounding "no," in large part because the lake was only formed 10,000 to 12,000 years ago. Yet, it wouldn't be the first time that scientists were wrong.

The 1981 Champ Conference began with an address by William Eddy, professor of environmental issues at the University of Vermont. Dr. Eddy mentioned the work of Baron Cuvier, who in the late 1700s published a scientific paper titled "The Discourse on the Theory of the Earth," which is famously quoted as concluding, "there is little hope that we shall find fresh species of large mammals." His miscalculation would become known as "Cuvier's Dictum." Over the next three decades of his life, Cuvier was forced to eat humble pie as dozens of animals were discovered for the first time by European explorers, from the koala bear to the spiny anteater to one of the largest mammals on earth: the African square-lipped rhino.[3] Eddy's point was made: It is important for scientists to keep an open mind to the possibility of Champ and kindred creatures as there are numerous historical precedents—lest they too be forced to eat their words.[4]

Without a body to offer definitive proof, no one can say whether or not there is a "monster" in Lake Champlain or other lakes for that matter. Some reports sound like exaggerations and many no doubt are. Others are likely hoaxes, although probably not many, for the vast majority of sightings appear to come from respectable people either vacationing or living along the lake and going about their daily lives, when they chanced upon something extraordinary. Many of the most detailed sightings come from multiple eyewitnesses. In at least one instance, two witnesses said it came so near their boat that they could have reached out and touched it. But what is "it?"

To the uninitiated, it would be easy to dismiss sightings as misidentifications of large fish that are known to reside in the lake. Sturgeon can grow up to and weigh hundreds of pounds. Garpike, the fish likely observed by Samuel de Champlain in 1609, routinely grow to more than two meters long. Yet, when one examines the reports more closely, the plot thickens.

There is little doubt that over the past two centuries, there have been *many more* than the few hundred witnesses who have reported something extraordinary in Lake Champlain. The lake surface is vast: Some 435 square miles with 587 miles of shoreline, so the chances of having a sighting are small.[5] Furthermore, few people venture out to swim or boat at night, and even if they did, visibility would be greatly diminished—and few go swimming or boating in the rain. Then there are the winter months when the lake is frozen—and in most years the lake is entirely frozen over. The point is: To have a sighting, one has to be in the right place at the right time during the right season, and even then they must make a record of their sighting and it must come to the attention of a newspaper reporter, who in turn, must then decide whether or not to publish the account. By reporting the story, the witnesses have to overcome their fear of ridicule. For these reasons, it is likely that the vast majority of encounters with mystery creatures go unreported. Biologist Gary Mangiacopra estimates that only 10 percent of possible Champ sightings are ever reported as a result of witness reluctance or apathy.[6] An example of the former category is provided by Leon Dean who was an English professor at the University of Vermont between 1923 and 1956, during which time he taught a course in folklore and collected reports of the Champlain sea serpent. Dean cites the 1960 sighting by his friend Harold Patch, observing that in the early nineteenth century "he wouldn't have been travelling, would not have had a pair of binoculars with him, would doubtless never have heard of the monster, would probably never have thought of notifying a paper about what he had seen. Even under present conditions, when everybody is going everywhere, seeing everything, and telling the world about it, he was some 15 years before breaking into print. What I am getting at is that an object like the monster is much more likely to be seen now and reported, than under former conditions."[7]

Every culture has its myths and legends, which are used to explain mysteries. Take Thunderbird tales that were once prevalent among Native American tribes of the Pacific Northwest. It may be difficult to take seriously accounts of gigantic birds with massive wing spans trolling the skies, yet such stories may have their origins in reality: the observation of pterodactyl fossils scattered throughout North America—in particular the Pacific Northwest, southwest, and Great Plains.[8] So these incredible tales may not have been created out of thin air after all. Could there be some truth to Champ?

Even Champ proponents concede that most sightings are mis-identifications of natural objects or phenomenon such as large fish, unusual light reflections, freak waves, and so on. Even if this is true, it doesn't explain the other 10 percent—especially when the observers are multiple witnesses who are well respected, and the object was at close range.

At first glance, the case for Champ seems compelling. How could so many witnesses be mistaken? Sober citizens, who are intimately familiar with the appearance and conditions of the lake, having grown up on it, make most reports. How does one explain the numerous sightings that are broadly similar in nature—essentially a large snakelike creature protruding several feet above the water? Certainly no otter or sturgeon is capable of such a feat, and neither are any of the eighty-one species of fish that are known to inhabit the lake.

Even if we were to entertain the possibility of such creatures in Lake Champlain, skeptics rightly point to the lack of definitive proof such as fossils or a carcass. One would think that throughout the time that humans have inhabited the region, definitive proof would have surfaced by now (pardon the pun). On the other hand, it often has been said that we know more about the surface of the moon than we do of our own oceans, and Lake Champlain, although not an ocean, is a vast body of water. As NASA scientist Gene Feldman observes, "even with all the technology that we have today—satellites, buoys, under-water vehicle and ship tracks—we have better maps of the surface of

Mars and the moon than we do the bottom of the ocean. We know very, very little about most of the ocean." Why is this so? Feldman explains: It is a notoriously difficult place to explore and work in as water exerts enormous pressure, and light doesn't shine very far, making the underwater world "a challenging place to study."[9]

Although most scientists remain skeptical of Champ, it is important to maintain an open mind and examine any new evidence without preconceived notions. We would do well to remember that in 1807, Thomas Jefferson, upon hearing an eyewitness account of meteorites, reportedly quipped: "I would sooner believe that two Yankee professors lied, than that stones fell from the sky."[10] Jefferson was mirroring the popular opinion of his day, and in the early nineteenth century, most learned people accepted as fact that such reports were the embellishments of some other phenomena. To his credit, in 1808, when faced with evidence that he could not explain, Jefferson called for scientists to examine the claim that stones fell from the sky, however bizarre. He wrote: "It may be very difficult to explain how the stone you possess came into the position in which it was found. But is it easier to explain how it got into the clouds from whence it is supposed to have fallen? The actual fact however is the thing to be established, and this I hope will be done by those whose situations and qualifications enable them to do it."[11] Not long after Jefferson wrote these words, scientists were able to establish the existence of meteorites. Despite numerous meteorites falling from the sky every day since humans have walked the earth (upwards of one hundred per hour during the Quadrantid meteor showers) and despite these objects being littered across the planet, and despite innumerable eyewitnesses descriptions, it took until the early nineteenth century before the scientific community finally accepted their existence. Before then, it was widely believed that "shooting stars" were natural atmospheric phenomena akin to rain or tornados. How did one explain the existence of rocks falling from the heavens? Why, they were spewed from volcanoes, of course![12] Even after the existence of meteors was accepted, for decades it was widely held that they were projectiles from lunar volcanoes![13] Like Jefferson, it is important to keep an open mind when confronted with detailed accounts from so many credible witnesses.

SOME UNLIKELY SUSPECTS

Let's begin by tackling the most improbable of candidates for Champ: lizards. There is no question that some Champ reports have been generated by these tiny critters. How so? The reports of baby Champs being captured. You will recall that in 1887, a group of soldiers based at Plattsburgh claimed to have captured a fourteen-inch long baby sea serpent. Further examination of the strange-looking creature revealed it to have been a specimen of Great Water Lizard.[14] The incident underscores the tendency for those on the lake who encounter anything unusual to think of Champ, in the same way that many people who see strange atmospheric phenomena may claim to have seen a flying saucer. These baby sea serpent claims are best summed up by the adage: "When you hear the sound of hoof beats in the night, first think horses, not zebras."

Chapter 1 discussed several old-timers who saw seals on the lake. Such creatures could easily be mistaken for the sea serpent from a distance. On July 23, 1874, a New York City reverend Dr. Cutting and his son were fishing in Westport Bay when they saw what appeared to be a log. Upon maneuvering their boat closer, it turned out to have been a large seal sticking its head above the waterline. The *Essex County Republican* noted, "with less coolness of head, and an elastic imagination, it would be easy to make quite a long serpent out of an innocent seal."[15]

As for eels being mistaken for Champ, we will recall that Phil Reines reported an encounter with a giant eel while scuba diving in 1975 off Valcour Bay. He said it was at least ten feet long and resembled a "big, white plastic pipe." He also noted that as it was just under the surface, the water could have a magnifying effect, making it appear larger to those observing from above the surface.[16] We also know that giant eels have been caught in other area lakes that are much smaller than Lake Champlain. A 1976 sighting by Orville Wells near Plattsburgh, was eel-like.

TWO PREHISTORIC SUSPECTS

When in early October 1884, a Champlain man named William Lavally reported spotting an alligator-like monster swimming in the lake, the

IN YOUR OWN WORDS, PLEASE DESCRIBE THE INCIDENT FROM THE
BEGINNING. BE SURE TO INCLUDE:
--WHERE AND WHAT YOU WERE DOING AT THE TIME...
--WHAT MADE YOU 1ST NOTICE THE CREATURE...
--DESCRIBE THE CREATURE & ITS ACTIONS...
--IN YOUR OPINION, WHAT DO YOU THINK YOU SAW...

During the afternoon, I was working near my home on the lake. I happened to look out over the water and noticed a strange object moving quite steadily from a northerly direction to a southerly direction. I had never observed anything like that before. I stood transfixed and yelled to a neighbor to observe, however he did not hear me. I was undecided whether to get a gun or a camera, however I just stood there until the object disappeared. I honestly believe I saw a huge animal or whatever swimming very steadily and slowly across our bay. It did not appear to be frightened or curious. Following is a sketch. It appeared as something out of the past or prehistoric monster. I would be happy to discuss this with others that may have seen the object. I've never spoken too much about it as I figured no-one would believe it. I did mention it to a friend, Gordie Little, when the conversation got around to the so called Lake Champlain Monster.

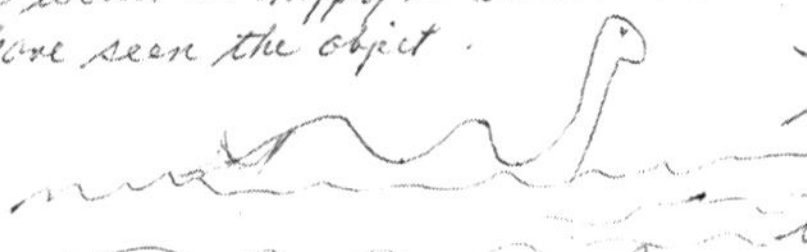

Figure 6.1. Orville Wells sketch of his 1976 sighting on Treadwell Bay just north of Plattsburgh, New York.

Glens Falls Star remarked that the "sea-serpent 'racket' has been worked too often to attract attention, and flagging interest had to be revived in some manner."[17] Mr. Lavally said he was returning home one evening in his rowboat along with his wife and child, when his wife cried out: "My God, what is that?" Mr. Lavally looked astern and spotted a strange-looking creature heading straight for the boat. "He stood up and for some minutes whacked with an oar what he supposes was an alligator," until the figure retreated and Mr Lavally pulled his boat to the safety of the shore. Had the party seen Champ? Could it have been a real alligator? According to one unconfirmed story that was making the rounds, two or three years earlier, a Mr. Channel was visiting Florida when he sent his son a baby alligator that soon escaped into the lake and grew to full size. Of course, such a creature could not possibly survive two winters let alone a few hours in the subzero temperatures found near the Canadian border.[18] It may be that in the darkness and confusion, the Lavally family mistook a garpike for an alligator. Far-fetched you say? Gar bear a striking resemblance to alligators, and another name for this odd-looking prehistoric fish is *the Alligator Gar.* These fish commonly reach a length of six feet and weigh more than one hundred pounds, and some ten feet long have been reported but not verified. Surely, garfish account for many sightings.

Figure 6.2. Depiction of the encounter by the William Lavally family who reported being attacked by a strange alligator-like creature during October 1884. (Sketch by Jamilah Bartholomew)

A more recent case of someone sighting an aquatic creature resembling a crocodile is also likely to have been a garfish. On a late November morning in 2000, Elizabeth Wilkins was enjoying breakfast in her summer home at Willsboro Bay, New York, when her eye spotted a strange form on the lake. The time was 7 AM; the date, November 26. Quickly grabbing her binoculars, she focused in for a closer look. What she saw left her stunned: a large creature, thirty to forty feet long, resembling a crocodile. After twenty minutes, it moved northward and disappeared near Klein's Marina. "What startled me first was the commotion all the seagulls were making out there. I thought 'What's going on here?' and I looked out. Then I saw it. Our camp is directly on the water. It's elevated; that's how I could see it so well. He lay there sort of still in the water for at least 15 minutes." She also noticed that a group of nearby ducks stayed away from the area. "The thing moved northward in a straight line. It humped up in the middle. Its skin looked just like crocodile skin; it was rough. As it moved, it left a little wake behind it."[19]

On the evening of July 11, 2005, two Vermont fishermen were in a boat trying to catch salmon at the mouth of the Ausable River east of Ausable, New York, when they spotted a log floating about one hundred feet away. As they maneuvered their vessel to get a closer look, they were astonished when the "log" submerged. About a half hour later, what appeared to be the same creature resurfaced and played cat and mouse with the men—Dick Affolter, a retired lawyer and Cornell Law School graduate, and Peter Bodette, his stepson. Bodette managed to videotape the object. The videotape was then aired on the ABC's *Good Morning America* the following year. Two FBI forensic experts who examined the video dubbed the image to be authentic although they could not identify the object.[20] Of course, "authentic" essentially means that it did not appear to have been hoaxed.

When *New York Times* journalist Peter Applebome viewed the video at the offices of the New Jersey-based intellectual property lawyer who is managing the images, he was less than impressed. "Unfortunately, the video shows nothing more than a long dark shape impossible to categorize that floats at a distance and at one point seems to go under their boat. The men can be heard talking excitedly, describing it as being like a serpent. But no head emerges from the water, and in the end it's impossible to be sure what was seen."[21] Melanie Stiassny of the American Museum of Natural History told Applebome that she was similarly unmoved when she was shown the video by Bodette's attorney. "The evidence I was presented was singularly unconvincing. We didn't see anything that led us to feel anything other than bemused as to what led these guys to think this was anything so special. It certainly wasn't any large vertebrate. We're sure of that." In defending the video, Bodette told Applebome: "I've fished all over the world. I've been on this lake since I was a little kid . . . I have no idea what it is. But I'm pretty certain what I saw isn't anything you'll find in any fish and wildlife books."

When a frame of the video appeared in the *Burlington Free Press*, a journalist noted: "In one frame it almost looks as if the head of an alligator-like animal breaks the surface. . . ." Investigator Joe Nickell observes that the description by one of the witnesses, Pete Bodette, was that the creature was as big as his thigh—echoing the comparison used by Samuel de Champlain in 1609. Nickell notes another remarkable coincidence: The fish described by Champlain was alligator-like right down to the long snout and double row of "dangerous teeth" and bears a remarkable resemblance to an Alligator Gar.[22]

The idea of an alligator or crocodile cavorting around in the lake is absurd. Even if one were to postulate that it was an escaped pet, by late November, such a creature would not survive long in the frigid waters. Although the mouth of a gar could easily be mistaken for an alligator, Ms. Wilkins did not report seeing such a feature, but crocodile-like skin. Is there any fish in the lake with skin that resembles a crocodile and appears to have humps? Yes, it's called a sturgeon. Here is a description of a sturgeon from a 1991 Associated Press report: ". . . its most unusual feature is an armored back. A series of bony plates—resembling the hide of a crocodile—replaced scales somewhere along the evolutionary line and protected the ancient fish from predators."[23]

Of all species known to inhabit the lake, the most likely creature to be mistaken for Champ is the sturgeon. Lake sturgeon can reach six feet in length and Atlantic sturgeon can grow to double that size. In 1993, Ervin Lang of Moriah reported seeing a fish that looked remarkably similar to an Atlantic sturgeon. On April 13, 1993, Lang was sitting quietly in his truck looking out on the lake, which was covered with mushy ice. Suddenly, a large fish, estimated to have been fourteen to sixteen feet long, crashed through the mushy ice and back into the lake. He was able to judge the size in relation to nearby ice fishing shanties. Theresa Magargee who grew up in the Plattsburgh area, believes that what Lang saw was an Atlantic sturgeon and notes the curious location of the sighting: "This sighting was in Port Henry, the hotbed for Champ sightings."[24] Atlantic Sturgeons are larger saltwater versions of their fresh-water counterparts, which also inhabit the lake. Mark Bain, professor of fish biology at Cornell University, believes that some Champ reports can be explained as sightings of Atlantic sturgeon, noting that their ribbed backs could easily be mistaken for humps.[25] Although Atlantic sturgeon are not native to Lake Champlain, Bain suspects that they occasionally make their way into the lake as they spawn in the St. Lawrence River near the Richelieu River, which is an outlet of Lake Champlain.

Consider a sighting that occurred on June 4, 2009. Carl Roberts was relaxing with friends at Wilcox Dock in Plattsburgh, fishing, catching up on the latest happenings, and hooking an occasional perch. After about two hours of casting, at about 8 PM, the fish stopped biting. The lake was dead calm. Then suddenly about one hundred yards off, a strange creature began making a commotion on the water. "It had to be 50 feet long, from what I could see of the humps" as they rose out of the water, Roberts recalled. Although he has tried to think of a logical explanation, he was stumped by what he saw. "There was no wind, no boats, no explanation whatsoever. It was so close that I could see the texture of the skin," he said describing it as "whale-like with a greenish-black tint that shined against the setting sun." Roberts and his friends watched as the creature moved toward the peninsula south of the dock before suddenly submerging. Roberts said: "It didn't move like a snake. It was not like a porpoise or dolphin, either. It moved straight and fast, with its bumps up high and then lower in the water." He was certain that it was no optical illusion or freak wave. "It was no log, no animal I've seen before. I just can't believe it." The encounter made such an impression on Roberts that he said, that night he "couldn't sleep because of it." Other witnesses included Randy Patnode and Lincoln Collins. Patnode pulled out her cell phone and aimed but couldn't get a picture because the phone was low on power. The creature seemed to have scared the fish away. They continued casting their lines for another hour after the sighting, but the fish had stopped biting.[26]

Roberts said it was unlike any aquatic creature he had ever seen on the lake, and listed several possible explanations. He never mentions sturgeon, perhaps because they are a protected species dwindling in number. Sturgeon can appear to be a prehistoric creature for good reason: They are a prehistoric fish! Remember, the creature was an entire football field away. Furthermore, the witnesses could not have been too rattled by the sighting. Instead of running off to tell friends of what they had seen or fetching a working camera and waiting for the creature to return, their reaction was to remain on the dock and continue fishing for another hour. No doubt they saw something unusual on the water, but their actions tell a different story; it simply could not have been overly compelling.

A favorite haunt of Champ over the years has been near the railroad bridge at Rouses Point, New York. In June 1949, several people were enjoying a picnic on the shore of Alburg Bay on the Vermont side of the lake opposite the village of Rouses Point, when they spotted an enormous creature churning up the water about one hundred feet away as thoughts quickly turned to the sea serpent. That's when Harold Taylor and Paul Narreau got in a boat and headed for the spot. They soon spotted a sturgeon just under the water "about 6 feet long, as big around as a man" and estimated to weigh upward of four hundred pounds. The encounter may never have reached the printed word if it hadn't been for Mr. Taylor working for *The North Countryman* newspaper, which published the account. That same day a 250-pound sturgeon was taken off South Hero, Vermont.[27]

Sturgeon can account for the several enigmatic reports where Champ was said to have slammed into boats on the lake. On the evening of August 5, 1982, three people were on the shoreline near the Kings Bay Campsite at Rouses Point when they said a huge, snakelike creature headed straight for a large sailboat, upward of thirty feet in length that was moored in the bay. The creature then slammed into the vessel with such force that it rocked back and forth, nearly tipping it over. Fourteen-year-old Shawn Elvidge said he was standing at the lake's edge talking with 58-year-old Edward Sheldon of Quebec and 13-year-old Dan Ormsby of Rouses Point, when "we saw these three big humps sticking out of the water. They were pure black. The thing looked like a giant snake . . . it was going north." He said the creature was not more than one hundred yards off shore and was hugging the shoreline.[28]

Reports of Champ ramming vessels on the lake date back to 1873 and have been noted on several occasions by credible witnesses. According to Dr. Bain, no one knows why but there are many reports on record from around the world of sturgeon "attacking" boats. Bain observes: "Because sturgeon are big and look primitive with bony plates and dark color, they can be seen in a surprising moment and look like a part of a monster. I think either lake or Atlantic sturgeon can appear as part of a monster in a brief moment of surprise."[29]

In June 1986, Scott Gifford and his grandmother Ida Gifford were fishing near Willsboro Point, New York, when their attention was drawn to splashing on the lake. Scott's description of the huge creature they saw is remarkably detailed and reminiscent of a scene from the movie *Jaws*. Scott spotted it first and said he "was stunned to see a series of large fins" about eighteen inches high protruding from the water, disappearing, then reappearing. Then his grandmother saw it. "Her jaw dropped" as the creature began moving toward them. "As we stood there in the boat, numbed, watching a creature that appeared to be 30 feet long, you could see the fins connected to the middle of its back, which was about the size of a 50 gallon barrel, a pea green color. We watched as the fins, about six to eight of them slid down into the water, and back up again, as it was swimming north at a slow pace [three to four miles per hour] toward the Four Brother Islands." The creature came to within thirty yards of the startled pair.[30] This account is remarkably consistent with a description of an Atlantic sturgeon, right down to the pea green color, sharklike fins, and slow pace. One Atlantic sturgeon taken in New Brunswick, Canada was fourteen feet long and weighed eight hundred pounds.[31] But how could a sturgeon be thirty feet long? Although this may sound impressive, we know that size estimates are notoriously exaggerated. Champ often is described as glittering in the sun. Both sturgeon and gar belong to the subclass of fish known as *Ganoidei*, from the Greek word *ganos* or "shiny."

Another problem is that few people are experts on all of the aquatic creatures that inhabit the lake. In 1931, several fishermen from West Swanton, Vermont were hauling a seine (a net that hangs in the water vertically with sinkers at the bottom end and floats at the top) for a hatchery. Suddenly, they saw a strange creature trapped in the net. According to the *Essex County Republican* of April 17: "It was 18 inches long with a back like alligator hide and a mouth tucked away back underneath a long and vicious looking snout. No one of the fishermen had ever seen its like, and they were about to hail it as the sea serpent's long lost child when John Niles, came along for inspection and pronounced it a rock sturgeon." Niles was the head of the local government fish hatchery and noted that such fish were "rare but not entirely unknown in the waters of Lake Champlain."[32]

A LIVING DINOSAUR?

Could Champ be a zeuglodon (a form of primitive whale) as postulated by some scientists? Not likely. Zeuglodons were air-breathing mammals that would not be able to survive when the lake freezes over. If Champ is a plesiosaur, there is a similar problem: They too were air-breathers and had to continually surface. Why aren't there more reports? Scott Mardis believes that plesiosaurs are the best candidate for Champ. An ancient carnivorous reptile resembling a long-necked turtle with four flippers but without a shell, they are thought to have become extinct 65 million years ago. He speculates that the creatures may have adapted over time, to be able to survive under the ice. "Reptiles and amphibians can absorb a significant amount of oxygen directly from the water through their skin," he notes.[33] Although some Champ accounts loosely resemble the long-necked plesiosaur or the more serpentine-appearing zeuglodon, it is most improbable that they are responsible for what is being seen in the lake. Once again, there would have to be a breeding community of these creatures and at some point through the law of averages, one would wash up on shore. Mardis points out that another strike against the plesiosaur theory is the apparent stiffness of their necks and their inability to assume a swan-shape that is so typical of Champ sightings. He postulates that some plesiosaurs may have evolved with more flexible necks. University of Vermont biologist Ellen

Marsden believes that there must be a minimum of fifty Champs to maintain a breeding population. That's a lot of Champs to be swimming around for a carcass to have never washed up.[34] If Champ is a living prehistoric creature, the most likely candidates are sturgeon and garpike: two species known to inhabit the lake.

OPTICAL ILLUSIONS

Most people think they can distinguish between waves, wakes, and a living object on the surface of the lake, but in reality it is not so simple. In 2002, a veteran deckhand on the Valcour Ferry remarked that it might be no coincidence that with the cessation of barge traffic in the late 1980s, there has been a corresponding decline in sightings. Skeptics contend that many reports are generated by just the right combination of wind and wakes. Consider an observation by an astute passenger in August 1902. The man wrote a letter to the *Burlington News* expressing great excitement, believing that he had singlehandedly

Figure 6.3. The plesiosaur (top) and zeuglodon (bottom) are thought to have been extinct for at least 60 million years. They are the two leading candidates put forth by cryptozoologists for Champ (Photo credit: Fortean Picture Library).

Figure 6.4. On the evening of June 14, 1983, Dick and Tim Noel reported seeing a dark snake-like creature upwards of twenty-five feet in length and four feet high. It bears little resemblance to a zeuglodon or plesiosaur. Is it an oversized eel, an unclassified species or an optical illusion? (Sketch by Jamilah Bartholomew)

solved the mystery of the Champlain sea serpent after an appearance off Thompson's point, a narrow peninsula about one mile south of Cedar Beach in southern Charlotte. The writer commented cynically that "the summer resorts will now do business" now that "His Majesty" is out and about. One day he was standing on the deck of the steamboat *Chateaugay* when he claims to have figured it out. "It was noticed that at certain times when the motion of the wind waves is in almost the contrary direction to the motion of the steamer's waves, their meeting produces a 'sea serpent'—that is, the meeting waves roll into a large curving wave about twenty feet long or more, which follows along in the direction of the steamer quite a distance behind. The wash from the steamer goes with considerable force and it moves some distance from the steamer before it meets enough resistance to pile up. The front wave rises a little above the [c]rest and meets the wind waves at an angle, the front wave constantly making progress in

the direction and the last one, with resistance exhausted, dying away."
He said the phenomenon only occurs "when the wind is in the right
direction and blowing with sufficient force to produce waves that will
resist the steamer's wash."[35] Of course, this theory doesn't explain the
vast majority of sightings that occur without any steamships or vessels
of any kind in the vicinity. Despite this, the editor of the *Plattsburgh
Sentinel* concurred with the writer's theory, observing: "Another myth
has been punctured by the spirit of scientific investigation. . . ."[36]

Many Champ sightings tax credibility in their length as descriptions, thirty, forty, fifty feet long are common. It is hard to image
a community of such large creatures making Lake Champlain their
home and remaining undetected, yet we face the conundrum: Many
encounters involve multiple observers who were well respected; credible people telling incredible stories. The typical sighting is twenty-five
to thirty feet long with two to three humps. Even Champ proponent
Joe Zarzynski believes that many witnesses are mistaken in their perceptions of what he thinks is most likely a plesiosaur. After examining
nearly three hundred sightings, he concludes that the creature is more
likely to be twelve to fifteen feet in length. This raises the possibility
that many sightings may be the result of a curious phenomenon called
a seiche, a theory supported by science writer Dick Teresi.[37]

Teresi notes that on one occasion, fifty-eight passengers on board
The Spirit of Ethan Allen spotted a creature between thirty and thirty-
five feet long with up to five humps. It is unlikely that so many people
could or even would make up such a tale, yet how could a community
of such enormous creatures reside in the lake and go undetected? The
monster was visible for five minutes, then made a ninety-degree turn
and vanished beneath the waterline. The vessel's experienced captain,
Michael Shea, estimated the weight of the creature at upward of 5,000
pounds! Teresi thinks that what the passengers may have seen that day
was a seiche, a little known wave phenomenon that occurs on certain
lakes including Champlain and Loch Ness.[38]

Research on the Champlain seiche is truly remarkable and bizarre.
There are two. One is about an inch high and travels up and down
the lake. Under the surface is a second monster wave that rolls up and
down the main section of the lake (some sixty miles), varying from
thirty to three hundred feet high! Scientists at Middlebury College

in Vermont have been studying the phenomenon for decades. The Champlain seiche may help to explain sightings like that of Sandi Mansi and others as people may have been seeing vegetation, logs, and tree stumps wrenched upward from the depths of the lake. As Teresi observes, the seiche "wreaks havoc on anything that tries to sit unperturbed in Lake Champlain" causing it to "spew up debris that is mistaken for monsters."[39]

THE MANSI PHOTO REVISITED: A SNAPSHOT IN TIME

Several "experts" claim that the best evidence for Champ—and arguably the best lake monster photo ever—is the Polaroid image snapped by Sandi Mansi back in 1977. Let us take a closer look at the photo and the circumstances surrounding it, weighing the pros and cons.

The Lost Negatives and What They Did With the Photo

Sandi Mansi said that she threw away the negatives. Yes, back in the time of predigital cameras when people routinely received negatives back from the local Fotomat after developing, some people threw them away, but *most* did not because everyone knew if you wanted to make extra copies, the negatives were essential—even if it was film of a day at the beach. In saving the negatives, priceless memories could be shared, and if a photo was ever lost or damaged, it was easily replaced. But this was no photo of a mundane picnic at the beach; by her admission it was believed to have been a prehistoric creature in the lake. If verified, it would have been one of the most important zoological pictures of the twentieth century—and what happens? She tosses the negative. Surely they should have realized that the negative would be valuable if for nothing other than to blow it up to get a better look.

In August 1980, the Vermont State Naturalist Charles Johnson noted that although the Mansi photo appeared to be authentic and not obviously faked or staged, and he was impressed by the Mansis' "apparent honestly and straightforwardness," he did see potential red flags. Johnson wrote: "One was a discrepancy over what happened to the negative: Mrs. Mansi said they threw it away, something they did with all the negatives of pictures they took; Mr. Mansi, talking to me

alone, said they buried it (or burned it . . .) since their experience
had been somewhat fearful. Second, they only took one photograph
despite the fact they said the monster remained surfaced for about
four minutes and they had enough film to take many shots."[40] How
do we account for this discrepancy in their story: Was it tossed away,
burned, or buried? Why would Anthony Mansi make such a statement?
It is not as if the creature was thought to have been some evil entity.
If the picture was so distressing as to prompt them to burn or bury
the negative—why even keep the photo itself, supposedly pinned on a
bulletin board no less, where they would potentially see it on a daily
basis?[41] In 1981, Ronald Kermani produced a series of feature articles
on Champ for the Albany *Times-Union*. He wrote: "For years, the color
print of a long-necked creature with one hump out of the water was
tacked to her [Sandra Mansis'] kitchen bulletin board."[42] Mr. Kermani
was a seasoned senior investigative reporter who has won numerous
journalistic accolades and who spoke directly to Sandra Mansi.[43] She
gave a similar account to Jeff Wright of the Plattsburgh *Press-Republican*,
who also interviewed her that same year. Wright wrote: "For two
years the color snapshot remained pinned to a Mansi family bulletin
board."[44] Two months later, Hal Smith of *Adirondack Life* wrote: "The
picture, still bearing a pinhole in a corner, remained tacked on a wall
in their home. . . ."[45] His article included a photo of Mansi that Smith
had taken, so he almost certainly interviewed her firsthand also. So
we have three journalists who interviewed Mansi directly, recounting
essentially the same story. Now jump ahead to 1992, when Glens Falls,
New York *Post-Star* journalist John Lerner had the opportunity to
spend the day with Sandi Mansi as she was observing a shoot for the
popular NBC TV show *Unsolved Mysteries*. He wrote that Mansi told
him that when the image came back from Fotomat, she "hid the photo
in an album behind another photo. And it stayed there for years."[46]
Then in 2003, researcher Ben Radford interviewed Sandi at her then
home in Bristol, Vermont. They sat down and conducted an extensive
interview. Radford would later write that Mansi told him "The photo
was tucked away in an album for four years."[47] Although memories
can become faulty with the passage of time, this is not exactly a ringing endorsement of her story. But it gets even stranger. When people
purchase rights to reprint the photo, the print is provided by Sandra

Mansi's attorney. What most people do not realize is that the original photo looks quite different than the image that the public sees. The original is sharper and has scratch marks and yellowing around the edges. Few people ever get to look at it firsthand because you have to go out of your way to do so. Several years ago, while conducting research for a study of the photo, Ben Radford flew to Washington DC and met with the attorney holding it and asked to examine it firsthand. He stood there as the photo was removed from a vault and was allowed to take a photo of the photo; and behold—there is no pin mark in it. What does this all mean? I can only say one thing for certain: It raises more questions than answers. Memories do become hazy but there is a big difference between pinning it on a bulletin board in your kitchen, and hiding it away in an album. If as Anthony Mansi reportedly asserted, the negative was disposed of as it evoked unpleasant memories, why keep it in your kitchen?

But wait, there's more. At the 1981 Champ Conference, Sandi said that after taking the picture, "I never told a soul about this. And then we told one of his cousins who had been to Loch Ness, to just go to Lake Champlain to see these things. And he told me I really ought to tell somebody about it." That was when they contacted Dr. Reines [in 1979].[48] In 1981, Sandra Mansi told journalist Jeff Wright that in the two and a half years before they showed the photo to Reines: "Our children would bring their friends in and show them the 2,000 pound duck we saw on vacation."[49] So, did they hide the photo away in an album and keep it a secret for years, or were their kids showing it off to their friends? The one man who has discussed with them the details of their sighting more than any other person—Joe Zarzynski—wrote in 1981 that the photo "remained a family secret until autumn, 1979" when they sought to authenticate it.[50]

The Single Shot

During the entire duration of the sighting, estimated by Mansi to have been between five and seven minutes, she snapped but one photo. It is certainly not your typical reaction. That's a long time for a "monster" to be in sight. And yes, there was more film left on the roll.[51] Again, this does not prove that the Mansis were untruthful, but it is unusual. It is not as if the object was coming at them or was moving around, making it difficult to focus on; they said it remained in the same location for the whole time.

The Inability to Find the Spot

Like the well-known real estate adage that location is the most important selling point of any house, the same is true of monster photos. It is vital to know where the photo was taken so that experts can go there. Knowing the location can help to determine the position and dimensions of nearby objects such as a sandbar, which the Mansi photo appears to show. Although Zarzynski writes that "the Mansi family can not exactly recall on which stretch of Lake Champlain's 587 miles of shoreline they took their now classic photograph," this does not tell the whole story.[52] There is only so much shoreline in the vicinity of St. Albans to the Canadian border, and only so many back roads. In her 1979 taped interview to Dr. Reines, Sandi said they stopped at the spot where the picture was snapped after driving for roughly an hour, north of St. Albans along the back roads. It is no more than twenty miles between St. Albans and the Canadian border, and despite a maze of back roads, it is not exactly a needle in a haystack scenario. Furthermore, traversing the nearby lakeshore by boat and scanning the shoreline, while tedious, is far from impossible. It seems to defy logic to think that the spot could not be located, given that the encounter had only happened in 1977, and four people were involved. Also, it was not as if Sandy was unfamiliar with the region; she spent part of her early life in the area as her parents lived in Brattleboro and her relatives had a camp near St. Albans. Given the extraordinary nature of the event (it is not every day that one reports seeing a prehistoric monster), one would think that at least one of the four would be able to recall a landmark in the vicinity, be it a house, mountain, farm, or sign that would allow them to narrow their search to within a few miles of where the photo was snapped. It was not as if their reported encounter happened decades earlier—it was two years earlier. After they drove off, Sandi said they got the kids a bite to eat. If they could remember where and how long it took to drive there, one would think they could drastically cut down the search area. Soon after a copy of the Mansi photo was given to

Dr. Reines, he and Zarzynski combed every inlet and bay between St. Albans and the Canadian border, without success. They even searched during July, the same time of year that Sandi said she took the photo. They were unable to find the spot despite the photo showing a distinct outcropping of rock on an equally distinct shoreline on the far shore. One would think that along just twenty miles of shoreline, the location would be easy to find. Even with the publicity surrounding the publication of the photo in *The New York Times*, still no one stepped forward to say they could recognize the stretch of New York shoreline where the picture was supposedly taken.

Their Disinterest in Finding the Location

Despite the importance of finding the spot from where she took the photo, neither Sandi nor Anthony Mansi ever expended much energy in trying to pinpoint the site, knowing full well that it would add credibility to their story—assuming it is true. During early July 1980, the Mansis spent ten days vacationing in the region and were to spend part of the time trying to identify the site. On July 17, Zarzynski would write to Reines that "the Mansis did not look for the site."[53] All people are different and have their own idiosyncrasies. Yet, it is hard to image why, given the importance of finding the location, the Mansis would treat finding it in such a lackadaisical way—unless they knew the photo was not taken on Lake Champlain or it was not in their best interests to find the spot.

The Object's Reaction to the Commotion

It is claimed that Anthony Mansi began shouting to get the kids out of the water. Yet, throughout all of the noise and commotion, the "creature" just sat there. "It never looked at us—never," Sandra said.[54] For five to seven minutes, the object made minimal movement—and never even turned toward shore despite the sound and movement. Then when it disappeared, it didn't swim away—it didn't swim at all—it just floated there before submerging.[55] It is certainly not your typical Champ sighting. In fact, one is hard pressed to find a similar recorded Champ sighting.

Fleeing in Fear

Sandi said that they left the shoreline fearing for their safety. "I thought that sucker had legs and was going to come up on shore," she recalled.[56] Although there are a handful of sensational Champ sightings from the nineteenth century when the creature purportedly came ashore, those sightings are dubious. Reports of Champ slithering on land are rare, and I am unaware of a single credible sighting where the witnesses have reported that they were fearful that the creature was going to chase after them on land. It is certainly not your typical reaction. Furthermore, it was not as if the figure was moving near the shoreline. By her own estimate it was 150 feet or half a football field away and was not moving toward her—in fact, it was not doing much of anything. It is difficult to understand why they would be in such a hurry to get away when in her description of the object appearing, she says that it wasn't swimming and appeared stationary, before quietly submerging. Sandi Mansi would later describe the scene with the word "serene" before getting caught up in the excitement. Although it is understandable that they wanted the children out of the water, they had them go up the bank and to the car, so they were clearly in no danger. If the object had begun moving toward shore, they could have simply walked up the embankment, gotten into their car and driven off—but it made no such move and never even faced the shore at any time. This is not to say that the Mansis were hoaxing, only that their actions are odd and not typical of Champ witnesses. In her original recorded interview of the incident, Sandi said when she first saw the object, she was scared: ". . . at that point, all I saw was the neck and the head and I was really frightened. I don't know what I was frightened about, but I was frightened."[57] In 2003, she told Ben Radford that when she first saw it: "I wasn't even scared, I'm just trying to figure out what I'm seeing."[58] Of course, later, she said she did become frightened.

The Sandbar and the Possibility of a Hoax

In his analysis of the photo at the Optical Sciences Center at the University of Arizona, B. Roy Frieden found no evidence of tampering but did see something "suspicious" that warrants further investigation: a brown horizontal streak that appears to be a sandbar. This has major implications for the possibility of a hoax either perpetrated on or by the witnesses, as it means the water would be much shallower and warmer. Frieden states that "if it is a sandbar then there is a distinct possibility that the object was put there by someone, either by the people who took the photo or by the people who were fooling them, because you could simply walk out on such a sandbar and tow the object behind you and hide behind it as you made it rise out of the water and so forth."[59] However unlikely, we should remember the Lake George hippogriff.

The Narrowness of the Lake

There also was suspicion about the narrowness of the body of water in the photo, which is uncharacteristic of most of the lake. It has even been suggested from the photo details that it may have been taken along The Narrows, a thirty seven-mile stretch of waterway at the extreme southern end of the lake, far away from where Mansi said the photo was taken. The Mansis are emphatic that the photo was not taken there. Frieden considers this suspicious "because if it is an uncharacteristically narrow portion of the lake, perhaps the picture wasn't taken at Lake Champlain but rather at some other body of water."[60]

The Structure of the Object

One expert argues that the anatomical structure of the object is biologically improbable. When the photo is enhanced, it becomes apparent that there are several lumps between the base of the neck and the body. British science writer and paleontologist Darren Naish specializes in studying aquatic creatures of prehistoric origin and is highly skeptical of the Mansi photo because of these lumps and the object's positioning. Naish says the lumps eliminate the possibility of the object being a plesiosaur or sauropod-like creature as the structure is wrong. "Logic and vertebrate morphology dictate that the tail will be out further to the right . . . (and) the chest and shoulder region will be more or less directly beneath the head, and thus the forearms will be more or less directly below the point at which the head is."[61] His bottom line: Based on the positioning of the object in the photo, it would be anatomically inconsistent with any known or extinct animal.

This also highlights the issue of bias. Most people are not experts in the biology of living or extinct aquatic creatures. Documentaries often have biases and working hypotheses. For instance, in the Discovery Channel's "Out of the Unknown" series, Naish observes that photographic analyst Peter Suthers concludes that the object is the tail of a whale and parts of the Mansi image were enhanced to try to highlight this theory. Naish describes this as "a bizarre and crazy idea apparently favored because Discovery wanted Champ to be a surviving basilosaurid whale."[62] It is important to remember that documentary makers often have a working hypothesis and try to get evidence to support it, often leaving out evidence to the contrary. This also is true of some of the print media. Phil Reines notes that some journalists have hyped the Champ story to make it sound more appealing. "There is a lot of irresponsible journalism. My name has been prominently mentioned by people who never called me . . . never checked the story with me. I have appeared in dozens of articles and a lot of magazines, and I kind of resent it."[63]

The Object Hardly Moves

Naish believes that the object in the photo is an illusion—that it is a piece of wood that looks like an animal but cannot be. This would help to explain why it hardly moved in the five to seven minutes that it appeared. He thinks that the object is most likely "a tree stump with branches or roots sticking out of it." How does he explain the movement as reported by Mansi? "Tree stumps which float to the surface may rotate, bob around and create the impression of a moving animal." Naish points out that decomposing vegetation can rise to the surface only to sink again as the gas is expelled.[64]

This would help to explain why Mansi said that the object did not swim, and another odd observation: When it appeared, she said that water poured out from where the mouth would have been and she could discern no animate details such as eyes.[65] This detail is inconsistent with all known reported sightings of Champ. Most witnesses report an object moving through the water. There are no other reports where the object slowly emerges several feet out of the water, remains in the same spot for several minutes, and then submerges. This description *is* consistent with a piece of driftwood breaking the surface of the water. Is it possible for someone to mistake a stump for a monster? People mistake Venus for a UFO all the time. Size and distance is notoriously difficult to judge on land, and even more challenging on water, even more so when the witness is in a panicky state. In 1959, Donald Mears of St. Albans, Vermont, was on the west side of South Hero Island when he said "a large snake-like head and neck lifted high out of the water." Mears grabbed his camera and was ready to snap a photo, when he decided to check the light meter. In those few seconds, the creature submerged. He added a curious observation: "It didn't dive like an ordinary animal—it just sank straight down."[66] This sighting echoes Sandra Mansi's description. Is it possible that Mears had misinterpreted a tree stump or driftwood?

Figure 6.5. Artist interpretation of a sighting by Donald Mears off South Hero Island in 1959 (Sketch by Jamilah Bartholomew).

Behavior During the Encounter

Occasionally, Sandra Mansi contradicts herself. For instance, in her 1979 taped interview, she said that her husband to be, Tony, returned to the car because "he wanted his sunglasses because it must have been around noon, one o'clock . . ." Just a few minutes later, they all hopped into the car but it would not start, frightening her because of the "dying light."[67] In fact, the longest day of the year in the northern hemisphere (the summer solstice) is June 21, plus or minus a day. The Mansi's reported sighting was just two weeks later, on one of the longest days of the year. How can it go from being noon or 1 PM to dusk? One could understand being off by an hour, but there is an eight- or nine-hour discrepancy.

Post-encounter Behavior

Sandi Mansi takes a photo of what she believes is a prehistoric animal on Lake Champlain and holds onto it for years without making it public, saying that she feared ridicule. She then contacts Dr. Reines (through an intermediary) and has it analyzed. If she was so worried about the ridicule, why not release the photo and keep her identity secret? Surely, keeping her identity under wraps would be no more harmful than stepping forward and then attempting to make money off the picture. Over the past two centuries, many witnesses have opted to remain anonymous. Revealing her identity was entirely unnecessary. The time lapse is troubling because if they had stepped forward shortly after the incident, it is highly likely they would have been able to find the location and the photo could have been further authenticated and more information revealed. For starters, the image could have been blown up with greater clarity and the distance from the object and the depth of the water could be determined. If it was, as some suspect, a tree stump, there was every chance it could have still been there. Mansi attorney Alan Neigher paints an unsophisticated picture of the Mansis, contending that they "could no more have constructed such a hoax than put a satellite in orbit."[68] After a lengthy interview with Sandi Mansi in 1994, journalist John Lenger portrays her as economically enterprising and anything but naive. "Sandra Mansi . . . was a tinsmith who helped build the 'Ohio,' the world's first nuclear submarine, and later took a small side business and built it into a million-dollar-a-year concern. Right now she owns an antique shop in West Swanzey, N.H."[69]

The Character Issue

First there is the issue of Anthony and Sandi Mansi contacting a lawyer and trying to profit from the photo. It is not a crime to do so, and many people in their shoes would no doubt have done the same. But their doing so does not promote their public image. It would have enhanced Sandi's image more if she had refused any money for the photo, especially given the questions surrounding it. A co-worker claims that Mansi talked about the photo at work and getting rich off it. Science writer Ben Radford interviewed Mansi and wrote: "Mansi says that all of them saw the creature and that her daughter had some difficulty dealing with the experience." This contradicts what was stated by Anthony Mansi, that the children never saw the creature.[70]

Figure 6.6. When noted fraud investigators Joe Nickell (left) and Ben Radford (right) interviewed Sandra Mansi, they could find no obvious evidence of a hoax, though many unanswered questions remain (Ben Radford photo).

The couple may be entirely truthful about what happened, as human memory can be fallible, but that does not necessarily mean that they saw Champ. The point here is that there are far too many question marks hanging over the Mansi photo and the circumstances under which it was taken. Clearly, if this is the best evidence, it leaves much to be desired.

Then there is Anthony's account. In his original interview after the sighting, Anthony told Phil Reines that he saw what appeared to be a long neck and a head.[71] The following year, he told a journalist for the *Palm Beach Post*: "It looks like a dinosaur without legs. It has flippers instead. The picture shows 8 feet of neck out of the water. You can see the back of the head, a hump and part of one flipper."[72] A similar transformation occurred with Sandi. By November 1980, after being exposed to the Champ literature, she told a reporter that it was "like seeing a dinosaur. It was big and black with a long neck and its head was like that of a horse with a hump, or back."[73]

Although Sandi Mansi expressed the belief that the object she had taken a photo of was prehistoric, Mary Watzin, an environmental biologist at the University of Vermont, is skeptical given the lake's very recent formation. ". . . [i]t's highly unlikely that there is anything here from prehistoric days . . . because this whole area was glaciated ten to twelve-thousand years ago . . . and it's very unlikely that anything could have survived those very traumatic changes."[74] As noted in Chapter 4, during her initial interview, Sandi never said it had a horselike head or resembled a dinosaur. In fact, she described it as "whatever it was we saw" and noted, "we talked about it a little bit after that like, you know, what was it? It could have been this, it could have been that, and we really didn't think much about it until the pictures came back. . . ." By August 1981, she told the Champ seminar: "You do not want to ask me if I think Champ exists—I know it does. I have seen Champ almost on a first name basis . . . (and) have photographed Champ." She ended her presentation by saying: "I'll tell you right now, Champ is there! It exists. It is really there!" Within the course of two years, the Mansis went from seeing something in the lake they were not sure of, to seeing Champ.[75] The description seems to have grown more elaborate over time. Although exaggeration and wish fulfillment are natural human tendencies, they also are a concern.

From the standpoint of social psychology, at the very least we can say that for many witnesses, stories of Champ allow people who have seen something unfamiliar on the lake, to place it into a familiar category.

In his original interview after the incident, Anthony Mansi said: "I threw her the camera and said, 'Take a picture and let's get out of here.'"[76] Later Sandi Mansi told the NBC TV *Unsolved Mysteries* program that Tony "handed me the camera," whereas in 2007 Mansi told Monster Quest interviewers: "I had the camera and I picked the camera up and I took the photograph."[77] So which was it? There is a big difference between throwing someone a camera, handing it to them, and picking it up. These three different stories may be a result of faulty memories; on the other hand, glaring discrepancies like this one are exactly what one could expect if the story was fabricated. It is certainly odd to have so many discrepancies in one story.

Researchers are fond of pointing out that the accounts by Anthony and Sandi Mansi have never wavered. On the contrary, they have wavered significantly in key details. The question to be answered is this: Is it due to confusion and faulty memories, or something more sinister—failing to get their stories straight after fabricating the tale? In 2010, 66-year-old Sandi Mansi described the photo as a life-altering event akin to a religious experience. She told journalist Mel Allen that she had asked God what he wanted her to do with the photo, and when there was no answer, she followed her heart. "I felt God gave us a gift," she said. "What we do with the gift will make a difference in our lives." Mansi says that when she passes on, she hopes to learn the secret. "I will go to God and stand before Him and say, 'God, why me? Now tell me what it was.'"[78] Is she a clever con artist, the innocent victim of a piece of floating driftwood, or a witness to something extraordinary? Each reader must weigh the evidence and decide for him or herself.

ANATOMY OF A MONSTER PHOTO

Radford conducted experiments at Lake Champlain after using Mansi's own estimates and camera type. His findings are in agreement with the assessment by Naish that the anatomy was wrong for it to have been a living creature. Radford observes that the "head" and "bump" on the picture are not connected. "If the photograph truly does depict the hump and neck of a lake monster, the actual body contortion is very unusual and unlikely for nearly any type of living animal."[79]

Radford's analysis of the photo did not stop there. He went so far as to drive to Connecticut to view the original, which he measured to see how it appeared in comparison to the entire photo, instead of using an image that had been cropped for a magazine or magnified. "With the camera held at the height Mansi had claimed (about 8.5 feet), Radford swam out exactly 150 feet to measure the object's size in that particular scale. "Any object of a claimed size at a certain distance (at a given focal length) will take up a given measurable space in the print. I measured the size of the one-foot scale at 150 feet on our photograph, marked that, and transferred the measurement to the Mansi image to the same size."[80]

Radford's finding: The object in the photo was half the size that Mansi had estimated, which is not surprising given that anyone taking Lake Monsters 101 will be aware that witnesses commonly overestimate the size and distance of aquatic objects. Radford concludes: "The 'neck' is nowhere near the previous estimates of six to eight feet or more; instead, the object is just over three feet out of the water, and both segments together are about seven feet across," he said.[81] Radford's findings place the object in the photo in an entirely different light as "the range of possible candidates becomes far larger—including perhaps a large bird, known animal, or a floating tree stump."[82] He concurs with Dr. Naish that the latter explanation is the most likely.

Although the Mansi photo may be genuine and depict an unknown species living in Lake Champlain, there are several unsettling questions surrounding it. Although any one point does not necessarily cast suspicion on the authenticity of the photo and the object in it, taken in their totality, it certainly does cast doubt among many scientists and as a result the scientific community and most mainstream scientists are unwilling to accept the photo as that of a lake "monster." This is perhaps best described by Dr. Reines, to whom Mansi first turned to get the photo analyzed. "That location must be found! There's no question about it!" Reines said. "I want that photograph to prove to me the existence of Champ. . . . but I have got to find that location. I have to satisfy my own criteria."[83] Science cannot simply take people's word for things. Honest, sincere people once reported seeing fairies and there was even The Fairy Investigation Society in England, which collected sightings just like Champ and UFO sightings are gathered today. Science cannot be based on someone's word or description. People hoax. People are imperfect observers. Science must be based on unemotional analysis of the available evidence. Dr. Reines is quick to point out that this doesn't necessarily mean that Mansi hoaxed the photo, but by her own admission she was in a "hysterical" state (her own word) and certainly strong emotions can lead to witnesses over-reacting. As Shakespeare wrote, "Or in the night, imagining some fear, How easy is a bush suppos'd a bear!"[84]

By Naish's analysis, it was a piece of wood that briefly rose to the surface, turned and sank again after several minutes. Mansi's panicked state may help to explain her interpretation of Champ. As a child, her grandfather would scare her with stories of Champ eating her. "If you don't sit still, I'm going to throw you over the side and Champ will eat you," she recalled.[85] It was natural for her to assume that the object was Champ. If one considers this too far-fetched, remember that prior to the twentieth century, there were hundreds and hundreds of sightings of mermaids by lonely sailors on long voyages; in many instances, describing them in great detail. People see what they expect to see.

Curiously, there appears to have been an influx of sightings at the start of the 1980s, almost certainly reflecting the intense media publicity with the protection legislation from New York and Vermont, the Mansi photo publication, and the Champ Conference. It had suddenly become vogue to see Champ. When Ben Radford visited the Champ sightings board in Port Henry in 2004, of the 132 sightings listed, nearly half were dated 1981 or 1982! Radford and fellow researcher Joe Nickell argue that the Mansi photo can be credited with single-handedly triggering a bandwagon effect "whereby widely publicized sightings lead to other reports independent of an actual creature's presence or absence."[86] It is also telling that as of 2012, the first sighting on the sighting board remains that of Samuel de Champlain in 1609, despite community officials knowing full well that it is of dubious origin. That it has remained unaltered for so many years underscores the fact that local officials are more interested in pulling in tourists than historical accuracy.

Figure 6.7. Captivated by the lure of Champ, Australian researcher Paul Cropper traveled to Port Henry to experience the legend firsthand. Cropper stands in front of the sighting board erected by the Village (Paul Bartholomew photo).

"SEEING" CHAMP

There is an interesting cautionary tale about the power of human suggestibility and the fallible nature of human perception. In 1992, Terry Megargee described an encounter that she had with a strange aquatic creature on the lake back in 1951. She spotted a snakelike creature about thirty feet long with at least three humps. "There was one hump like an overturned boat. There was a middle hump like an overturned boat, and a third one. And I thought, this has to be truly something . . . [extraordinary]." At this point, she took aim with her rifle and fired, confident that it had found its mark. The description of a snakelike creature about thirty feet long with three humps is a classic. Was it Champ? Several days later a sturgeon was found washed ashore—with a bullet hole! Judging distances and the size of objects, are notoriously difficult, especially on water.[87]

Even experienced fishermen and boaters can be deceived if they are in the right place at the right time. Consider the following illustration. On Sunday evening July 11, 1948, two residents of Rouses Point, New York, Robert Rochester and Arnold Scales, spotted what they took to be the Champlain Monster heading south, a few hundred feet from shore. In a scene reminiscent of a 1950s monster movie, what Scales did next was enough to make most environmentalists cringe: He fetched a rifle from his house and the two men jumped in a motorboat and gave chase! *The North Countryman* newspaper describes what happened next: "As they overtook the 'monster' it split, however, and the boat was soon in a school of big sheephead, a species of carp, that were evidently migrating up the Lake."

Another classic example of how witnesses' eyes can deceive them occurred on July 5, 1988 at Shelburne Falls, Vermont, when a couple reported seeing a humped creature in the water. Sandra Tappan was adamant that she saw the creature's head and neck rise out of the water, and then submerge. It was a classic sighting of a head and neck, including an observation of a hump and would probably go down in history as such if not for one key detail: her husband Frank who videotaped the encounter. Experts who have looked at the video are confident that it is a school of fish: most likely carp spawning. In fact, it is hard to imagine anyone looking at the tape and concluding otherwise! So how did Mrs. Tappan come to report seeing a head, neck, and hump? She contends that what she saw was not on the tape.[88]

BUGS BUNNY, ORSON WELLES, AND CHAMP

What do Bugs Bunny, actor Orson Welles and the Champlain Monster have in common? More than you might think. Human perception is notoriously unreliable and people have a tendency to see what they want or expect to see. A good Champ-related example of this occurred on July 9, 1981, when Kelly Williams of Port Henry was standing on shore when she snapped photos of something vague in the water. In August 1982, her images appeared in *Life Magazine*. Although Richard

Deuel of ChampQuest pronounced them as being of good quality,
Ben Radford observed, "they could be of just about anything in the
water."[89]

In recent decades with advancements in DNA evidence, hundreds
of people who were imprisoned—and in some cases executed—on the
weight of eyewitness testimony, have been exonerated. In most cases,
the witnesses weren't lying, but the human eyes and mind do not work
together like a video recorder, simply taking in everything that is seen;
the mind interprets what it sees and is preconditioned by one's mental
outlook.[90] Furthermore, the more ambiguous the situation, the more
likely the information will be distorted, and most Champ sightings
occur at a distance and on water—not the best of viewing conditions.
When many people visit Lake Champlain and see anything unusual
on the water, the thought of Champ immediately arises. Hence, what
people see is often based more on inference than reality as witnesses
begin "filling in missing information in instances where perception is
either inefficient or inadequate."[91] But what about the many sightings
by police officers dating all the way back the Clinton County Sheriff
Nathan Mooney's remarkably detailed report from 1883? Despite often
being described as "trained observers," law enforcement personnel are
no more reliable than the person on the street. The same holds true
for the testimony of doctors, lawyers, priests, scientists, teachers and
yes, even authors!

There are two classic examples of how poor humans are in observing their environment—especially under stress—and most Champ witnesses would admit to having been excited during their sighting. Both
examples occurred not far from the shores of Lake Champlain.

On Halloween Eve in 1938, actor Orson Welles produced a radio
play at the studios of WCBS in New York City. The broadcast was
heard across the country. It was an adaptation of the famous science
fiction novel *War of the Worlds* by H.G. Wells, rewritten to be read as
a radio drama. It has been estimated that more than 1 million listeners
who tuned in late, thought for a brief time that Martians were invading
earth. According the broadcast, the aliens were attacking parts of New
York and New Jersey with heat rays and in giant cylinders towering
twenty-five feet into the air. Incredibly, some people reported that they

could feel the heat rays or see the towering Martian machines on the horizon—as was being described on the radio.[92]

A second example comes from Adirondack historian Fred Stiles who describes an incident that occurred not far from Lake Champlain with a Bigfoot encounter in the Adirondacks. The incident involves his neighbor Hail Hall, who was searching for lost coins using a metal detector at the same time there had been a series of area Bigfoot sightings. One day Hall was digging when he glanced upward to see "a giant form about 10 feet tall with a great bushy head." He galloped off with the speed of a sprinter, only to realize moments later that his expensive machine was lying in the woods. Frightened but determined, he stealthy made his way back the scene of the "encounter." "Glancing towards the place where Bigfoot had been, there he was and he was wiggling his head back and forth—it was a very large porcupine, munching on a limb about 10 feet up a tree. And I guess he believes as I do, if the people who see Bigfoot had time to look more closely, they would find something which could be explained."[93]

So where does Bugs Bunny fit into this? Even after people recall something that happened, they do not play it back as it had occurred, but as how they think it occurred. A dramatic example of this process took place when psychologist Elizabeth Loftus of Washington State University and her colleague Jacquie Pickrell decided to do an experiment using America's favorite cartoon rabbit, Bugs Bunny. They were able to get about one-third of the subjects involved in their study, all of whom had visited Disneyland, to believe that they had shaken hands with Bugs Bunny when in fact, they could not have because Bugs is a trademark of Warner Brothers. Mickey Mouse? Yes. Bugs Bunny? Impossible. Pickrell found the study "frightening" as it shows how easily memories can be manipulated. "Memory is very vulnerable and malleable. People are not always aware of the choices they make. This study shows the power of subtle association changes on memory."[94]

The history of sailing is filled with examples of the eyes and mind playing tricks on even the most experienced sailors. For instance, on one sunny afternoon in the nineteenth century, sailors and officers on a French Frigate spotted a life raft. Everyone on the vessel "clearly saw

a raft covered with men towed by boats." A rescue craft was lowered
and they rushed toward the distressed men who were "clearly seen
stretching out their hands and clearly heard." Upon reaching the "raft"
the rescuers were astounded. The escape raft turned out to have been
"nothing but a few branches of trees covered with leaves" that had
been swept out to sea from the nearby land mass.[95]

On several occasions in this book we have documented sightings
by so-called trained observers from military personnel to state police
and sheriff's deputies. There is no such thing as a trained observer and
his or her descriptions hold no greater weight than that of anyone else.
Dr. Reines, a trained nautical observer with several decades of experience, is aware of the fallibility of the human eye and brain. "I have
been fooled many, many times by things that looked like grey heads
coming out of the water which have turned out to be the heads of
ducks, loons, sticks, and you know, I can shake my eyes because this
can't happen to me. . . . So, if trained observers have difficulty—and
boy we do—you can imagine how much difficulty people [have]
whose frame of reference basically is land."[96]

In 1898, there was a sensational, multiple sighting of a huge sea
serpent off a North Country bridge. The story shows how easily people
can get carried away with excitement. Rosel Couture, a Delaware &
Hudson Railroad engineer, would later recount the "encounter" for
The North Countryman. He and his Uncle Jim Barrie were working with the "Central Vermont bridge gang" on the span connecting
Rouses Point with Vermont. When the old ties were replaced, the pair
would take them down. It so happened that on this occasion there were
so many unusable ties, that they built a raft and loaded it down with
ties that were to be chopped up and used for firewood. On the front
of the raft, they attached a log to close up a hole on the raft. With
dusk approaching, they attached a 1,100-foot rope to the raft and tied
the other to a boat and ever so slowly pulled the raft along. It was a
strange-looking sight as it was moving through the water and bobbing
up and down. "Uncle John and Mr. Couture finally got their raft load
of timber as far as the old shanty that was just east of the long pier.
They had noticed two fellows fishing from the pier when they passed
in the boat but the fishermen apparently hadn't spotted them. When
the submerged raft with its load of old ties and apparently progressing

under its own power, was sighted by the two fishermen they hastily pulled in their lines, rubbed their eyes and pinched themselves to see if they were really awake, and made tracks for town."

Couture says that he and his uncle hadn't given the matter much thought until they arrived on the shore of Rouses Point with their cargo, where they "heard the astounding news, which had spread rapidly, that two men had seen a huge sea monster on the bridge. It seemed that the two men hadn't remained on the bridge long enough to find out the size or shape of the 'sea serpent' but from the splashing they had heard they judged it was of monstrous proportions."[97]

Could misidentifications account for the enigmatic patterning of Champ sightings, such as how there could be a dozen one year, followed by none for the next three? Decade after decade, there are periods of not one single report, followed by a flurry of observations. After the dozens of sightings in the Whitehall and Dresden area in 1873, there was not a single report in the regional papers until 1878. Time and again we see this same pattern, which may be a function of newspapers whipping up interest with a single high-profile sighting, followed by others who are actively looking for and expecting to see the creature.

Scientists are as fallible and prone to making mistakes as everyone else. Analysis of anything by scientists with all of their sophisticated equipment often can be a highly subjective process. Sure, the machinery does not lie, but data can be open to broad interpretations, and scientists can be fooled like anyone else. In 1981, J. Richard Greenwell of the University of Arizona said that when the Mansi photo was superimposed onto the famous 1934 surgeon's photo at Loch Ness, there were remarkable similarities. He noted that the ratio between the head and neck was "very close," suggesting that the two species were related.[98] It is well known that Loch Ness and Lake Champlain are glacial lakes that were cut off from the ocean about 10,000 years ago, and there has long been speculation that Champ and Nessie are the same species. Earlier, Vermont State naturalist Charles Johnson made a similar observation: "I was immediately struck by how much the head and neck resembled the 'surgeon's photo' of the Loch Ness Monster."[99] The Nessie photo fell into disrepute in 1994 when Christian Spurling revealed that the picture was a hoax involving a toy submarine that had been fitted with a sea serpent head in an effort to fool the *Daily Mail*.[100] Scientific analysis is often more subjective than not; that is why doctors give second opinions!

Several years ago at Loch Ness, historian Richard Frere decided to conduct an experiment, so he and a friend stood by a road near the loch and began snapping photos and gesticulating excitedly before passing motorists. Soon people accumulated at the lakeside and pulled out their own cameras, training them on the loch. The pair said they spotted a big hump in the water. At one point several boats passed by, creating wakes in the choppy waters. Several witnesses claimed to see humps in the loch, and two men sharing binoculars even claimed to discern flippers and a tail! An adept artist even sketched a picture of an object in the loch, bearing a remarkable resemblance to a plesiosaur.[101]

Noted American monster hunter Loren Coleman has been researching Champ sightings for more than forty years and is surpris-

Figure 6.8. Famous "Surgeon's Photo" snapped in the 1930s, was long held to have been the best lake monster photo in existence until it was unveiled as a hoax in 1994. It was actually a toy submarine fitted with a serpent's head. Source: Fortean Picture Library.

ingly cautious about the likelihood of Lake Champlain harboring a new or "extinct" species, although he says, it is not out of the question. He believes that most reports "are explainable as known animals (e.g., beaver, deer, moose, sturgeon, other large fish, otters, muskrats, and dogs) and natural phenomena (e.g., rogue waves, fog, tree limbs, floating peat)." Coleman notes that in the scientific literature, there have been several reports of out-of-place seals in the lake that could give rise to sightings.[102]

So, after weighing all of the evidence, does Champ exist as a new or long-thought extinct creature? If I had to wager $100, I would bet $10 on the affirmative, $40 that people are seeing known fish and optical illusions; I would take the remaining $50 and put it in my pocket.[103] Why? Because to know would kill the mystery and would be the equivalent of shooting the Easter Bunny or Santa Claus. Even if Champ does not exist, the monster saga is a fascinating chapter in the history of human psychology.

THE POWER OF A SYMBOL

When one glances at a topographical map of Lake Champlain, its glacial symmetry is reminiscent of a Rorschach inkblot test that psychiatrists use to help their patients describe what they are thinking. Ironically, a close reading of the history of the elusive Champlain Monster, may tell us more about us than him. It is a message about the beauty, awe and mystery of nature and the importance of preserving it. It is a message of excitement and adventure in our otherwise mundane lives. Ultimately, Champ sightings may represent an anti-scientific symbol in a skeptical age, a reminder with each new sighting, that scientists do not know everything. As science gains a greater foothold in the modern world and religious beliefs decline, the spiritual side of the human psyche may suffer. If Champ turns out to be a collective fiction based on expectation and hope, it is no less real for having been a human creation. If as most scientists assert, Champ is a creation of the human mind, we may do well to heed the words of Walter Lippmann: "For it is clear enough that under certain conditions men respond as powerfully to fictions as they do to realities, and that in many cases they help to create the very fictions to which they respond."[104] Lippmann documented how the news media creates and sustains "reality."

Peter Dendle believes that the search for "hidden animals" such as Champ may reflect an attempt to resurrect "magic and wonder in a world many perceive as having lost its mystique."[105] The ultimate arbitrator of truth was once religion. There was a time, many centuries ago, when no one questioned the word of a priest or "enlightened" kings who were widely believed to have a direct connection to God. Next came the justice system, which became the new arbitrator of disputes: judges, juries, and legal statutes. We now live in an age of specialist scientists who solve technical problems. Yet, many people feel uneasy given that scientific findings are open to interpretation, as evidenced by the continuing debate over the nature of global warming. In this regard, many people may feel that their power to influence certain issues has been taken over by scientists. Subconsciously, Champ may allow us to question the validity of those scientists and feel like we have regained some control over decisions that affect our lives. In the words of Dendle: "To be on to something that even the professors of Harvard do not know about, or to benefit from a cure of which the National Institutes of Health are ignorant, can be very empowering in an age of routine deference to higher bodies of institutional knowledge."[106]

If Dendle is right, Champ may represent a form of collective wish fulfilment on par with religious followers who think they see the Virgin Mary appear in the clouds or the eyes of a statue in her likeness, moving during Sunday mass. In October 1977, Maria Rubio was cooking a meal in Lake Arthur, New Mexico when she noticed skillet burns on her tortilla bearing a remarkable resemblance to the face of Jesus. Soon, thousands of faithful came to see the "miracle" for themselves to confirm their faith. By November, the skillet of a housewife in Phoenix, Arizona, had produced a similar tortilla and before long, similar miracle tortillas were popping up across the country.[107] No one knows what the face of Christ looked like, but we have a popular image. Conversely, no one knows what Champ looks like. Yes, we have the Mansi photo (an undefined form with no facial features—the so-called "best" evidence) and a number of blurry photos and videos. The Mansi photo, like the tortilla, is open to interpretation, and whether one believes that it is the genuine article is ultimately a matter of faith. Clearly, publicity from the first incident had prompted people to begin scrutinizing their cooking creations and some began to see what they expected to see. Lake Arthur, New Mexico, home to the Original Tortilla, is forty miles from Roswell, home of the popular myth that space aliens crashed landed in June 1947. Whatever the answer to the Champ mystery, it is likely to tell us more about us as a species, than a possible new species in the lake.

There is a certain spiritual mystique surrounding Champ. Humans seem to have a deep spiritual longing, and in an age where religious belief and devoutness is waning, perhaps monsters and saviors from our skies in the form of UFOs are filling that void. It is worth remembering that to many witnesses, they *did* see Champ. A common theme in the UFO/Bigfoot/lake monster literature involves witnesses being transformed by their encounter with the unknown. The observers often are left with an enhanced spirituality, more in touch with the cosmos, and more at peace with themselves, even to the point of undergoing a personality change and new outlook on life. There also seems to be a connection with the environmental movement and Champ: so many witnesses and researchers talk about shooting Bigfoot with a camera and not a gun, the importance of Champ as an environmental symbol and barometer of the lake's health, and that space aliens are here to save humanity from itself. Each of these mysteries has a similar spiritual thread running through it that may be more of a reflection of the human mind than of any external reality.

During the 1990s, Champ became an important symbol for the environmental health of the lake and was used in a series of protests. One memorable incident took place on November 19, 1991, at a heated public hearing by International Paper (IP) Company Mill in Ticonderoga. After longstanding criticism of its discharge of pollution into the lake, the hearing was on whether to renew IP's wastewater discharge permit. One by one, people stepped up to express their disapproval. That's when someone dressed in a green Champ costume walked up to speak in favor of the renewal, the implication being that the many Champ sightings were evidence that the lake was healthy.[108] Before the meeting, Vermont members of the group Earth First!, had held a protest against IP on the Crown Point Bridge using a mock coffin bearing the word "Champ." A counter rally by IP supporters included "a full-size replica of Champ to show the creature is OK."[109]

These events show how Champ is a malleable icon that can be used to symbolize many different perspectives.

In the absence of a carcass or DNA evidence, the existence of Champ will continue to be debated. Given the vast number of sightings, some may wonder why scientists are being so stubborn amid such overwhelming evidence. During the eighteenth and nineteenth centuries, there were scores of FE3s: Fairy Encounters of the Third Kind. Many respected people claim to have seen fairies, typically at night in the woods. Several said they had spoken with the little people. How can so many people be wrong? That is why, although compelling, scientists must have hard evidence. Nothing short of a body will satisfy the scientific community. In this sense, perhaps Champ, Nessie, and Bigfoot may be seen as modern-day fairies. The existence of fairies is no longer widespread, and people rarely see them anymore. Why? They do not expect to see them because in the eyes of most people, their existence is no longer plausible. Hundreds of years ago, many people in England believed in fairies and witches and there were hundreds of fairy sightings each year. At the height of the witchcraft fear in the Middle Ages, people routinely reported seeing witches flying about the skies. They saw what they expected to see as a reflection of their mindset. Another way of saying it is, "believing is seeing."

Harvard biologist Edward Osborne Wilson thinks that part of the human fascination and fear of snakes, sharks and other predators, lies in our genes. People have built-in preoccupations with monsters because it was to our evolutionary advantage, he argues. Throughout human existence, large predators who saw us as a meal, often lurking in the dark, waiting to pounce, have surrounded us. In this sense, we may be preprogramed to see monsters such as Champ as a vestige of our past, and that may be a major reason why we are still around today.[110] Of course, most sightings can be explained as fish, logs, wakes, and the like, but what Wilson appears to be saying is that out of self-preservation, humans tend to think predators. The observers mind set (created by the environment and their previous experiences) may have more to do with it—people boating on Lake Champlain, then seeing something they cannot explain, interpreting it as Champ.

The Champlain Monster is many things to many people. To some biologists it is part of our evolutionary heritage that preprograms us to see mythical beasts. To environmentalists it is a green symbol. To sports lovers it is a baseball mascot. Local politicians and shopkeepers view it as a symbol of economic revival. For parents it is a cautionary tale and a way to scare children ("Don't go to the lake alone or Champ will get you!"). For children it is a comforting stuffed toy, a friendly monster, and a dead set certainty. For believers, it is an anti-scientific symbol epitomising the view that science does not have all the answers, whereas for skeptics, depending on their temperament, it is either a humorous legend or an annoying myth. For everyone, Champ is a poster child of what may lie undiscovered because it is scientifically plausible. Champ may be a new or long-thought extinct creature. Some day sophisticated technology will settle the debate, and even if the answer is nay, the legend will endure because it is a legitimate part of our regional identity and national history. All but the most hardened cynics want to believe, yet its existence is almost irrelevant. Even if the creature is not real, the legend lives on. For the many residents who believe that it exists, it *is* real.

Champ is a symbol of beauty, awe and mystery that titillates the psyche of humanity about the mysteries of human existence and what could be. Albert Einstein said it best: "The most beautiful thing we can experience is the mysterious. It is the source of all true art and science." The Champlain Monster is a symbol with many meanings that resonate with a broad audience. Real or imaginary, that is why it endures.

NOTES

CHAPTER 1

1. Fort, Charles Hoy. (1941). *Lo!* New York: Garland Publishing.

2. Fish, Charles. (2006). *In the Land of the Wild Onion: Travels Along Vermont's Winooski River.* Hanover, NH: University of New England Press, 169.

3. Tsonakwa, Gerald Rancourt, and Wapitaska, Yolakia. (2001). *Seven Eyes, Seven Legs: Supernatural Stories of the Abenaki.* Walnut, CA: Kiva Publishing, 74.

4. Hill, Ralph Nading. (1995). *Lake Champlain, Key to Liberty.* Woodstock, VT: Countryman Press, 16.

5. Linguist Gordon M. Day, after painstaking research, believes that the literal Abenaki translation of Split Rock is "the go-through rock." See, Day, Gordon M. (1998). In *Search of New England's Native Past. Selected Essays by Gordon M. Day.* Ed. Michael K. Foster and Gordon Cowan. Amherst, MA: University of Massachusetts Press, 256.

6. Glenn, Morris F. (1977). *The Story of Three Towns: Westport, Essex and Willsboro, New York.* Alexandria, VA: The author, 82. For this very reason, Gordon Day states that Split Rock was also known to the Abenaki as "picture rock" or "portrait rock." See p. 256.

7. Wiseman, Frederick Matthew (2001). *The Voice of the Dawn: An Autohistory of the Abenaki Nation.* Hanover, NH: University Press of New England, 128.

8. Zarzynski, Joseph W. (no date, circa 1984). "'Champ' A Zoological Jigsaw Puzzle." *Adirondack Bits 'n Pieces Magazine* 9(1):16–21, 45, 48. See p. 18.

9. Griffis, William Elliot. (1897). *The Romance of Discovery: A Thousand Years of Exploration and the Unveiling of Continents.* Boston, MA: W.A. Wilde and Company, 129.

10. Zarzynski, Joseph W. (no date, circa 1984). "'Champ' A Zoological Jigsaw Puzzle." *Adirondack Bits 'n Pieces Magazine* 1(1):16–21, 45, 48. See p. 18. I acknowledge that the term *Native American* is more accurate than *Indian*, which is a misnomer, but is used for ease of language.

11. Based on information recounted by astronomer Gerard Tsonakwa, a member of the Abenaki tribe of Southern Québec, chronicled by the Fairbanks Museum and Planetarium, St Johnsbury, Vermont, Pathways to History Curriculum Guide II, "Misingwe ta Gitaskogak: The Masked Hunter and the Great Serpent (Mars and Scorpio) Abenaki Nation." Reprinted from a Special Section of the *Arizona Daily Star* entitled "Return to Mars," April 6, 2001. There were many other Abenaki names for Lake Champlain including *bitawbágw* (double lake) and *Sitoâmbogook (double bay)*. See Day. (1998). Op. cit., 240–41.

12. Bruchac, Joseph. (1998). "Introduction." *The Waters Between: A Novel of the Dawn Land*. Hanover, NH: University Press of New England, xiv.

13. Sea serpents have been spotted in several small glacial lakes in Western New York including Cayuga Lake near Ithaca ("The Sea Serpent Again." *The Daily Journal* [Ogdensburg], August 9, 1886), Owasco Lake in 1900 which was tentatively identified by an experienced fisherman as a sturgeon ("The Hook is Gone." *Auburn-Democrat Argus*, July 24, 1900, 8), and in Lake Keuka ("Sea Serpent Reported in Lake Keuka." *The Auburn Citizen*, July 18, 1921, 8). The Silver Lake sea serpent in Wyoming County during the nineteenth century was reported to have been a hoax (Kimiecik, Kathy, "The Strange Case of the Silver Lake Sea Serpent," *New York Folklore* 9[2]:10–11). A 1937 sighting in Seneca Lake turned out to be three carp tied together and pulled by a line to give it an undulation motion (see, "Sea Serpent." *Union Springs Advertiser* (Union Springs, New York), August 5, 1937, 1). Northern New York sea monsters include Schroon Lake in the Adirondacks (Zarzynski 2009, personal communication), Sylvia Lake in St. Lawrence County ("Claim Sight of Sea Serpent." *Gouverneur Northern Tribune*, June 14, 1916), and Chateaugay Lake in 1925 (Undated letter appearing in the *Chateaugay Record and Franklin County Democrat*, September 18, 1925, 2). The Hudson River sea monster of 1886 was later identified as a burnt timber from the steamship *Daniel Drew* ("The Sea Serpent: He Appears in the Hudson River Below Albany." *The New York Times*, September 4, 1886; "Local News." *The Daily Journal* [Ogdensburg, NY], September 13, 1886). Lake monsters also have been reported in the Baldwinsville Mill Pond (see: "The Last Snake Story," *The New York Times*, May 27, 1871). Then there is the St. Lawrence River Monster ("'Monster' Seen in St. Lawrence. Motor Boatmen Believe They Saw a Man Eater." *St. Lawrence Republican*, September 24, 1913, 9). Sea serpents in Vermont lakes

include Memphre, who is said to frolic in Lake Memphremagog ("Topics of To-Day," *Brooklyn Daily Eagle*, August 14, 1868) and Willy in Lake Willoughby (Fisher, Harriet F., *Willoughby Lake Legends and Legacies*. Rutland, VT: Academy Books, 1988). An aquatic monster also has been spotted in Lake Bomoseen (Smith, Dwight, and Mangiacopra, Gary [2003]. "Rumors of an Unknown Vermont Lake Monster: The Lake Bomoseen Cryptid." *North American Bio-Fortean Review* 5[2]:7–9).

14. For a comprehensive survey and discussion of lake monster reports in nearby Quebec and Ontario provinces, see *Lake Monster Traditions: A Cross-Cultural Analysis* by Michel Meurger and Claude Gagnon. (1988). London: Fortean Tomes. This book is remarkable for its in-depth analysis of lake monster folklore and original research.

15. Rands, Robert L. (1954). "Horned Serpent Stories." *The Journal of American Folklore* 67 (263):79–81; Stanton, M. (1947). "Pictographs from Tramping Lake, Manitoba." *American Antiquity* 13(2):180–81; Townsend, Richard F. (2004). *Hero, Hawk, and Open Hand*. New Haven, CT: Yale University Press. The Chickasaw, for instance, believed in *Sint-holo*, a horned snake that resided in caves and creeks. See Willoughby, Charles. (1936). "The Cincinnati Tablet: An Interpretation." *The Ohio State Archaeological and Historical Quarterly* 45:257–64.

16. Day, Gordon M. (1998). In *Search of New England's Native Past. Selected Essays by Gordon M. Day*. Ed. Michael K. Foster and Gordon Cowan. Amherst, MA: University of Massachusetts Press, 256. In his 1854 book on snakes of New York State, Spencer Baird made a point to note the abundance of rattlers near Split Rock. See, Baird, Spencer F. (1854). *On the Serpents of New York with a Notice of a Species Not Hitherto Included in the Fauna of the State*. Albany, NY: C. Van Benthuysen, 120.

17. Zarzynski, Joseph W. (1984). *Champ: Beyond the Legend*. Port Henry, NY: Bannister Publications, 52–53.

18. Newton, Michael (2009). *Hidden Animals: Guide to Batsquatch, Chupacabra, and Other Elusive Creatures*. Santa Barbara, CA: Greenwood Publishing, 52–53.

19. One pioneer letter describes the adventures of a Mr. Price, a traveller forced ashore by bad weather near Westport and threatened by rattlesnakes. See, Letter from Dr. Reines to J. Robert Dubois (then editor of *Adirondack Bits n'Pieces* magazine), Port Henry, New York dated November 15, 1983, 2.

20. Beagle, Peter S. (1991[1968]). *The Last Unicorn*. New York: Penguin Books.

21. Steckley, John. (2007). *Words of the Huron*. Ontario, Canada: Wilfred Laurier University Press, 23. See also, Englar, Mary, and Duden, Jane (2001).

The Iroquois: The Six Nations Confederacy. Mankato, Minnesota: Capstone Press, 8.

22. Laurent, Stephen. (1956). "The Abenakis: Aborigines of Vermont Part II." *Vermont History* 24(1):3–11. See p. 5.

23. See, *Vermont History*, January 1956, 24(1):24.

24. Masta, Henry Lorne (2008). *Abenaki Indian Legends, Grammar and Place Names*. United States (no location): Global Language Press, 83.

25. Haviland, William A., and Power, Marjory W. (1994). *The Original Vermonters: Native Inhabitants Past and Present*. Hanover, NH: University Press of New England, 194; Bassett, Thomas D.S. (2000). *The God of the Hills: Piety and Society in Nineteenth Century Vermont*. Montpiler: Vermont Historical Society, 5; Parker, Philip M. (2008). *Webster's Abenaki-English Thesaurus Dictionary*. ICON Group International, 5. In the book *Lewis Creek Lost and Found* (Hanover, NH: University of New England Press), Kevin T. Dann makes reference to a serpent-like creature that roamed the marshland that the Abenaki referred to as *wiwiliamecq* (40).

26. Mayor, Adrienne (2005). *Fossil Legends of the First Americans*. Princeton, NJ: Princeton University Press, 12.

27. Ibid., 13.

28. Smith, Dwight, and Mangiacopra, Gary. (2003). "Rumors of an Unknown Vermont Lake Monster: The Lake Bomoseen Cryptid." *North American BioFortean Review* 5(2):7–9. See p. 9.

29. Haviland, William A., and Power, Marjory W. (1994). *The Original Vermonters: Native Inhabitants Past and Present*. Hanover, NH: University Press of New England, 194–195.

30. Porter, Marjorie L. (1970). "The Champlain Monster." *Vermont Life* 24(4):47–50. Most historians list his birth as 1567, although a few contend that it is open to debate. See for instance, Castillo, Susan, and Schweitzer, Ivy (2001). *The Literatures of Colonial America An Anthology*. Malden, MA: Blackwell, 99.

31. Porter, Marjorie L. (1970). "The Champlain Monster." *Vermont Life* 24(4):47–50.

32. (1966). *Voyages of Samuel de Champlain*. Translated from the French by Charles Pomeroy Otis. With historical illustrations and a memoir by Charles F. Slafter. New York: Ben Franklin. Volume 2, 1604–1610. http://www.canadachannel.ca/champlain/index.php/Samuel_de_Champlain%2C_Voyages%2C_Vol._II_1608–1612. Accessed September 12, 2010.

33. Connie Pope publicly pointed this out in: "Rotary News: Unusual Topic Chosen by Guest Speaker." *Chateaugay Record*, June 17, 1971. John Ross followed this in his 1978 article: "Sidelight on History." *The North Country-*

man, August 23, 1978, 16. This was noted by Michel Meurger and Claude Gagnon their 1982 book, *Monstres des Lacs du Quebec: Mythes et Troublantes Realites.* Montreal: Stanke. In 1988, the book was updated and translated into English as *Lake Monster Traditions: A Cross Cultural Analysis.* London: Fortean Tomes Publishing.

34. Occasionally spelled Chaousaroo. See, Gray, Richard J. (2004). *A History of American Literature.* Malden, MA: Wiley-Blackwell, 20. The etymology is Huron (Iroquois). Green states that 'Chow-sa-roo' is the correct pronunciation. Refer to: Green, Susan. (1996). "Tales from the Cryptozoologists. Are we keeping Champ's Legacy Afloat?" *Vox* (Vermont's Voice of Arts and Culture) 2(16):1, 3. See p. 3.

35. Morgan, Christopher, and O'Callaghan, Edmund B. (1850). *The Documentary History of the State of New York, Volume III.* Albany, NY: Weed, Parsons & Company, 5,6, citing a translation of Champlain's original log.

36. Morgan, Christopher, and O'Callaghan, Edmund B. (1850). *Volume III,* Op. cit., 6.

37. "Migraine Treatment: From Trepanation to Magnetic Stimulation." Presentation given by Yusof Mohammed, assistant professor of neurology, Ohio State University (mohammad-1@medctr.osu.edu), undated; Vandrei, Charles (2009). "Samuel de Champlain, Intrepid Explorer." *New York State Conservationist* (August):10–13. See p. 12.

38. Heidenreich, Conrad E. (2004). "'Champ': The Lake Champlain 'Monster.'" *Pen & Paddle: The Newsletter of the Champlain Society* 1(1):1, 3.

39. Warkentin, Garmaine (2010). "Aristotle in New France Louis Nicolas and the Making of Codex Canadiensis." *French Colonial History* 11:71–107. The Richelieu River is sometimes referred to in historical maps and writings as the Sorel River and the Iroquois River.

40. Nicolas, Louis. (1930). *Les Raretes des Indes.* Paris: Maurice Chamonal, 61. Only 110 copies were printed from the original album, although it has been reprinted since.

41. Ross, John (1978). "Sidelight on History." *The North Countryman,* August 23, 1978, 16.

42. The account of this "monster" is taken from an English translation from the logs of Samuel de Champlain of the experiences he recorded while exploring the St. Lawrence Valley in 1604. They appeared in Volume 1 of a six-volume set, *The Works of Samuel de Champlain, reprinted, translated and annotated by six Canadian scholars under the general editorship of H.P. Biggar.* Volume 1 covers 1599–1607, translated and edited by H.H. Langton and W.F. Ganong, with the French texts collated by J. Home Cameron. Reprinted by the University of Toronto Press, 1971. The narration appears on pp. 186–188

in Chapter XII, titled, "Of a frightful monster which the savages call *Gougou*, and of our short and favourable passage back to France."

43. Ross, John (1978). "Sidelight on History." *The North Countryman*, August 23, 1978, 16.

44. Hoffman, Bernard G. (1961). "The Codex Canadiensis: An Important Document for Great Lakes Ethnography." *Ethnohistory* 8(4):382–400.

45. Nicolas, Louis. (1930). Op. cit., 55.

46. Meurger, Michel, and Gagnon, Claude. (1988). *Lake Monster Traditions*. London: Fortean Tomes, 196.

47. Nicolas, Louis. (1930). Op. cit., 40.

48. Meurger, Michel, and Gagnon, Claude. (1988). Op. cit., 212–13.

49. Both "waterhorses" and mermen are common figures of British and Irish folklore, and Nicolas would have certainly been familiar with stories of such mythical creatures.

50. Anderson, Alan Orr, and Anderson, Marjorie Ogilvie (Eds.) (1991). *Adomnán's Life of Columba* (Oxford Medieval Texts). Oxford: Oxford University Press, 133–34.

51. Bauer, Henry. (1987). "Common Knowledge about the Loch Ness Monster: Television, Videos, and Films." *Journal of Scientific Exploration* 16(3):455–77. See p. 460.

52. There are a handful of vague accounts that have been uncovered since 1933, but they were not publicized until long after 1933. For all intent and purposes, the Loch Ness "Monster" did not exist on the world stage until 1933.

53. "Lake Champlain." *Public Advertiser* [New York], May 18, 1808, 2. See also, "Lake Champlain." *Republican Star* [Maryland], May 31, 1808, 2.

54. Scows on Lake Champlain at this time were square, flat-bottomed wooden boats that were typically used to transport goods.

55. "Cape Ann Serpent on Lake Champlain." *Plattsburgh Republican*, July 26, 1819, 2.

56. See, for example: Revai, Cheri, and Wiggins, Heather Adel (2005). *Haunted New York: Ghosts and Strange Phenomena of the Empire State*. Mechanicsburg, PA: Stackpole, 11; Newton, Michael (2009). *Hidden Animals: Guide to Batsquatch, Chupacabra, and Other Elusive Creatures*. Santa Barbara, CA: Greenwood Publishing, 76.

57. Personal communication between Dr. Phillip Reines and Robert Bartholomew circa August 2010. Reines notes that the definitive volume on the subject of sea serpents was by Belgian zoologist Dr. Bernard Heuvelmanns and first appeared in 1968, under the title, *In the Wake of the Sea Serpent*. New York: Hill and Wang.

58. According to the King James version, in Isiah 27:1, "In that day the LORD with his . . . strong sword shall punish leviathan the piercing serpent . . . and he shall slay the dragon that is in the sea."

59. See for example: "The Sea Serpent." *Plattsburgh Republican*, October 4, 1817. See also, Brown, Chandos M. (1990). "A Natural History of the Gloucester Sea Serpent: Knowledge, Power and the Culture of Science in Antebellem America." *American Quarterly*, 402–36 (September).

60. Oudemans, Anthonid Cornelis (2009[1892]). *The Great Sea Serpent*. New York: Cosimo, 160–61.

61. The panel was created by The Linnaean Society of New England, established at Boston in 1814 with the purpose of studying and promoting natural history.

62. (1817). *Report of a committee of the Linnaean Society of New England: relative to a large marine animal, supposed to be a serpent, seen near Cape Ann, Massachusetts, in August 1817*. Boston, MA: Cummings and Hilliard.

63. Silverberg, Robert (2007). *Scientists and Scoundrels: A Book of Hoaxes*. Bison Books (an imprint of the University of Nebraska), 53–54; Babson, John James, Chandler, Samuel. (1860). *History of the Town of Gloucester, Cape Ann: including the town of Rockport*. Gloucester, MA: Procter Brothers, 523; McDougall, Dan, and Reed, Meredith. (1981). "Marblehead Monsters! The Truth about an Ancient Legend." *Marblehead Magazine* 2(1). http://www.legendinc.com/Pages/MarbleheadNet/MM/Articles/MarbleheadMonsters.html. Accessed December 12, 2010

64. Anderson, Gregory J. (1978). "America's Loch Ness Monster." *Argosy* (July):19–22. See pp. 20–21. The witnesses were ages 20 and 15.

65. "Yachting on Lake Champlain." *Argus and Patriot*, June 16, 1886, 1.

66. Pope, Connie. (1978). "The Lake Champlain Sea Serpent. Anatomy of a Legend." *The Valley News* [Elizabethtown, New York], August 9, 1978, 3–4. See p. 3.

67. Brookesmith, Peter. (1989). *Creatures From Elsewhere: Weird Animals that No-One Can Explain*. London: MacDonald and Company, 51.

68. Citro, Joseph A. (1994). *Green Mountain Ghosts, Gouls, and Unsolved Mysteries*. Christensen, Bonnie (illustrator). New York: Houghton Mifflin Company, 115; Porter, Marjorie L. (1970). "The Champlain Monster." *Vermont Life* 24(4):47–50. See p. 47.

69. Porter, Majorie. (1966). "Essex County Notes." *Plattsburgh Press-Republican*, February 4, 1966.

70. No one knows how Whitehall got its name. The original settlement was named after Philip Skene, but when he sided with the British during the Revolutionary War, residents decided that a name change was in order.

Unfortunately, all village records documenting the change to Whitehall were destroyed by fire.

71. *Whitehall Times*, July 9, 1873.

72. "Westport." *Essex County Republican* [Keeseville, New York], July 21, 1873.

73. "The Lake Champlain Serpent." *The Evening Telegram* [New York], August 4, 1873, 1, citing the *Whitehall Times*.

74. "The Champlain Sea Serpent." *Fort Wayne Gazette* [Indiana], July 29, 1873, citing the *Whitehall Times* (New York).

75. Ibid.

76. Ibid.

77. "The Lake Champlain Serpent." *The Evening Telegram* [New York], August 4, 1873, 1, citing the *Whitehall Times*.

78. Pope, Connie. (1978). "The Whitehall Chapter." *The Valley News* [Elizabethtown, NY], August 9, 1978, 5.

79. Ibid.

80. Ibid.

81. Ibid.

82. "The Lake Champlain Serpent." *The Evening Telegram* [New York], August 4, 1873, 1, citing the *Whitehall Times* of July 30.

83. Ibid.

84. "A Serpent in Lake Champlain." *The Palladium* [Malone, NY], August 7, 1873, citing the *Burlington Free Press*. See also, "Over the Lake." *Plattsburgh Sentinel*, August 1, 1873, 3.

85. "A Serpent in Lake Champlain." *The Palladium* [Malone, NY], August 7, 1873, citing the *Burlington Free Press*.

86. "The Lake Champlain Serpent." *The Evening Telegram* [New York], August 4, 1873, 1, citing the *Whitehall Times*.

87. Ibid.

88. Pope, Connie. (1978). "The Whitehall Chapter." *The Valley News* [Elizabethtown, NY], August 9, 1978, 5–6, citing the *Whitehall Times* of August 13, 1873. A check with the Whitehall Historical Society reveals that the original copy of this issue of the paper is no longer in existence therefore we are relying on Pope's transcription of this issue and other accounts reprinted in papers of the time which confirm this.

89. Some accounts have it on the 8th and others have it on the 9th. The *North Countryman* of September 9, 1937, reprinted a supposedly verbatim story from the *Whitehall Times* describing the encounter as taking place on the 8th. Historian Connie Pope has it on the 9th ("The Whitehall Chapter." *The Valley News*, August 9, 1978). As the search party had been organized for

several days previously, it may very well be that both accounts are correct in that the creature was reportedly found on the 8th and attacked on the 9th. Without the original *Whitehall Times* article, we must rely on reprints.

90. Pope, Connie. (1978). "The Whitehall Chapter." *The Valley News* [Elizabethtown, NY], August 9, 1978, 5–6, citing the *Whitehall Times* of August 13.

91. This source specifically notes that the vessel was chartered. See, "The Lake Champlain Sea Serpent is *Dead!*" *The Daily Journal* [Ogdensburg, NY], August 18, 1873.

92. Pope, Connie. (1978). "The Whitehall Chapter." *The Valley News* [Elizabethtown, NY], August 9, 1978, 5–6, citing the *Whitehall Times* of August 13.

93. Ibid.

94. "The Killing of Young Long." *The New York Times*, July 30, 1878.

95. "The Dead Snake. Search for its Carcass." The *Whitehall Times*, circa November 1873.

96. http://www.circusinamerica.org/public/corporate_bodies/public_show/13. Accessed September 2, 2010.

97. Betts, John Rickards. (1959). "P. T. Barnum and the Popularization of Natural History." *Journal of the History of Ideas* 20(3):353–68.

98. "The Dead Snake. Search for its Carcass." The *Whitehall Times*, circa November 1873. Grappling irons of the period were characterized by a rope to which one end was attached to several metal hooks that were used to hold ships together.

99. "That Snake." *Plattsburgh Sentinel*, August 8, 1873., citing the *Herald*.

100. Pope, Connie. (1978). "The Whitehall Chapter." *The Valley News* [Elizabethtown, NY], August 9, 1978, 6.

101. "That 'Sea Sarpint.'" *Argus and Patriot*, August 21, 1873, 2.

102. Pope, Connie. (1978). "The Whitehall Chapter." *The Valley News* [Elizabethtown, NY], August 9, 1978, page 6.

103. "A Serpent in Lake Champlain." *The Palladium* [Malone, NY], August 7, 1873.

104. "Whitehall." *Essex County Republican* [Keeseville, NY], August 21, 1873.

105. *Vergennes Messenger*, August 13, 1873, 3.

106. "Camp Life in 1873." *Argus and Patriot* [Vermont], September 11, 1873.

107. Pope, Connie. (1978). "The Whitehall Chapter." *The Valley News* [Elizabethtown, NY], August 9, 1978, 6; "Washington County." *Plattsburgh Sentinel*, September 19, 1873.

CHAPTER 2

1. "Westport." *Essex County Republican*, July 30, 1874.

2. Miller, George Frederick. (1922). *The Academy System of the State of New York*. Doctoral thesis, Columbia University. Albany, NY: J.B. Lyon Company.

3. My thanks to the University Archives and Record Center of the University of Pennsylvania.

4. Mangiacopra, Gary. (1978). "Lake Champlain: America's Loch Ness." *Of Sea and Shore* 9(1):21–28, citing the *Port Henry Herald*. See pp. 21–22. See also, Anderson, Gregory J. (1978). "America's Loch Ness Monster." *Argosy* (July):19–22. See p. 20, citing the *Port Henry Herald*, September 1878. See also, "The Sea Serpent in Lake Champlain." *Worcester Daily Spy* (Massachusetts), October 4, 1878, 2; "That Lake Champlain Sea-Serpent." *Springfield Republican*, August 3, 1878, 8.

5. "Local All Sorts." *Franklin Gazette* [Malone, NY], June 18, 1879. See also, *Lowville Times*, May 29, 1879.

6. One rod is equal to 16.5 feet or 5.5 yards.

7. *St. Louis Globe-Democrat* [Missouri], May 31, 1879, citing the St. Albans *Advertiser*.

8. "Local Matters." *Lowville Times*, May 29, 1879.

9. "A Lake Monster." *Plattsburgh Sentinel*, May 16, 1879, citing the *St. Albans Messenger*. See also, "A Lake Monster." *Norwood News*, May 20, 1879, citing the *St. Albans Messenger*.

10. Ibid.

11. "The Lake Serpent." *St. Albans Daily Messenger*, June 12, 1879, 3.

12. "The Lake Serpent Again." *Plattsburgh Sentinel*, September 19, 1879, citing the *Burlington Free Press*.

13. "Paragrams." *Plattsburgh Sentinel*, September 26, 1879.

14. "A Vermont Sea-Serpent." *New York Times*, November 10, 1879, citing a report from the *Burlington Free Press* of November 7, 1879.

15. "The Sea Serpent Again." *Plattsburgh Sentinel*, November 14, 1879, 2.

16. "Home Matters." *St. Albans Daily Messenger*, November 8, 1879, 3.

17. "Paragrams." *Plattsburgh Sentinel*, November 21, 1879.

18. "Old Timer's Column by 'Rufus.'" *Tupper Lake Press* (New York), June 5, 1934. See also, "Writer Believes Lake Champlain Serpent Exists." *Courier Freeman* [Potsdam, NY], July 18, 1934, 1.

19. Zarzynski, Joseph. (1978). "The Search for the Lake Champlain Monsters." *International Fortean Organization Journal* 28:2–4, citing the *Swanton Cou-*

rier [Vermont], July 31, 1880; "State News Items." *Vermont Argus and Patriot*, July 28, 1880.

20. "Sea Serpent Discovered Petrified." *Ogden Standard Examiner* [Utah] September 23, 1881, 1, citing the *Springfield Telegram*.

21. Letter from Charlotte Mehrtens to Robert Bartholomew dated March 23, 2010.

22. Letter from Mary Watzin to Robert Bartholomew dated March 22, 2010. She is dean and professor of the Rubenstein School of Environmental and Natural Resources.

23. Letter from Pat Manley to Robert Bartholomew dated January 17, 2011.

24. My thanks to Jonathan Downes for uncovering this press report. Mr. Downes, a writer and researcher who is held in high esteem within the cryptozoological community, is director of the Centre for Fortean Zoology.

25. My thanks to Jonathan Downes for uncovering this information.

26. Thompson, Zadock. (1850). "An account of some fossil bones found in Vermont, in making excavations for the Rutland and Burlington Railroad." *American Journal of Science*, Series 2 (9):256–63.

27. Pope, Connie. (1978). "The Lake Champlain Sea Serpent. Anatomy of a Legend." *The Valley News* [Elizabethtown, NY], August 9, 1978, pages 3–4.

28. "Across the Lake." *Plattsburgh Sentinel*, September 28, 1881, 2.

29. "Paragrams." *Plattsburgh Sentinel*, August 4, 1882, 1; "Grand Isle. Another Sea Serpent." *Plattsburgh Sentinel* circa August 1, 1882 (exact date unreadable).

30. "Across the Lake." *Plattsburgh Sentinel*, October 27, 1882, 1.

31. "The Sea Serpent Again." *The Daily Journal* (Ogdensburg, New York), October 25, 1882, citing the St. Albans *Messenger*.

32. "The Champlain Sea Serpent. Distinctly Seen at Last and by a Reliable Witness." *St. Albans Daily Messenger*, August 1, 1883, 3, citing the *Plattsburgh Telegram*. See also, "That Sea Serpent." *Watertown Daily Times*, August 4, 1883.

33. Zarzynski, Joseph. (1978). Op. cit., 3, citing the *Plattsburgh Republican*, August 4, 1883.

34. Pope, Connie. (1978). "The Lake Champlain Sea Serpent. Anatomy of a Legend." *The North Countryman*, August 16, 1978, 12, 17. See p. 12.

35. According to the *Plattsburgh Sentinel*, August 17, 1883, 1, the following month, a Westport, New York man claimed to have spotted the serpent but no details are available.

36. "Paragrams." *Plattsburgh Sentinel*, August 3, 1883, 1.

37. Ibid., August 24, 1883, 1.

38. "The Woman Pilot." *Burlington Free Press and Times*, May 5, 1887; "A Female Pilot." *The New York Times*, May 5, 1887.

39. "Across the Lake." *Plattsburgh Sentinel*, September 7, 1883.

40. "Paragrams." *Plattsburgh Sentinel*, August 10, 1883, 1, citing the *Montreal Star*.

41. Ibid.

42. "The Champlain Sea Serpent." *Plattsburgh Republican*, May 21, 1887. This account does not explicitly say that he was in a buggy or a wagon, but as he was a physician we assume that it was a buggy.

43. Prior to 1900, there are scattered references to "Willsborough," which was used interchangeably by some with the name "Willsboro" and "Wilsboro." In about 1905, the "ugh" appears to have been dropped. During the nineteenth century, occasionally the term "Willsboro' Point" was employed, with an apostrophe after the 'o.' It also was referred to as Willsborough Point. Willsboro—the modern-day spelling—is used for consistency and to avoid confusion.

44. Letter dated December 7, 1886 from Mr. E. Brown of Willsboro Point (a proprietor of the firm E. Brown and Son) to the *Plattsburgh Republican*, December 11, 1886.

45. Ibid.

46. "Lake Champlain's Sea Serpent." *Burlington Free Press*, July 16, 1886.

47. Pope, Connie. (1978). "The Lake Champlain Sea Serpent. Anatomy of a Legend." *The Valley News* [Elizabethtown, NY], August 9, 1978, 3–4. See p. 3.

48. Ibid.

49. "Nonsense." *Plattsburgh Sentinel*, September 10, 1886.

50. Pope, Connie. (1978). "The Lake Champlain Sea Serpent. Anatomy of a Legend." *The Valley News* [Elizabethtown, NY], August 9, 1978, 3–4. See p. 3.

51. Ibid.

52. "$1000 Reward." *Plattsburgh Sentinel*, October 15, 1886, 1.

53. Clark is almost certainly referring to the *Vermont II*, in service between 1871 and 1903. The *Vermont I* sank in 1815 and was 120 feet long. The *Vermont II* was of comparable length to *Vermont I*, so the creature was sizeable.

54. "The Sea Serpent in Lake Champlain." *Boston Journal*, December 4, 1886, 2.

55. "The Champlain Sea Monster." *Plattsburgh Sentinel*, December 10, 1886, 1. For secondary sources, see also, Rosenkranz, Marty. (1983). "Sea Monster Made Historic Stop at Willsboro." *Chateaugay Record*, November 9, citing the *Essex County Republican*, December 9, 1886.

56. "The Lake Champlain Monster." *Plattsburgh Sentinel*, May 6, 1887.

57. "The Lake Champlain Sea Serpent." *The Daily Journal* [Ogdensburg, NY], May 6, 1887.

58. "The Lake Champlain Monster." *Plattsburgh Sentinel*, May 6, 1887.

59. "Matters and Things." *Plattsburgh Republican*, May 14, 1887, 1; "Neighboring Counties." *Plattsburgh Sentinel*, May 13, 1887, citing the *Port Henry Herald*.

60. Pope, Connie. (1978). "The Lake Champlain Sea Serpent. Anatomy of a Legend." *The North Countryman*, August 16, 1978, 12, 17. See p. 12.

61. Murray, W.H.H. (1887). "The Sea Serpent has Wings." *New York Times*, May 22.

62. "The Sea Serpent in Lake Champlain." Letter. *New Hampshire Sentinel*, May 18, 1887.

63. Clark, S.W. (1887). "Lake Champlain's Monster." *New York Times*, May 29.

64. Ibid.

65. Italicized for emphasis.

66. "Franklin County." *The Ogdensburg Advance and St. Lawrence Weekly Democrat*, May 26, 1887, 1.

67. "Paragrams." *Plattsburgh Sentinel*, May 27, 1887, 1.

68. "Paragrams." *Plattsburgh Sentinel*, September 2, 1887, 1; "A Baby Sea Serpent." *Plattsburgh Sentinel*, August 26, 1887, 1.

69. Personal communication dated June 16, 2010, between Michael Lange, head of behavioral sciences at Champlain College, Burlington, Vermont, and Robert Bartholomew.

70. Anonymous. (1887). "A Milk and Lemonade Serpent." *The New York Times*, July 11, page 1; "Across the Lake." *Plattsburgh Sentinel*, July 15, 1887. See also, *Franklin Gazette* [Malone, NY], July 15, 1887.

71. "Still the Wonder Grows." *Albany Journal*, July 12, 1887, 7; "Where Canoes Will Float." *New York Times*, August 2, 1891.

72. "Neighboring Counties. Essex." *Plattsburgh Sentinel* (specific date unreadable but based on the dates listed on the page, between July 20 and July 27, 1887).

73. "Paragrams." *Plattsburgh Sentinel*, August 5, 1887, 1.

74. "Barnum wants the Sea Serpent." *The Sun* (New York), August 4, 1887, 1. According to "Paragrams." *Plattsburgh Sentinel*, August 5, 1887, 1, the minimum length was fifty-six feet.

75. Saxon, A.H. (1998). "P. T. Barnum and the American Museum," 34–46. *In Media in America: The Wilson Quarterly Reader* ed. Douglas Gomery. Washington DC: Woodrow Wilson Press Center, 40.

76. "Across the Lake." *Plattsburgh Sentinel*, September 2, 1887, 1; "Local." *St. Lawrence Herald* [Potsdam, NY], September 9, 1987, 1.

77. "The Sea Serpent Seen Again." *Plattsburgh Sentinel*, July 1, 1887.

78. Now spelled Shelburne.

79. "The Sea Serpent Again." *Plattsburgh Sentinel*, September 27, 1889, 1.

80. Bond, Hallie E. (1995). *Boats and Boating in the Adirondacks*. Blue Mountain Lake, NY: The Adirondack Museum, 111.

81. "In Frail Canoes. A 'Sea Serpent' and Good Races on Lake Champlain." *New York Herald Tribune*, August 18, 1891, 8.

82. Italicized for emphasis.

83. "The Lake Champlain Sea Serpent Heard From." *Plattsburgh Sentinel*, August 28, 1891, citing the *Whitehall Times*.

84. *The Brooklyn Daily Eagle,* April 24, 1915, 1.

85. Gregory, John. (1971). "'Monster' Reported in Lake Champlain." *Anderson Daily Bulletin* [Anderson, Indiana], January 14, 1971, 32. Gregory's article was syndicated as part of the *Los Angeles Times/Washington Post* News Service.

86. Baldwin, Elizabeth Robinson. (1997). *The Reconstruction of the Lake Champlain Sidewheel Steamer Champlain II*. Texas A & M University. Department of Anthropology, master's thesis, 140.

87. Citro, Joseph A. (1994). *Green Mountain Ghosts, Gouls, and Unsolved Mysteries*. Christensen, Bonnie (illustrator). New York: Houghton Mifflin Company, 115.

88. "Sea Monster." December 11, 1975, letter to the editor of the *Burlington Free Press*, citing an incident from 1892, signed by F.B. Haggerty of Burlington. Moses Blow was the man's father.

89. Citro, Joseph A. (1994). *Green Mountain Ghosts, Gouls, and Unsolved Mysteries*. Christensen, Bonnie (illustrator). New York: Houghton Mifflin Company, 115–16.

90. "The Champlain Sea Serpent Again." *Plattsburgh Sentinel*, September 21, 1894.

91. Letter from L. M. DeLamater, Long Island, New York to A.W. Lansing dated October 1, 1894 and published in the *Plattsburgh Sentinel*, October 5, 1894, 1; "The Champlain Sea Monster Accounted For." *Plattsburgh Sentinel*, October 5, 1894, 1.

92. *Plattsburgh Republican*, October 6, 1894.

93. "A Live Seal in the St. Lawrence." *Plattsburgh Sentinel*, January 23, 1891, 1.

94. "How are the Mighty Fallen." *Plattsburgh Republican*, March 2, 1895.

95. "Not a Muskrat." *Plattsburgh Republican*, March 9, 1895.

96. "Lake Champlain Sea Serpent Done Up in Ice." *The Plattsburgh Sentinel*, April 5, 1895, citing the St. Albans *Messenger*.

97. "Additional Local," *Chateaugay Journal*, November 12, 1896; "The Sea Serpent Again." *Essex County Republican* [Keesville, NY] November 19, 1896.

98. "Vermont Gets into Line." *The Brooklyn Eagle*, August 10, 1899, 6, citing the *Burlington Daily News*; "Lake Champlain Sea Serpent Heard From." *Plattsburgh Sentinel*, August 18, 1899.

99. "Lake Champlain Sea Serpent Heard From." *Plattsburgh Sentinel*, August 18, 1899.

100. "Vermont Gets into Line." *The Brooklyn Eagle*, August 10, 1899, 6, citing the *Burlington Daily News*; "Lake Champlain Sea Serpent Heard From." *Plattsburgh Sentinel*, August 18, 1899.

CHAPTER 3

1. "Of Local Interest." *Malone Farmer* [New York], July 25, 1900, 1.

2. "Vicinity News." *Ticonderoga Sentinel* [New York], September 19, 1901, 8, citing the *Plattsburgh Republican*.

3. Pope, Connie. (1978). "The Whitehall Chapter." *The Valley News* [Elizabethtown, NY], August 9, 1978, 5.

4. Radford, Benjamin, and Nickell, Joseph (2006). *Lake Monster Mysteries*. Lexington, KY: University of Kentucky Press, 101.

5. "Lake George Sea Serpent in 1904 Hoax by Watrous." *Ticonderoga Sentinel*, May 3, 1934, 1, 5.

6. "Lake George Sea Serpent in 1904 Hoax by Watrous." Op. cit., 5.

7. Ibid.

8. Ibid.

9. Ibid.

10. Mr. Watrous said that he had heard the couple had divorced over the incident but he was unable to verify this. See, "Watrous Estate Property Razed by Fire Sunday." *Ticonderoga Sentinel*, July 2, 1936, 1.

11. "Lake George Sea Serpent in 1904 Hoax by Watrous." Op. cit., 1, 5.

12. Ibid.

13. "Local Department." *Malone Farmer*, July 20, 1905.

14. "Monster which Frightened L. George Residents 30 Years Ago to Re-appear." *The Lake Placid News*, June 1, 1934, 4.

15. "Lake Champlain Serpent seen near Crown Point." *Essex County Republican*, April 23, 1915, 4.

16. "Champlain Sea Serpent." *Potsdam Courier-Freeman* [New York], April 28, 1915.

17. "Railroad Drawboat Documented." (2001). *Lake Champlain Maritime News* (Spring): 9.

18. "Champlain Sea Serpent Tale is Still Recalled." *Ticonderoga Sentinel*, February 8, 1934, 2, citing the *Albany Evening News*.

19. "Sea Serpent or Submarine?" *Plattsburgh Daily Republican*, July 25, 1918, 7.

20. "Famous Sea Serpent is Again on the Job." *Adirondack Record*, August 23, 1918, 1.

21. This is an approximate date.

22. "Champlain Sea Serpent Back in the News." (1945). *The North Countryman*, May 31, 1945.

23. Glavin, Marney. (1976). "Lake Rumored Domain of Man-Eating Monster." *Press-Republican*, October 9, A9.

24. "Island Refuge of Arctic Gulls Given to Zoological Society . . . Lake Champlain Serpent to be Hunted." *New York Tribune*, October 9, 1922, 3.

25. Letter from Mary H. Humiston, president, Chateaugay Historical Society, to Robert Bartholomew dated January 15, 2011, including a letter appearing in the *Chateaugay Record and Franklin County Democrat*, September 18, 1925, 2,"Thirty-Five Years Ago. Week of Sept. 19, 1890."

26. "Doubtful if Bodies will be Recovered." *Adirondack Record*, November 1, 1928.

27. "Sea Serpent Seen, Fishermen Assert." *Charleston Daily Mail* [West Virginia], July 16, 1929; "Claim Sea Serpent in Lake Champlain." *Ticonderoga Sentinel*, July 18, 1929.

28. "Ibid. See also, "Sea Serpent Scares Three Men Fishing." *Chateaugay Record*, July 19, 1929, 3.

29. Tape recording by Paul Bartholomew of a seminar presentation by Joseph Zarzynski at the "Does Champ Exist?" Conference in Shelburne, Vermont on August 29, 1981; *Albany Times Union* of July 21, 1929.

30. "Sea Serpent Bids Science." Expedition is Planned to Seek Famous 'What Is It?'" *The Billings Gazette* [Montana], July 20, 1929, 2.

31. "Sea Serpent Again." *Tupper Lake Free Press*, September 20, 1934, 5.

32. "'There Ain't No Such Animal.'" *Plattsburgh Daily Press*, March 3, 1934, 4.

33. "Strange Lake Creature Caught in Lapan Bay." *Essex County Republican*, May 11, 1934.

34. "Bit Early in the Season, But Here's a Fish Story." *Ticonderoga Sentinel*, March 12, 1936, 7, citing the *Malone Farmer*.

35. "Lake Champlain's 'Sea Serpent' Now Seen at Whitehall." *Ticonderoga Sentinel*, July 15, 1937.

36. "Lake Champlain Sea Serpent 'Seen' Again Near Rouses Point Bridge Last Thursday." (1937). *The North Countryman*, September 9, 1937.

37. Ibid.

38. "Lake Champlain Sea Serpent 'Seen' Again Near Rouses Point Bridge Last Thursday." (1937). *The North Countryman*, September 9, 1937.

39. "Perhaps You Didn't Know." Hear Ye! Hear Ye! A Fish Story that is a Fish Story." (1937). *The North Countryman*, circa mid-November. Exact date unreadable due to poor microfilm.

40. "Champlain Sea Serpent Back in the News." (1945). *The North Countryman*, May 31, 1945.

41. Porter, Marjorie L. (1970). "The Champlain Monster." *Vermont Life* 24(4):47–50. See p. 49.

42. Ibid.

43. "Lake Champlain Sea Serpent Seen Once More [at] Rouses Point." *Essex County Republican* [Keeseville, NY], July 5, 1946, citing *The North Countryman*.

44. "War Over; Sea Serpent Comes Back." *The North Countryman*, June 27, 1946, 1.

45. Ibid.

46. "Fish Story From Whitehall." *Schenectady Gazette*, March 3, 1947, 15 or 16 (number blurred), citing the *Whitehall Times*.

47. Vachon, Brian. (1977). "In Search of the Champlain Monster." *Yankee Magazine* (November):134–39, 210, 212–13, 215–16. Quote on pp. 210, 212; Porter, Marjorie L. (1970). "The Champlain Monster." *Vermont Life* 24(4):47–50. See pp. 49–50. The same account by Jones also appears in its entirety in Rayno, Paul. (1978). "Champlain Monster." *The Post-Star* [Glens Falls, NY], September 13, 2.

48. Ibid.

49. Ibid. "The segments alternately appeared and disappeared from view. The coordination of movement leading us all to believe that it must be one single inhabitant," Jones said.

50. Smith, Hal. (1981). "Myth or Monster?" *Adirondack Life* (November–December), 22–26, 44–45, 47. See p. 44.

51. "'The Thing' Back in Lake Champlain." *Burlington Free Press*, July 10, 1952.

52. Frost, Alfred H. (1953). "Willsboro-Essex." *Plattsburgh Press-Republican*, June 19, 5.

53. "L. Champlain Monster Gains Renewed Interest." *Press-Republican*, December 29, 1975, 7.

54. Copy of a letter from Harold Patch, date unknown.

55. Duffy, John J., Hand, Samuel B., and Orth, Ralph H. (2003). *The Vermont Encyclopedia*. Burlington, VT: University of Vermont Press, 304.

56. "L. Champlain Monster Gains Renewed Interest." *Press-Republican*, December 29, 1975, 7.

57. Zarzynski, Joseph W. (1984). *Champ: Beyond the Legend*. Port Henry, New York: Bannister Publications, 80, citing a letter from Thomas E. Morse dated September 20, 1980.

58. Cowperthwait, Richard. "The Lake Champlain Monster. Looking for Champ." *The Vermont Vanguard Press*, circa August 1977.

59. Jordan, Laurie (circa 1981). "Is There a Sea Monster in Lake Champlain?" *National Grit*, June 7.

60. Zarzynski, Joseph W. (circa 1982). *Adirondack Bits 'n Pieces Magazine*. "'Champ' A Zoological Jigsaw Puzzle." 16–21, 45–46, 48. See p. 21.

61. Interview between Tony Healy and the man during March 1979. The man wishes to remain anonymous. My thanks to Mr. Healy for allowing me access to this interview.

62. Interview between Tony Healy and the woman during March 1979.

CHAPTER 4

1. Porter, Marjorie L. (1970). "The Champlain Monster." *Vermont Life* 24(4):47–50.

2. "Speaking of Sea Monsters? Now Hear This!" *Watertown Daily Times* [Watertown, NY], September 8, 1970, 4.

3. The first to publicly do so was Connie Pope. See, "Rotary News: Unusual Topic Chosen by Guest Speaker." *Chateaugay Record*, June 17, 1971. For later examples of calling into question Porter's claims, see: Ross, John. (1978). "Sidelight on History." *The North Countryman*, August 23, 1978, 16; Meurger, Michel, and Gagnon, Claude. (1982). *Monstres des Lacs du Quebec: Mythes et Troublantes Realites*. Montreal: Stanke; Meurger, Michel, and Gagnon, Claude. (1988). *Lake Monster Traditions: A Cross Cultural Analysis*. London: Fortean Tomes Publishing.

4. Personal interview between Joe Nickell and Robert Bartholomew, circa August 22, 2002.

5. Spear, Richard. (1978). "A USO Seen from the Ferry. Two Independent Accounts of the Same Sighting." *Valley News* [Elizabethtown, NY], August 9, 1978, 14.

6. Spear, Richard. (1978). "A USO Seen from the Ferry. Two Independent Accounts of the Same Sighting." Op. cit., 14.

7. Ibid.

8. Smith, Warren. (1976). *Strange Secrets of the Loch Ness Monster*. New York: Zebra Books.

9. MacNeil, Deirdre. (1980). "Lake Champlain Monster. Hudson Falls Man Describes Sighting." *The Saratogian* [Saratoga Springs, NY], September 28, 5C. In August 1973, a Hudson Falls, New York family was excited after recently buying a new boat, and decided to all pile in and head up to Montreal via Lake Champlain: Ray Williams, his wife Alice and their daughter. On their return trip they were slowly making their way down the lake. After clearing customs, they decided to mosey on over to Barton's Island near St. Albans and spend the night. Alice was scanning the horizon with a pair of field glasses when she gasped. "What IS that?" Some two hundred yards away "something had raised itself three to five feet out of the water. The head seemed to be horse-shaped with smooth greyish skin like that of a snake," he said, followed by a large hump. The creature maintained a parallel course with their boat for five minutes before submerging back into the depths of the lake. Stunned by what they were witnessing, Williams said, "All we could do was stare."

10. Smith, Hal. (1981). "Myth or Monster?" *Adirondack Life* (November–December), 22–26, 44–45, 47. See p. 26.

11. Ibid.

12. It may be that there are pre-1970 accounts of witnesses claiming to have seen a creature with a horselike head, but they would not nullify this thesis if these stories were *collected and recalled after 1970*. Witness memories could have been altered by the flurry of magazine and newspaper articles beginning in the 1970s, describing Champ with a horselike head.

13. Warren Billy Smith was a prolific writer who published dozens of popular books on topics ranging from UFOs to Bigfoot and ESP, sometimes under the pseudonym Eric Norman. The author of numerous romance and western novels, his other pseudonyms included David Norman, Norma Warren, Joanna Warren, and Barbara Brooks.

14. Smith, Warren. (1976). *Strange Secrets of the Loch Ness Monster*. New York: Zebra Books; See also, *The Cardinal Points* [student publication of the State University of New York at Plattsburgh], February 18, 1988, 15.

15. When Lucia says that the creature cocked its head out of apparent curiosity, he is engaging in anthropromorphism, that is, attributing human characteristics to non-humans. When humans cock their head, it may often indicate that they are curious, but of course, not always. Head cocking by a large aquatic creature may indicate a very different intention!

16. Vachon, Brian. (1977). "In Search of the Champlain Monster." *Yankee Magazine* (November):134–39, 210, 212–13, 215–16.

17. Ironically, Vachon would later recall that the *Yankee* article paid $500, a fair sum for the late 1970s, while *Reader's Digest*, with its massive readership,

paid a paltry $100. Why the discrepancy? *Reader's Digest* has historically paid little as their articles are reprints and the authors are not required to do anything. No author in his or her right mind is going to turn down a chance to be published in *Reader's Digest* (telephone interview by Robert Bartholomew with Brian Vachon, March 2010).

18. Vachon, Brian. (1978). "Is There a Champlain Monster?" *Reader's Digest* 9–10, 14, 16. See also, Walter, Emilia. (1978). "Lk. Champlain Monster? Featured in Apr. *Reader's Digest*." April 20.

19. Anderson, Gregory J. (1978). "America's Loch Ness Monster." *Argosy* (July):19–22. See pp. 20–21. The witnesses were ages 20 and 15.

20. Mangiacopra, Gary. (1978). "Lake Champlain: America's Loch Ness—Part Two." *Of Sea and Shore* 9(2):89–92, citing Sawchuk, Pamela. (1975). *The Sunday Times Union* [Albany, NY], November 23, 1, 10, 11.

21. Interview between Tony Healy and Janet Tyler, March 1979.

22. Oserowsky, N. (1978). "Lake Champlain's Spacemen in Green Caps." *True Flying Saucers & UFO's Quarterly* (Winter):54–59.

23. Tape recording by Paul Bartholomew of a seminar presentation by Sandi Mansi at the "Does Champ Exist: A Scientific Seminar" held at Shelburne, Vermont on August 29, 1981. Wright, Jeff. (1982). "Photo of 'Creature' Means Headaches for Mansi." *Plattsburgh Press-Republican*, September 2, 1981, 5.

24. Tape recording by Paul Bartholomew of a seminar presentation by Sandi Mansi at the "Does Champ Exist: A Scientific Seminar" held at Shelburne, Vermont on August 29, 1981.

25. Wilford, John Noble. (1981). "Is It Lake Champlain's Monster?" *The New York Times*, June 30.

26. Tape recording by Paul Bartholomew of a seminar presentation by Sandi Mansi at the "Does Champ Exist: A Scientific Seminar" held at Shelburne, Vermont on August 29, 1981.

27. Ibid.

28. (1992). *Unsolved Mysteries*. NBC TV.

29. Tape recording by Paul Bartholomew of a seminar presentation by Sandi Mansi at the "Does Champ Exist: A Scientific Seminar" held at Shelburne, Vermont on August 29, 1981.

30. "Worker Claims he has Photo of Lake Monster." *The Ledger* (Lakeland, Florida), November 27, 1980, 14C.

31. Tape recording by Paul Bartholomew of a seminar presentation by Sandi Mansi at the "Does Champ Exist: A Scientific Seminar" held at Shelburne, Vermont on August 29, 1981.

32. Ibid.

33. The earliest known recorded statements from the Mansi's was a 1979 tape describing their alleged sighting of July 1977, and later transcribed by Sean Reines. Transcriber's note: Underlined text is to emphasize important parts of the Mansi's descriptive account. It does not connote exclamation on the part of the Mansi's.

Sandra Mansi

So, anyway, the children and I were down at the lake and the children were off a little distance and I was sitting on a rock and I looked out across the lake . . . [when I saw] some bubbles . . . coming up and I think in—I thought, at first, that maybe there was some scuba divers under there or something. And, so, I really wasn't concerned about it at that point—and I kept watching and it was like getting, rough out there. The wind was blowing anyway. It was a nice sunny day, warm and clear, but the water was kind of rough because there was a wind blowing. But it was getting—I looked out there and, like I said, the bubbles were coming up and then it was like, getting dark out there . . . not the sky or anything, but the water. And, at this point, I could see like, something coming out of the water. . . . And, and then I kept watching and looking and then, I heard Tony screaming up on the bank and so, he kept saying, and was hollering down, 'get the kids out of the water. Get up here.' And I looked out again and that's when I saw this [big pause], mammal, or whatever it was we saw. It was, big. It was like, a big neck on it, it was like a big neck and a he—the head, and a hump. But at that, I don't think I, no, I didn't see the hump at that point, all I saw was the neck and the head and I was really frightened. I don't know what I was frightened about, but I was frightened. So he was hollering to get the kids out. So, I went over and I, I hollered to my son, 'come on we're going, we're gonna go get something to eat!' So, he got out of the water and headed up the bank. And I went over and got my daughter, by the arm, and told her, 'come on, we're gonna go,' cause they had been hollering they were hungry anyway, so they were anxious to go and get something to eat, so they didn't give me any opposition. They ran up the bank and by then, I looked out again, and it was full out of the water. The whole neck and the back. So, the kids got up the bank and I came up. Tony grabbed my hand, helped me up the bank. And by then, the kids were heading across the field going towards the car. I stood there with Ton[y], and I looked out, and, it was a frightening experience, you have to realize that. It was, probably, I'd say, the neck was maybe, and the head, out of the water, was maybe—six feet—from where it came out of the water to the head. And, it was looking to the left and the neck and the head turned and it, looked, started looking, towards the right. And, at this point, it was just, sort of like, sitting there, you know. And then, it just sort of, went back down. It didn't swim or anything like that, it just went back down. And after that, after say, after it got down, it wasn't even under the water fully. We heard the motor boat coming . . . and then, it was just gone. I was really frightened, I'm telling ya . . . Anyway, before it went down, Tony handed me the camera and said, 'take a picture of it!' So, I took a picture and, so anyway, we got back to the car. We're both very shaken up about this thing. And of course, the car, you know, couldn't start the car, was worried, you know, dying light, and then we, you know, we were really rattled. We . . . get the kids something to eat and I said [to Tony], you know, you wanna go home or what? He decided, 'let's go home.' He really didn't like our Vermont after that, I'm afraid.

It really shook us up and I, I think, at the, at the time, we didn't discuss it because, the kids were in the car and we just decided if we didn't talk about it, maybe didn't happen . . . And, so, we talked about it a little bit after that like, you know, what was it? It could have been this, it could have been that, and we really didn't think much about it until the pictures came back and then, we saw the picture and we decided that we'll just put it away because if you don't think about it, you don't talk about it, it really doesn't happen you know. And I don't think I ever really would have . . . thought about it again but, where I was working, there was a bunch of us in the room and one of the girls, Diane, says, 'Gee, I'd like to go to Scotland . . . so I can see the Loch Ness monster!' And I said to her, 'Well, you really don't have to go to Scotland you know. All you have to do is go to Lake Champlain. There's Loch Ness type monsters up there!' And she said, 'No there isn't,' and they [the people present] were laughing and joking. And I said, 'No really, I saw one. I got a picture of it.' And I [she means, Diane, her co-worker] said, 'oh sure you did, okay!' Sandi replied: '. . . I really did, I'll bring it in and show it to you.' And so anyway, that's how this thing came about and Roy [Kappeler] was there and Roy said, 'you know, you really ought to tell people about [it?]. I said, 'they'll think we're crazy.'

You know, they'll just think we're nuts. And he convinced me that we really should do this [send Phil Reines the photo].

Tony Mansi

This is Tony Mansi. I will try to tell you what I saw that day, pertaining to the pictures we sent you. . . . We pull over the side of the road, in view of the lake, the lake was over side there. Let the kids go wading or something like that. Run across this field, down an embankment, kids were wading, we were sitting off to the side, sun was pretty bright and I had forgotten my sunglasses in the car, so I, so I had to go back to the car, get my sunglasses and also pick up my camera. We hadn't taken any pictures. So, I did so [meaning, he got the camera from the car]. On the way back [from the car], I came to the top of the embankment and I walked out and I saw this weird thing sort of coming out of the water. Oh, I wager to say, I saw it started to come out, it just didn't look right, and I yelled down to the wife to grab the kids and get up there. Just, it just, was weird. And big. And so, as the kids came running, she sent the kids up—they came running up the bank, she [Sandra] coming up, I gave her a hand, pulled her up, brought her up, [we] were just looking at it while the kids were heading to the car. Oh, I wager to say, just came up very gentle . . . It sort of turned, then, looked to the left, looked like a long neck with a head on it. And, uh, then, it gradually started to turn to the right. At this stage, it was out of the water a little bit more. Seemed to have a hump on the back. Sorta [i.e., 'sort of']. As it turned to right, I says to my wife, 'Here's the camera, snap a picture.' She snapped one picture. And it started to disappear down into the water. Just as it disappeared, around the bend, a motor boat came. And we just got outta there, because it just didn't look good to us and we didn't know what it was, and we just took off. Got in that car, finally got it started, cause when you're shook [and] in a hurry, the car, a lot of times, don't want to start. And we just headed away. That's about it. And, as for what type of camera [that they used to take the photograph of what was in the lake], it was a Kodak 708 with uh, 110 color film. Thank you.

Now that I told you the way I saw it, let me add a couple of details. Oh, I wager to say, it was approximately [a] hundred to a hundred and fifty feet out into the water. As for the depth of the water, I do not know. And, that's mainly why the children are wading and not swimming. We didn't know how deep it was there. And, the water was on the rough side. There was a good breeze blowing so the water was ripply. And, as for size . . . [it] . . . came out of the water six to eight feet, approximate, very hard to say but, then, it varied because it was moving, not fast, very gradual like and [long pause], of course, the head was moving because evidently, it looked one way, which was to the left. Then, evidently, that motorboat that came around the bend must have [sounds like either 'stirred' or 'disturbed'] it and it [the motorboat] must have heard it, and it just disappeared.

34. Reines also asked Kappeler to request that Sandi and Tony Mansi (by now, her husband) put their detailed account of the incident in a signed statement, and also, separately, on tape, with each one recording a detailed oral account of their individual experiences, which they did.

35. Undated letter from Roy Kappeler to Phil Reines, fall 1979.

36. Personal communication from Phil Reines to Robert Bartholomew, August 2010.

37. On April 14, 1980, Zarzynski wrote: ". . . I am waiting until the Mansi's and Roy K. [Kappeler] find the site. . . . It is just so frustrating . . ." Letter from Joe Zarzynski to Phil Reines.

38. Letter from Joe Zarzynski to Phil Reines dated July 10, 1980.

39. Letter from Joe Zarzynski to Phil Reines dated July 17, 1980, 2.

40. Letter from Joe Zarzynski to Phil Reines dated 10 July 1980.

41. In his earlier correspondence on the Mansi photo, Zarzynski was in agreement that they should not go public before the site could be found. For instance, on July 14, 1980, he wrote to Reines, "I think it is best to wait until we get the site before we proceed."

42. Letter from Phil Reines to Joe Zarzynski dated November 17, 1983.

43. Letter from Phil Reines to Robert Bartholomew dated June 24, 2010, 3.

44. Personal communication from Joe Zarzynski to Phil Reines dated July 17, 1980.

45. Personal communication from Joe Zarzynski to Phil Reines dated July 12, 1980.

46. Personal communication from Phil Reines to Robert Bartholomew dated September 15, 2010.

47. Ibid.

48. Working copies were used for fieldwork.

49. Letter from Dr. Reines to Joe Zarzynski dated August 8, 1980. As Dr. Reines recalls, this August letter was the last correspondence from Joseph Zarzynski until December 1980.

50. Letter dated December 23, 1980, from Alan Neigher of Byelas and Neigher, attorneys at law, 1804 Post Road East, Westport, Connecticut 06880, acknowledging receipt of a certified package containing the two prints that were sent by Dr. Reines on December 18, 1980.

51. Letter from Alan Neigher to Dr. Reines dated December 11, 1980.

52. Personal communication between Phil Reines and Robert Bartholomew dated September 15, 2010.

53. Letter from Joe Zarzynski to Dr. Reines dated December 24, 1980.

54. Ibid.

55. Handwritten letter from Phil Reines to Joe Zarzynski dated December 26, 1980.

56. Ibid., see 3. The article referred to appeared in the November 28, 1980, Albany *Times Union*.

57. Three days prior to his letter to Zarzynski, Dr. Reines returned the Mansi's original photo to their attorney, and in his December 23 reply, Neigher wrote: "This is to acknowledge receipt of two photographic prints of the creature in Lake Champlain. One of them an unmarked copy three inches by five inches [the original]; the other five by seven inches had certain writings at the top with the creature circled in pen [working field copy]. I appreciate your cooperation and I hope we can get you some permanent copies in the near future. Sincerely, Alan Neigher."

58. Wright, Jeff. (1980). "Monster 'Champy' Subject of TV's 'Real People.'" *Press-Republican* [Plattsburgh, NY], September 13, 15; Wright, Jeff. (1980). "Monster 'Champy' Subject of TV's 'Real People.'" *Press-Republican* [Plattsburgh, NY], September 15, 1980, 21. Oddly, both articles have the same exact titles.

59. Personal communication between Phil Reines and Robert Bartholomew dated September 2010.

60. Letter from Reines to Zarzynski dated December 26, 1980, 3.

61. Letter from Fred Wilson to Phil Reines dated September 3, 1981, at p. 2; Two separate news stories broadcast on WIRY, Plattsburgh, on June 29 and June 30 1981, including two audio interviews with Phil Reines.

62. Wilford won a Pulitzer Prize in 1984 for a series of articles on planetary exploration and science, and shared another prize three years later for his coverage of the Challenger space shuttle disaster. See also, Wilford, John Noble. (1981). "Is It Lake Champlain's Monster?" *The New York Times*,

June 30; Wilson, Fred. (1981). "'Champ' and the 1977 Mansi Photo." *Pursuit* 14(2):50.

63. Wright, Jeff. (1982). "Photo of 'Creature' Means Headaches for Mansi." *Plattsburgh Press-Republican*, September 2, 1981, 5.

64. Allen, Mel. (2011). "The Gift: Lake Champlain's Mysterious Photo." *Yankee Magazine* (March/April). http://www.yankeemagazine.com/issues/2011-03/features/champ-sighting/1. Accessed July 21, 2011.

65. Carter, E. Graydon. (1981). "People." *Time*, July 13.

66. "Over 100 See Champ on Lake Champlain." *The North Countryman*, July 8, 1981, 11.

67. Letter from George R. Zug to Joseph Zarzynski dated July 9, 1980.

68. Letter from George R. Zug to Joseph Zarzynski dated August 15, 1980.

69. Letter from Joseph Zarzynski to J. J. Kronenwetter, administrative assistant, Kodak Films, dated August 21, 1980.

70. Letter from Charles W. Johnson, Naturalist for the State of Vermont, to Joe Zarzynski dated August 22, 1980. See p. 2.

71. Robert Bartholomew, a former stringer for UPI, saved the original wire copy that was sent on April 18, 1981. I was reminded of this article by fellow researchers Ben Radford and Joe Nickell.

72. "'Champy' Photo Called Authentic." *Press-Republican* [Plattsburgh, NY], March 28, 1981, 17.

73. Letter from Roy Mackal to Joe Zarzynski dated December 2, 1983.

74. Letter from Dr. Reines to Frederick S. Wilson, Production Editor of *Pursuit* (publication of the Society for the Investigation of the Unexplained), 601 Bergen Hall, Suite 28, Paramus, New Jersey 07652, dated September 3, 1981, see page 3.

75. Letter from Dr. Reines to Frederick S. Wilson, Op. cit., 3.

76. Ibid.

77. Personal communication between Phil Reines and Robert Bartholomew, September 2010.

78. Tape recording by Paul Bartholomew of a seminar presentation by Philip Reines at the "Does Champ Exist: A Scientific Seminar" held at Shelburne, Vermont on August 29, 1981.

79. Letter from SUNY science professor James C. Dawson to Acting Vice President Charles Warren of SUNY College at Plattsburgh, NY, September 3, 1981. In commenting on the event, Dawson wrote (in part): "It was my pleasure on August 29 . . . to attend an all day seminar on "Champ" our Lake Champlain phenomenon. Along with over 200 paying participants. The presentations were very interesting, and the attached clippings from *The*

New York Times accurately summarize the points of view. No doubt you saw additional news reports in our Press Republican. The seminar . . . was well done. The general tone was very serious . . . the program was billed as a 'scientific seminar' and the organizers did their best to present an objective viewpoint. . . . In this respect it was very successful."

80. Letter from Barnard R. Carman to Dr. Reines dated September 10, 1981, 2.

81. "Does Champ Exist? A Scientific Seminar." Memorandum from James C. Dawson, director, Institute for Man and the Environment, SUNY Plattsburgh, to Charles Warren, acting vice president for academic affairs, dated September 3, 1981 (cc to Dr. Phil Reines).

82. Reines says that the issue was given to him by *Pursuit* editor Fred Wilson at the seminar, with the intention of clarifying questions that he had about its accuracy. Impressed by the conference, he wrote to Reines that it "was like nothing I have ever seen or felt before. For this, you should take much credit."

83. Zarzynski, Joseph W. (1981)."'Champ'—A Personal Update." *Pursuit* 14(2):51–52. *Pursuit* is the official publication of the Society for the Investigation of the Unexplained.

84. Letter from Dr. Reines to Frederick S. Wilson, Production Editor of *Pursuit*, 601 Bergen Hall, Suite 28, Paramus, New Jersey 07652, dated September 3, 1981.

85. Wilson, Frederick. (1981). "'Champ' and the 1977 Mansi Photo." *Pursuit* 14(2):50.

86. Letter from Dr. Reines to Frederick S. Wilson, production editor of *Pursuit*. See p. 1.

87. Ibid. Zarzynski's reference to Reines as a "non-expert" and his statement that he could not work with what he did not have, were obvious references to their lack of cooperation in Reines' refusal to accepting the photo (on faith) without knowing the location.

88. Letter from Frederick S. Wilson to Dr. Reines, dated September 17, 1981. See p. 1.

89. Reines would later write that his letter to the editor of *Pursuit* was personal and intended to square the record, but that he had no intention of publishing it. With the conference over, Reines was hoping that Zarzynski would become more inclusive of those holding opposing views, and that the Mansis would reopen relations. Neither happened. Reines saw the situation as a clash of approaches: One open and scientific, the other based on faith and inadequate evidence. Besides, with the possibility of a 1982 conference at his college, he did not want to give critics any reasons to deride and cancel it. The idea of holding another conference ultimately fizzled.

90. Letter from Dr. Reines to Barnard R. Carman, editor of *Adirondack Life*, dated September 8, 1981, 1.

91. Ibid.

92. Smith, Hal. (1981). "Myth or Monster?" *Adirondack Life* (November–December), 22–26, 44–45, 47.

93. Letter from Dr. Reines to Barnard R. Carman, editor of *Adirondack Life*, dated September 8, 1981.

94. Letter from Barnard R. Carman to Dr. Reines dated September 10, 1981, 2.

95. Anonymous. (1981). "Americana: The Champ of Champlain." *Time* (March 31).

96. "Is There a Sea Monster in Lake Champlain?" *Grit*, June 7, 1981, 1.

97. "Port Henry Plans Monster of a Celebration," *Press-Republican*, July 31, 1997, D1; McKinstry, Lohr. (1996). "PBS Crew Looks for Champ in Moriah," *Press-Republican*, October 7, B1.

98. "Rotary News: Unusual Topic Chosen by Guest Speaker." *Chateaugay Record*, June 17, 1971; See for later examples of calling into question Porter's claims: Ross, John. (1978). "Sidelight on History." *The North Countryman*, August 23, 1978, 16; Meurger, Michel, and Gagnon, Claude. (1982). *Monstres des Lacs du Quebec: Mythes et Troublantes Realites*. Montreal: Stanke; Meurger, Michel, and Gagnon, Claude. (1988). *Lake Monster Traditions: A Cross Cultural Analysis*. London: Fortean Tomes Publishing.

99. McKinstry, Lohr (2009). "Something Fishy Seen in Lake Video, but is it Champ?" (June 5). http://pressrepublican.com/0100_news/x155079490/Something-fishy-seen-in-lake-video-but-is-it-Champ-nbsp-img-src-http-static-cnhi-zope-net-images-icons-videoiconbullet-gif-width-19-height-12-border-0-alt-Includes-video?keyword=topstory. Accessed January 5, 2011; McKinstry, Lohr. (2009)." Could Burlington Video be Champ?" (June 3). http://pressrepublican.com/0100_news/x155079428/Could-Burlington-video-be-Champ. Accessed January 5, 2011. For examples: "Champ was first sighted in the lake in 1609, by Samuel de Champlain." (McKinstry, Lohr [1993]. "Sonar Readings Being Studied in Champ Hunt." Plattsburgh *Press-Republican*, September 4, 15); "In 1609, explorer Samuel de Champlain was the first known person to report seeing Champ. He described the sea serpent's sighting in his writings" (McKinstry, Lohr [1997]. Port Henry Plans Monster of a Celebration." Plattsburgh *Press-Republican*, July 31, D1).

100. Foulke, Patrica and Robert. (1994). *Day Trips, Getaway Weekends, and Vacations in New England*. Chester, CT: Globe Pequot Press, 287.

101. Letter from Dr. Reines to J. Robert Dubois (then editor of *Adirondack Bits n'Pieces* magazine), Port Henry, New York dated November 15, 1983, 1.

102. Letter from Dr. Reines to Joe Zarzynski dated November 17, 1983, 1. Reines then tried to patch up their differences, mindful that a public dispute could be harmful given the recent seminar and the attempts that were underway to get protective legislation passed. "Don't you think that unless we resolve our differences and can at least function on an *objective* and *professional* level that our . . . (cryptozoological) colleagues will think it not a bit strange that virtually *no* communication or shared information exists between the two recognized 'Champ' researchers who live so close to each other and *once did* have a relationship? Is it an accepted fact that your 'Lake Champlain Phenomena Investigation' group is the *only* responsible or professional organization dedicated to the saving and preserving of our elusive local ecological treasure? What is 'select' about it? And, how is it respectfully credentialed? What [are] the criteria for membership?"

103. Handwritten letter from Phil Reines to Robert Bartholomew dated June 24, 2010, at p. 3.

104. Ibid.

105. Wright, Jeff. (1982). "Photo of 'Creature' Means Headaches for Mansi." *Plattsburgh Press-Republican*, September 2, 1981, 5.

106. Ibid.

107. Letter from John Noble Wilford to Robert Bartholomew dated March 10, 2010.

108. Letter from Fred Wilson to Phil Reines dated September 3, 1981, at p. 2; Two separate news stories broadcast on WIRY, Plattsburgh, on June 29 and June 30 1981, including two audio interviews with Phil Reines.

109. Wright, Jeff. (1982). "Photo of 'Creature' Means Headaches for Mansi." *Plattsburgh Press-Republican*, September 2, 1981, 5.

110. Lenger, John. (1992). "Bright Lights, Big Mystery: TV's 'Unsolved Mysteries' to Retell Champ Legend." *The Post-Star* (Glens Falls, NY), July 5, C1 and C8. See p. 8.

111. Koepper, Ken. (1981). "Champ: About the Money and a Monster." *The Day* (New London, Connecticut), October 18, 1981, 1, 14. Quoted on p. 1.

112. Ibid.

113. Ibid. Quoted on p. 14.

114. Ibid.

115. Around the Towns. Banking on the Champ." *The Day* (New London, CT), December 19, 1982, A3.

116. Ibid.

117. Ibid.

118. Telephone conversation between Ben Radford and Robert Bartholomew, January 2011.

119. Around the Towns. Banking on the Champ." Op cit.

120. Lenger, John. (1992). "Bright Lights, Big Mystery: TV's 'Unsolved Mysteries' to Retell Champ Legend." *The Post-Star*, July 5, C1 and C8. See p. 8.

121. Copy of the resolution passed by the Village of Port Henry, October 6, 1980.

122. "Lake Off Limits to 'Monster' Harassers." *New York Times* syndicated article appearing the *Palm Beach Post*, December 2, 1980, B3.

123. Kermani, Ronald. (1981). "In Search of Champ." *Times-Union* [Albany, NY], July 5, 1981, 1, A8.

124. "Loch Ness Monster Sightings Down." Associated Press report dated October 1, 2007.

125. Felton, Bruce (2007). *What Were They Thinking? Really Bad Ideas Throughout History*. Guilford, CT: Lyon Press, 174.

126. Kermani, Ronald. (1981). "In Search of Champ." *Times-Union* [Albany, NY], July 5, 1981, 1, A8.

127. Geist, William E. (1981). "Village on Lake Champlain Seeking Its Fortune in Tale of a Fabulous Sea Monster." *The New York Times*, November 29, 25, 28.

128. Zarzynski, Joseph W. (1981). "'Champ'—A Personal Update." *Pursuit* 14(2):51–52. See p. 51.

129. Elkin, Larry. (1981). "Don't Scoff at Sea Monster in this Town." *The Ledger* [Lakeland, FL], July 8, D6; Manchester, Lee. (1984). "Iron Center Museum Tells the Story of Moriah Mines and Mills." *Lake Placid News*, October 24.

130. Kermani, Ronald. (1981). "In Search of Champ." *Times-Union* [Albany, NY], July 5, 1981, 1, A8. Quoted on p. A8.

131. Kermani, Ronald. (1981). "In Search of Champ." *Times-Union* [Albany, NY], July 5, 1981, 1, A8. Quoted on p. A8.

132. Geist, William. (1981). "Port Henry Protective of its 'Sea Monster.'" *The Winchester Star* [Virginia], December 27, 1981, 18.

133. Zarzynski, Joseph W. (1981). "'Champ'—A Personal Update." *Pursuit* 14(2):51–52. See p. 51.

134. Geist, William E. (1981). "Village on Lake Champlain Seeking Its Fortune in Tale of a Fabulous Sea Monster." *The New York Times*, November 29, 25, 28.

135. Legislative Assembly Resolution 112, State of New York, Albany, sponsored by A. W. Ryan and colleagues Harris, Casale, Conners and McCann and signed by Catherine A. Carey, Clerk, April 18, 1983. See also, "Lake Monster Debated in New York Assembly." *The Victoria Advocate* [Victoria, TX], March 20, 1983, 10B.

136. "Protection for Monster Urged." *Tri-City Herald* [Washington], April 18, 1982, 23; Zarzynski, Joseph W. (circa 1982). *Adirondack Bits 'n Pieces Magazine.* "'Champ' A Zoological Jigsaw Puzzle." 16–21, 45–46, 48. See p. 21.

137. Donnelly, John. (1987). "Vermont's New Lake Monster Protected." *Press-Republican*, March 18, 1; Donnelly, John. (1987). "Legislators Seek Monster Support." *The Citizen* [Auburn, New York], March 19, 4.

138. Cottage industries are small-scale enterprises where products and services are home-based rather than produced in factories.

139. Zarzynski, Joseph. (1989). *Champ Channels* 6(1):7.

140. McKinstry, Lohr. (1995). "Champ Day Commorates Port Henry's Mascot." *Plattsburgh Press-Republican*, July 26, 13.

141. "Farah Yurdozu Interviews Frank Soriano." http://www.ufocasebook.com/soriano.html. Accessed December 25, 2010; "Frank Soriano, Alien Abductee." http://beyondthedial.wordpress.com/2007/10/11/frank-soriano-alien-abductee/. Accessed December 25, 2010.

142. Green, Susan. (1996). "Tales from the Cryptozoologists. Are we keeping Champ's Legacy Afloat?" *Vox* (Vermont's Voice of Arts and Culture) 2(16):1, 3. Quoted on p. 1.

143. Ibid., 3.

144. In early 2000, Champ appeared in court. Well, not exactly. At this time there was a burglary trial of ex-Ticonderoga police chief John Wade. In an attempt to discredit a key witness against Wade, it was noted that she had reported not one, but three sightings of "Champy." The prosecution countered by reminding jurors that former President Jimmy Carter once reported seeing a UFO. In the end, a mistrial was declared as the jurors were deadlocked 10 to 2. Although there may be less of a stigma than there once was, clearly there remains a stigma for witnesses of Champ, and many witnesses have noted this over the years. See, McKinstry, Lohr. (2000). "Judge Declares Mistrial." *Press-Republican*, January 15; McKinstry, Lohr. (2000). "Wade Jurors Struggle with Deadlock." *Press-Republican*, January 14.

145. *Weekly World News*, February 12, 2002.

CHAPTER 5

1. http://www.northernbigfoot.net/. Accessed April 5, 2011.

2. Ibid. Accessed April 27, 2011.

3. Other tenants of the society are "WONDER that such a magnificent and elusive creature co-exists with us . . ."; "DISCOVERY of who or what Sasquatch is, what its purposes are, how to contact and communicate with it . . ."; "EDUCATION of the general public to accept that Sasquatch exists . . ."

4. Louv, Richard. (1978). "Bigfoot Follies." *Human Behavior* 7(9):18–24. See p. 20.

5. Ibid. See pp. 21–22.

6. Ibid. See p. 20.

7. *Champ Channels*. (1984), 2(3): 1.

8. Clark, Tim. (1986). "The Believer." *Yankee Magazine* (June). See pp. 85–92, 142, 145. Quoted on p. 86.

9. "Photo Revives Champlain Monster Mystery." *The Valley Voice* [Middlebury, VT], December 9, 1980, 1, 7; Wright, Jeff. (1980). "Monster 'Champy' Subject of TV's 'Real People.'" *Press-Republican* (Plattsburgh, New York), September 13, 15; Paul Bartholomew recording of the *Real People* episode circa 1981.

10. Clark, Tim. (1986). "The Believer." *Yankee Magazine* (June). See pp. 85–92, 142, 145.

11. Citro, Joseph A., and Christensen, Bonnie. (1994). *Green Mountain Ghosts, Ghouls & Unsolved Mysteries*, 109–10.

12. Clark, Tim. (1986). "The Believer." *Yankee Magazine* (June). See pp. 85–92, 142, 145.

13. Ibid. See pp. 91–92, 142, 145.

14. Zarzynski, Joseph W. (1984). *Champ: Beyond the Legend*. Port Henry, NY: Bannister Publications.

15. Four years later, Zarzynski self-published an updated edition. In 2010, the world's largest network of library content, the WorldCat catalogue, lists 1,037 libraries holding copies of Roy Mackal's 1976 book, *The Monsters of Loch Ness* (Chicago: Swallow Press) in U.S. libraries including subsequent reprints. In comparison, the 1984 edition of Zarzynski's book was held by 55 participating U.S. libraries; just 4 in the state of Vermont. His 1988 edition was held in 66 U.S. libraries; 3 in Vermont. Of course, this is not a true picture of the number of libraries holding the book, but it gives an idea as to its limited commercial success. See, Zarzynski, Joseph W. (1988). *Champ: Beyond the Legend*. Wilton, NY: M-Z Information; Zarzynski, Joseph W. (1984). *Champ: Beyond the Legend*. Port Henry, NY: Bannister Publications; WorldCat Catalogue. www.worldcat.org. Accessed March 7, 2010.

16. Hartnett, Tim. (1981). "Zarzynski in Pursuit of Champ." *Plattsburgh Press-Republican*, September 6, 1984, 8.

17. Downs, Jack. (1984). *Press-Republican*, "'Champ' Blends Opinion, Scientific Data." December 17, 5.

18. Zarzynski wrote in his preface that the evidence for Champ was "Far from definitive . . ." though the case he presented was "tantalizing" and "intriguing" (21).

19. Zarzynski, Joseph W. (1984). *Champ: Beyond the Legend*. Port Henry, NY: Bannister Publications. See back cover.

20. Ibid.

21. Clark, Tim. (1986). "The Believer." *Yankee Magazine* (June). See pp. 85–92, 142, 145. Quote appears on p. 145.

22. Citro, Joseph A., and Christensen, Bonnie. (1994). *Green Mountain Ghosts, Ghouls & Unsolved Mysteries*. New York: Houghton Mifflin Company, 109.

23. Ibid., 108.

24. Vachon, Brian. (1977). "In Search of the Champlain Monster." *Yankee Magazine* (November):134–39, 210, 212–13, 215–16. Quote on p. 136.

25. Telephone interview between Phil Reines and Sandi Mansi circa May 2010.

26. Simanek, Donald E. "Arthur Conan Doyle, Spiritualism, and Fairies." http://www.lhup.edu/~dsimanek/doyle.htm. Accessed December 20, 2010.

27. http://web.archive.org/web/20060517031714/www/champquest. com/champquesthist. htm.

28. Hall, Dennis Jay (2000). *ChampQuest: The Ultimate Search*. Jericho, VT: Essence of Vermont, xiii.

29. "Baby Champ?" Letter from Dennis Hall to Ben Radford dated February 1, 2003.

30. Kirk, John, *In the Domain of the Lake Monsters*. Toronto, Canada: Key Porter Books, 132–33; "What Lies in the Depths of Lake Champlain." Interview with Dennis Jay Hall.

http://www.uhaul.com/supergraphics/states/vermont/champ/expertqa. html; Eberhart, George. (2002). *Mysterious Creatures: A Guide to Cryptozoology, Vol. 2*. Santa Barbara, CA: ABC-CLIO, 97; the last ChampQuest.com website archive from May 14, 2006 from the wayback archive://web.archive.org/web/20060517031714/www. champquest. com/champquesthist.htm.

31. Archives of Loren Coleman's Cyptomundo website and personal communication between Robert Bartholomew and Loren Coleman, March 2010.

32. Email from Dennis J. Hall to Loren Coleman dated July 22, 2003.

33. Ibid.

34. Email from anonymous Champ Trackers blog member to the group dated May 23, 2006. The actual poll was under the URL: http://groups. yahoo.com/groups/champ-trackers/surveys?id=2237191.

35. Email from Dennis J. Hall to anonymous Champ Trackers blog member dated May 23, 2006.

36. "Port Henry's Champ Day Celebrates Lake Champlain's Most Enduring Mystery." *Press-Republican*, August 4, 1997, B1.

37. McKinstry, Lohr. (1992). "Lake Monster Champ Focus of Port Henry Fete." *Press-Republican*, August 2, 1992, A4.

38. "Port Henry's Champ Day Celebrates Lake Champlain's Most Enduring Mystery." *Press-Republican*, August 4, 1997, B1.

39. Dennis Hall repeatedly states that he has been searching for Champ for thirty years in his emails to the Champ Trackers News Group. See for example, Hall's email dated July 20 and August 9, 2000.

40. http://web.archive.org/web/20060514032010/http://www.champquest.com/. Accessed May 12, 2010.

41. Munro, Stan (Host) (2003). "Sightings Week." WRGB Channel 6, Schenectady, NY, May 15. See, http://web.archive.org/web/20060517031714/www/champquest.com/champquesthist.htm

42. http://web.archive.org/web/20060517031714/www/champquest.com/champquesthist.htm, Accessed May 12, 2010.

43. Ibid.

44. Hall, Dennis Jay. (1999). *Champ Quest 1999 Field Guide and Almanac for Lake Champlain.* Jericho, VT: Essence of Vermont.

45. Heinselman, Craig (2001). "Testing the New Moon Theory at Lake Champlain." *North American BioFortean Review* 3(1):76–79.

46. Heinselman, Craig (2001). "Testing the New Moon Theory at Lake Champlain." *North American BioFortean Review* 3(1):76–79.

47. Hewitt, Ben (2000). "Q & A: Champ-Chasing Champ Tells All." *Sports Afield* 233(2):19.

48. Hall, Dennis Jay, (2000). *ChampQuest: The Ultimate Search.* Jericho, VT: Essence of Vermont, 30.

49. Hall, Dennis Jay, (March 2000). *Champ Quest 2000: The Ultimate Search Field Guide and Almanac of Best Search Dates for Lake Champlain.* Panton, VT: Essence of Vermont.

50. Dennis Hall letter to the Champ Chasers newsgroup dated July 15, 2000.

51. Ibid., dated August 9, 2000.

52. Ibid., dated October 4, 2000.

53. Ibid., dated October 11, 2000.

54. "What Lies in the Depths of Lake Champlain?" A website promotion by U-Haul International which appeared in 1999 in an effort to publicize the U-Haul Company. See, http://www.uhaul.com/supergraphics/states/vermont/champ/expertqa.html. Accessed May 2, 2010.

55. Radford, Ben (2001). "U-Haul Moves into the Paranormal." *The Skeptical Inquirer* 11(4). http://www.csicop.org/sb/show/u-haul_moves_into_the_paranormal. Accessed December 17, 2010.

56. Hall, Dennis Jay (2000). *ChampQuest: The Ultimate Search.* Jericho, VT: Essence of Vermont, 15.

57. Email from Ruby Anderson on the Champ Trackers Blog September 14, 2009; phone interview between Scott Mardis and Robert Bartholomew on December 22, 2010. Mr. Mardis said he had recently seen and talked to Mr. Hall, who was still living in the Vergennes area.

58. Inexplicably, a MonsterQuest documentary gives the date as June 2002. See, http://www.history.com/shows/monsterquest/videos/lake-champlains-monster#lake-champlains-monster. Accessed July 12, 2010.

59. Ober, Lauren (2009). "A Bioacoustician records, well, Something in Lake Champlain." *Seven Days: Vermont's Independent Voice* (July 15). http://www.7dvt.com/2009making-sound-waves. Accessed December 23, 2010.

60. Ober, Lauren (2009). "A Bioacoustician records, well, Something in Lake Champlain." *Seven Days: Vermont's Independent Voice* (July 15). http://www.7dvt.com/2009making-sound-waves. Accessed December 23, 2010.

61. Ibid.

62. Radford, Benjamin, and Nickell, Joseph (2006). *Lake Monster Mysteries.* Lexington, KY: University of Kentucky Press, 64–65.

63. Emails from Elizabeth von Muggenthaler to Robert Bartholomew dated August 7, 12, and December 8, 2010.

64. Letter from Steve Daniel, editor of *Old Dominion Magazine,* to Robert Bartholomew dated January 13, 2011.

65. Muggenthaler, Elizabeth, Gregory, Joseph, and Mardis, Scott H. (2010). "Echolocation in a Freshwater Lake." Paper presented to the Acoustical Society of America, April 21, 2010; Ober, Lauren (2009). Op. cit.

66. Letter from Susan E. Parks to Robert Bartholomew dated January 11, 2011.

67. Letter from Dr. Simone Baumann-Pickering to Robert Bartholomew dated January 12, 2011.

68. Fauna Communications website. http://www.animalvoice.com/lake-champlain.htm Accessed December 24, 2010.

69. Ibid.

70. Letter from Pat Manley to Robert Bartholomew dated January 16, 2011.

71. Letter from Dr. David Mann to Robert Bartholomew dated January 11, 2011.

72. Ibid.

73. Letter from Dr. Peter Teglberg Madsen, associate professor of zoo-physiology, Aarhus University, Denmark, to Robert Bartholomew dated January 12, 2011.

74. Letter from Dr. Kristian Beedholm, postdoctoral fellow, Institute of Biology, Aarhus University, Denmark, to Robert Bartholomew dated January 12, 2011.

75. Letter from James T. Fulton to Robert Bartholomew dated January 16, 2011.

76. Letter from Erich Hoyt to Robert Bartholomew dated January 12, 2011.

77. Two separate letters from Craig Radford to Robert Bartholomew dated January 20, 2011.

78. Letter from Dr. Kuczaj to Robert Bartholomew dated January 17, 2011.

79. Mullen, Jennifer (2002). "If We Could Talk to the Animals." *Old Dominion University Magazine.* http://www.odu.edu/ao/alumni_magazine/spring02/stories/dolittle.html. Accessed January 12, 2011.

80. Leavitt, Kirk. "Monster Quest Look at the Lake Champlain Monster." July 9, 2009. http://www.associatedcontent.com/article/1928182/the_monsterquest_ look_ at_the _lake_champlain_pg3.html?cat=2. Accessed April 20, 2010.

81. Hemmingway, Sam. (2003). "Lake's First 'Champ-Hearing' Recorded." *Burlington Free-Press*, published approximately July 19. Press report appeared on the Jeff Rense Radio Show website. http://www.rense.com/general39/champ.htm. Accessed January 12, 2011.

82. Ms. Pope was the head of the New York State Special Collections section at the college's Feinberg Library and specialized in documenting the history of nineteenth-century and early twentieth-century "ghost towns" of the Adirondacks, communities that came into existence and became prosperous because of an industrial base (like iron mines and granite quarries) but were later abandoned and forgotten. She was well known in the region as a columnist for the Plattsburgh *Press-Republican*.

83. Personal communication between Dr. Reines and Robert Bartholomew, August 2010.

84. This weight is an estimate by Reines that was "at least a ton and a half."

85. Telephone interview between Robert Bartholomew Phil Reines circa July 28, 2010.

86. Tape recording by Paul Bartholomew of a press conference at the "Does Champ Exist?" Conference in Shelburne, Vermont on August 29, 1981.

87. Telephone interview between Robert Bartholomew Phil Reines circa July 28, 2010.

88. Smith, Carolee. (1982). "Champy—Fantasy, Fact or Fable?" *Chronica* 2(1):15. *Chonica* is a publication of the State University of New York, detailing faculty research within the SUNY system.

89. Letter from Dr. Reines to Robert Bartholomew dated August 23, 2010.

90. Detullio, Andrew (2009). "What Might Lie Beneath." *Phoebe Magazine* (focusing on Burlington, Vermont culture) 36–39. See p. 39.

91. Ibid., 36–39.

92. Mardis's claim is indeed true. See Bauer, Henry H. (1986). *The Enigma of Loch Ness: Making Sense of a Mystery*. Urbana, IL: University of Illinois Press, 123–124.

93. Mangiacopra, Gary. (1992). *Theoretical Population Estimates of the Large Aquatic Animals in Selected Freshwater Lakes of North America*. Master's thesis, Department of Biology. New Haven, CT: Southern Connecticut State University.

94. Mangiacopra, Gary, Smith, Dwight, and Avery, David. (1994). "A Champ Trilogy: Part Three. But Hunting What?" *Of Sea and Shore* 16(4):209–12, 243–46. Quote on p. 244.

95. Mangiacopra, Gary, Smith, Dwight, and Avery, David F. (1994). "A Champ Trilogy: Part Two, A Checklist and Statistics on Champ Sightings: 1609–1990." *Of Sea and Shore* 16:3:169–72.

96. Ibid.

97. Mangiacopra, Gary. (1993). "A Champ Trilogy: Part One, Hunting for Champ." *Of Sea and Shore* 16:1:43–52.

CHAPTER 6

1. "Champlain Fisherman saw Champy on Father's Day." *Press-Republican*, July 18, 1992, 17.

2. Personal communication between Dr. Bain and Robert Bartholomew, March 30, 2010.

3. Tape recording by Paul Bartholomew of a seminar presentation by William H. Eddy Jr., at the "Does Champ Exist?" Conference in Shelburne, Vermont on August 29, 1981.

4. Tape recording by Paul Bartholomew, Op. cit.

5. These figures vary slightly depending on the source.

6. Mangiacopra, Gary, Smith, Dwight, and Avery, David. (1993). "A Champ Trilogy Part Two, A Checklist and Statistics on Champ Sightings: 1609–1990." *Of Sea and Shore* 16(2):95–102. See p. 99.

7. Letter from Leon W. Dean to journalist N. Oserowsky, circa 1978. Born in Bristol, Vermont in 1898, he founded the Green Mountain Folklore Society in 1948 and served as its first president. He died in 1982.

8. Mayor, Adrienne (2005). *Fossil Legends of the First Americans*. Princeton, NJ: Princeton University Press.

9. National Aeronautics and Space Administration Homepage. Interview with NASA scientist Gene Feldman. "Oceans: the Great Unknown." Interview by Daniel Stillman of the Institute for Global Environmental Strategies. http://www.nasa.gov/audience/forstudents/5–8/features/oceans-the-great-unknown-58.html. Accessed January 17, 2010.

10. The source of this often-cited quotation continues to elude scholars, prompting some to suggest that he never uttered these words. The first-known citation can be traced to G. Brown Goode, "The Beginning of American Science," Annual Address of the President, G. Brown Goode, *Proceedings of the Biological Society of Washington*, Vol. 4, February 20, 1886–January 28, 1888, 35.

11. Randi, James. (2003). "Thomas Jefferson on Stones and Perpetual Motion, Crystal Homeopathy . . ." SWIFT, newsletter of the James Randi Educational Foundation, March 7.

12. Burke, John G. (1991). *Cosmic Debris: Meteorites in History*. Berkeley, CA: University of California Press.

13. Ibid., 63.

14. "Paragrams." *Plattsburgh Sentinel*, May 27, 1887, 1.

15. "Westport." *Essex County Republican*, July 30, 1874.

16. Tape recording by Paul Bartholomew of a seminar presentation by Philip Reines at the "Does Champ Exist: A Scientific Seminar" held at Shelburne, Vermont on August 29, 1981.

17. "A Champlain Man's Combat with an Alligator." *The Daily Journal* [Odgensburg, NY], October 10, 1883, citing the *Glens Falls Star* [Glens Falls, NY].

18. Ibid.

19. McKinstry, Lohr (2000). "Mystery Resurfaces: Champ Spotted: Presence Remains Deep, Dark Secret." Plattsburgh *Press-Republican*, December 21.

20. Avila, Jim (2006). "Creature Feature: A Monster in Lake Champlain." ABC TV News report featuring FBI forensic analyst Gerald Richards. http://www.youtube.com/watch?v=NHpsqfWTvx8&feature=player_embedded. Accessed December 25, 2010.

21. Peter Applebome, "Our Town: A Serpent, Or at Least its Tale, Resurfaces." *The New York Times*, October 12, 2005.

22. Nickell, Joe (2006). "North America's 'Loch Ness' Monster Spotted Again." Live Science. http://www.livescience.com/animals/060307_lake_monster.html. Accessed April 18, 2010.

23. "Save Sturgeon? It May be too Late." Associated Press report appearing in *The Daily News Weekend* [Moscow, ID and Pullman, WA], January 19 and 20, 1991, 8E.

24. Meyers, Jeff. (1997). "Researchers Consider Theory that Champ is Sturgeon." *Plattsburgh Press-Republican*, September 2, A3.

25. Personal communication between Dr. Bain and Robert Bartholomew, March 30, 2010.

26. Meyers, Jeff. (2009). "Unusual Creature Seen in Lake Champlain." *Plattsburgh Press-Republican*, June 6, 2009.

27. "Lake Champlain 'Sea Serpent' May be a Leviathian Sturgeon." *Ticonderoga Sentinel*, June 23, 1949.

28. "3 See Champy Ram Sailboat in King's Bay." *Plattsburgh Press-Republican*, August 7, 1982, 15.

29. Personal communication between Dr. Bain and Robert Bartholomew, March 30, 2010.

30. Letter from Scott Gifford to Phil Reines dated November 19, 2010.

31. Scott, William B. (1967). *Freshwater Fishes of Eastern Canada.* Toronto, Canada: University of Toronto Press, 8; "New York's Sturegon." New York State Department of Environmental Conservation website. http://www.dec.ny.gov/animals/7025.html. Accessed December 22, 2010.

32. "Rock Sturgeon Threw Scare into Fishermen." *Essex County Republican*, April 17, 1931.

33. Mardis, Scott. (1996). "Sealing Champ's Fate: More Thoughts on the Lake Monster." *Vox* (Vermont's Voice of Arts and Culture) 2(25):7.

34. "The MonsterQuest Look at the Lake Champlain Monster," July 9, 2009. http://monsterquestreview.blogspot.com/2009/07/monsterquest-look-at-lake-champlain.html. Accessed December 35, 2010.

35. "Albany Day by Day." *The Albany Evening Journal*, August 15, 1902, 6, citing the *Burlington News*.

36. "Champlain's Sea Serpent." *Plattsburgh Sentinel*, August 15, 1902, 1.

37. Teresi, Dick. (1998). "Monster of the Tub." *Discover* 19(4):87–92.

38. Ibid.

39. Ibid.

40. Letter from Charles W. Johnson, Naturalist for the State of Vermont, to Joe Zarzynski dated August 22, 1980. See p. 2.

41. Wright, Jeff. (1982). "Photo of 'Creature' Means Headaches for Mansi." *Plattsburgh Press-Republican*, September 2, 1981, 5.

42. Kermani, Ronald. (1981). "In Search of Champ." *Times-Union* [Albany, NY], July 5, 1981, 1, A8. See p. A8.

43. Letter from Ronald Kermani to Robert Bartholomew dated January 14, 2011.

44. Wright, Jeff. (1982). "Photo of 'Creature' Means Headaches for Mansi." *Plattsburgh Press-Republican*, September 2, 1981, p. 5.

45. Smith, Hal. (1981). "Myth or Monster?" *Adirondack Life* (November–December), 22–26, 44–45, 47. See pp. 23 and 44.

46. Lenger, John. (1992). "Bright Lights, Big Mystery: TV's 'Unsolved Mysteries' to Retell Champ Legend." *The Post-Star* [Glens Falls, NY], July 5, C1 and C8. See p. 8.

47. Radford, Benjamin, and Nickell, Joseph (2006). *Lake Monster Mysteries*. Lexington, KY: University of Kentucky Press, 45.

48. Tape recording by Paul Bartholomew of a seminar presentation by Sandi Mansi at the "Does Champ Exist: A Scientific Seminar" held at Shelburne, Vermont on August 29, 1981.

49. Wright, Jeff. (1982). "Photo of 'Creature' Means Headaches for Mansi." *Plattsburgh Press-Republican*, September 2, 1981, 5.

50. Zarzynski, Joseph W. (1981). "'Champ'—A Personal Update." *Pursuit* 14(2):51–52.

51. "Pictures of Famed Champlain Monster." Associated Press report appearing in the *Oswego Palladium*, circa November 1980 (microfilm of specific date is damaged).

52. Zarzynski, Joseph W. (1984). *Champ: Beyond the Legend*. Port Henry, NY: Bannister Publications, 67.

53. Letter from Joe Zarzynski to Phil Reines dated July 17, 1980, 2.

54. Interview with Sandra Mansi by Jordan Warner appearing in the video "Cryptid Hunt," under the episode heading: "America's Loch Ness Monster." (October 31, 2007). http://www.youtube.com/watch?v=zpBjx_Kj9gc. Accessed July 22, 2011.

55. Radford, Benjamin, and Nickell, Joe (2006). *Lake Monster Mysteries: Investigating the World's Most Elusive Creatures*. Lexington, KY: University of Kentucky Press, 44.

56. "Lake Champlain 'Monster' Makes Believers." *The Pittsburgh Press*, August 30, 1981, A22.

57. A 1979 tape recording by Sandra and Anthony Mansi, describing their alleged sighting of July 1977, and later transcribed by Sean Reines. The recording was made for and mailed to Phil Reines, along with the original photo.

58. Radford, Benjamin, and Nickell, Joseph (2006). *Lake Monster Mysteries*. Lexington, KY: University of Kentucky Press, 157–58.

59. Frieden, B. Roy. (1981). "Interm Report/Lake Champlain 'Monster' Photograph" issued by the Optical Sciences Center, University of Arizona, April 30, and recorded by J. Richard Greenwell.

60. Ibid.

61. Arment, Chad (2003). "C–Z Conversations: Darren Naish on Plesiosaurs, Basilosaurs, and problems with Reconstructions." *North American Bio-Fortean Review* 5(3):10–19. See p. 18.

62. Naish, Darren (2008). "Best Lake Monster Image Ever: The Mansi Photo."Tetrapod Zoology. http://scienceblogs.com/tetrapodzoology/2008/06/mansi_champ_photo.php. Accessed March 21, 2010.

63. Tape recording by Paul Bartholomew of a seminar presentation by Philip Reines at the "Does Champ Exist: A Scientific Seminar" held at Shelburne, Vermont on August 29, 1981.

64. Arment, Chad. (2003). "C–Z Conversations: Darren Naish on Plesiosaurs, Basilosaurs, and problems with Reconstructions." *North American Bio-Fortean Review* 5(3):10–19. See pp. 17–18.

65. Radford, Benjamin, and Nickell, Joseph. (2006). *Lake Monster Mysteries*. Lexington, KY: University of Kentucky Press, 55.

66. Interview between Tony Healy and St. Albans chiropractor Donald Mears, March 1979. This date could have been off slightly, earlier or later than 1959.

67. The 1979 tape-recorded statements of Sandra Mansi and her husband, Tony Mansi, describing their alleged Lake Champlain monster sighting of July 1977. Transcribed by Sean Reines, August 11, 2010. Transcriber's note: Underlined text is to emphasize important parts of the Mansi's descriptive account. It does not connote exclamation on the part of the Mansis.

68. Zarzynski, Joseph W. (1988). *Champ: Beyond the Legend*. Wilton, NY: M–Z Publications, 64.

69. Lenger, John (1992). "Bright Lights, Big Mystery: TV's 'Unsolved Mysteries' to Retell Champ Legend." *The Post-Star* [Glens Falls, NY], July 5, C1 and C8. See p. 8.

70. Radford, Benjamin, and Nickell, Joseph (2006). *Lake Monster Mysteries*. Lexington, KY: University of Kentucky Press, 158.

71. A 1979 tape recording by Sandra and Anthony Mansi, describing their alleged sighting of July 1977, and later transcribed by Sean Reines. The recording was made for and mailed to Phil Reines, along with the original photo.

72. "The Monster in the Lake. Kin of Loch Ness Creature in Vermont?" *The Palm Beach Post*, November 27, 1980, A13 (Associated Press article).

73. Reilly, John. (1980). "Lake Champlain Monster—Caught on Film," *Burlington Free Press*, November 22.

74. (1999). "Lake Monsters." BBC Worldwide Unlimited. Discovery Channel.

75. Tape recording by Paul Bartholomew of a seminar presentation by Sandi Mansi at the "Does Champ Exist: A Scientific Seminar" held at Shelburne, Vermont on August 29, 1981.

76. A 1979 tape recording by Sandra and Anthony Mansi, describing their alleged sighting of July 1977, and later transcribed by Sean Reines. The recording was made for and mailed to Phil Reines, along with the original photo.

77. "Champ." *Unsolved Mysteries* TV program narrated by Dennis Farina accessed from the *Unsolved Mysteries* homepage on January 8 2011.http://www.unsolved.com/legends.html. "America's Loch Ness Monster." MonsterQuest TV documentary (2007). Narrated by Stan Bernard and produced by Whitewolf Entertainment Incorporated and Bosch Media LLC for The History Channel. For the excerpt in question, see, http://www.youtube.com/watch?v=D9IL-d9R2lE&feature=related. Accessed July 21, 2011.

78. Allen, Mel. (2011). "The Gift: Lake Champlain's Mysterious Photo." *Yankee Magazine* (March/April). http://www.yankeemagazine.com/issues/2011-03/features/champ-sighting/1. Accessed July 21, 2011.

79. Radford, Ben (2003). "The Measure of a Monster: Investigating the Champ Photo." *The Skeptical Inquirer* 27(4):24–28.

80. Ibid.

81. Ibid.

82. Ibid.

83. Tape recording by Paul Bartholomew of a seminar presentation by Philip Reines at the "Does Champ Exist: A Scientific Seminar" held at Shelburne, Vermont on August 29, 1981.

84. Shakespeare, William, "A Midsummer Night's Dream." Act 5, scene 1, lines 21–22.

85. Lenger, John. (1992). "Bright Lights, Big Mystery: TV's 'Unsolved Mysteries' to Retell Champ Legend." *The Post-Star*, July 5, C1 and C8. See p. 8.

86. Radford, Benjamin, and Nickell, Joe (2006). *Lake Monster Mysteries: Investigating the World's Most Elusive Creatures.* Lexington, KY: University of Kentucky Press, 45.

87. (1999). "Lake Monsters." BBC Worldwide Unlimited. Discovery Channel.

88. "Lake Champlain Monster," December 4, 1992, TV documentary.

89. McKinstry, Lohr. (1992). "Fox TV to Broadcast Episode on Champ Later this Month." *Press-Republican*, November 4, 13; Radford, Benjamin, and Nickell, Joseph (2006). *Lake Monster Mysteries.* Lexington, KY: University of Kentucky Press, 41.

90. Buckhout, Robert. (1980). "Nearly 2000 Witnesses can be Wrong." *Bulletin of the Psychonomic Society* 16: 307–310. Buckhout, Robert. (1974). "Eyewitness Testimony." *Scientific American* 231(6):23–31. Ross, David Frank, Read, J. Don., and Toglia, Michael P. (1994). *Adult Eyewitness Testimony: Current Trends and Developments.* Cambridge: Cambridge University Press.

91. Massad, Christopher M., Hubbard, Michael, and Newston, Darren. (1979). "Selective Perception of Events." *Journal of Experimental Social Psychology* 15:513–32. See p. 531.

92. See, Bartholomew, Robert E., and Evans, Hilary. (2004). *Panic Attacks: Media Manipulation and Mass Delusion.* Gloucestershire, UK: Sutton Publishing.

93. Stiles, Fred Tracy. (1984). *Old Day–Old Ways: More History and Tales of the Adirondack Foothills.* Hudson Falls, NY: Washington County Historical Society.

94. "'I Tawt I Taw' A Bunny Wabbit At Disneyland: New Evidence Shows False Memories Can Be Created." *Science Daily News* Release, University of Washington, June 12, 2001.

95. "Mirage at Sea." *The Fulton Patriot* [Fulton, NY], March 4, 1937.

96. Tape recording by Paul Bartholomew of a seminar presentation by Philip Reines at the "Does Champ Exist: A Scientific Seminar" held at Shelburne, Vermont on August 29, 1981.

97. "Rosel Couture Tells of Champlain 'Sea Serpent' in '98." *The North Countryman*, September 27, 1934.

98. "Belua Aquatica Champlainiensis—Does it Exist? The Scientific Viewpoint." *The North Countryman*, September 16, 1981, 1, back page.

99. Letter from Charles W. Johnson, Naturalist for the State of Vermont, to Joe Zarzynski dated August 22, 1980. See p. 1.

100. Bauer, Henry. (1986). *The Enigma of Loch Ness: Making Sense of a Mystery.* Champaign, Illinois: University of Illinois Press.

101. Emer, Rick (2010). *Loch Ness Monster: Fact or Fiction?* New York: Chelsea House Publications, 80.

102. Letter from Loren Coleman to Robert Bartholomew dated 1 January 2011.

103. I recall Arthur C. Clarke making a similar statement years ago as to the reality of time 'slips' time travel.

104. Lippmann, Walter. (1922). *Public Opinion.* New York: Harcourt, Brace, cited in MacDonnell, F. (1995). *Insidious Foes.* New York: Oxford University Press, 2.

105. Dendle, Peter (2006). "Cryptozoology in the Medieval and Modern Worlds." *Folklore* 117(August):190–206, see 200.

106. Dendle, Peter (2006). "Cryptozoology in the Medieval and Modern Worlds." Op cit., see p. 200.

107. *Newsweek*, August 14, 1978.

108. "Rallies, Vandalism Puncture IP Permit Hearing." *Plattsburgh Press-Republican*, November 21, 1991, 12.

109. "Multi-Agency Investigation of Spill at IP Begins." *Plattsburgh Press-Republican*, November 19, 1991, 13.

110. Teresi, Dick. (1998). "Monster of the Tub." *Discover* 19(4): 87–92 (April).

INDEX